Investigating small firms

Investigating Small Firms presents a unique, 'real-life' analysis of the organisation of production in small firms. The research is qualitative, involving actual work experience by Ruth Holliday in three small firms, and the discussion centres around three detailed case studies. These are organised around themes ranging from issues such as layout, scheduling, quality and inventory management to aspects such as recruitment, training and control. A fascinating account emerges, of the production process, the often turbulent small firms' environment and of the experience of managers and employees.

A detailed coverage of the qualitative research process brings to light the problems, responsibilities and ethical questions involved. Ruth Holliday shows that in this type of research the importance of the human element in production processes cannot be ignored. In showing the impact of workplace cultures and social relations upon the 'rationality' of management, the author overcomes the traditional boundary between production and human resource management in the literature.

Providing a gripping insight into qualitative research techniques and small firms' organisation of production, this volume will be of great interest to students and researchers in small business, industrial sociology, operations management and related areas.

Ruth Holliday is a lecturer in human resource management at Staffordshire University.

Routledge Small Business Series
Edited by David J. Storey

Small Firms Grow: An implementation approach
Christopher J. Hull and Benny Hjern

Barriers to Growth in Small Firms
J.S. Barber, S. Metcalfe and M. Porteous

The Performance of Small Firms
David Storey, Kevin Keasey, Robert Watson and Pooran Wynarczyk

Small and Medium-size Enterprises and Regional Development
Edited by Maria Giaoutzi, Peter Nijkamp and David Storey

The Entrepreneurial Personality: Concepts, cases and categories
Elizabeth Chell, Jean Haworth and Sally Brearley

Managerial Labour Markets in Small and Medium-sized Enterprises
Pooran Wynarczyk, Robert Watson, David Storey, Helen Short and Kevin Keasey

The Small Firm and the Labour Market
Edited by J. Atkinson and D.J. Storey

Small Firms in Urban and Rural Locations
Edited by J. Curran and D.J. Storey

Finance and the Small Firm
Edited by A. Hughes and D.J. Storey

Investigating small firms
Nice work?

Ruth Holliday

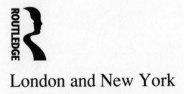

London and New York

First published 1995
by Routledge
11 New Fetter Lane, London EC4P 4EE

Simultaneously published in the USA and Canada
by Routledge
29 West 35th Street, New York, NY 10001

© 1995 Ruth Holliday

Typeset in Times by LaserScript, Mitcham, Surrey
Printed and bound in Great Britain by
TJ Press (Padstow) Ltd, Padstow, Cornwall

British Library Cataloguing in Publication Data
A catalogue record for this book is available from the British Library

Library of Congress Cataloguing in Publication Data
A catalogue record for this book has been requested

ISBN 0–415–12305–4

To Daisy

Contents

List of figures   viii
Acknowledgements   ix

1 **Introduction**   1

2 **Working the field**   17

3 **Wellmaid Clothing – all sewn up?**   31

4 **Logos Ltd – engineered for success**   56

5 **FranTech Ltd – soldering on!**   86

6 **Small firms and production management**   114

7 **Recruiting, training and flexibility**   140

8 **Management control and family culture**   150

9 **Quality, rationality and bureaucracy**   161

10 **Conclusion**   173

Bibliography   176
Index   184

List of figures

3.1 Layout of Wellmaid Clothing   33
4.1 Layout of Logos Ltd   58
5.1 Layout of FranTech Ltd   88
6.1 Rational versus irrational organisation of workflow   118
6.2 Small firms' funding: the vicious circle   128

Acknowledgements

I would like to thank the following people for their help and guidance during the writing of this book: David Bell, James Curran and Monder Ram for their very constructive comments and criticisms; Laura Large, Frania Weaver, Rebecca Garland and John Bell at Routledge for their wisdom and moral support; and especially the participants in this study from Wellmaid, Logos and FranTech.

1 Introduction

I would like to begin by describing how I started the empirical research which forms the basis of this book. I had been told and had read in much of the literature that accessing the small business sector was troublesome – small firms were notoriously difficult to get in to. I was rather worried about this for obvious reasons, but after putting off the inevitable start of my fieldwork for as long as possible I phoned my first case study company. I started working there as a pattern cutter the following week. Access to my second case study was equally smooth. I started writing job descriptions in the company about a week after my first phone call. I phoned the last firm in my study about two weeks before I wanted to start. 'Oh,' said the owner-manager, 'why can't you start tomorrow?' This simple illustration epitomises some of the major themes of this book. Firstly, there are ways of studying small firms which are more amenable than others – access may be less of a problem if it is not requested by men with clipboards (there is no room for freeriders in small firms); and secondly, perhaps this illustrates the desperate and frantic nature of the small firms which I studied, where the promise of an extra pair of hands can cause some excitement.

RESEARCHING SMALL FIRMS

Turning away from the stories of my fieldwork for a moment, I now want to look at some of the literature on small firms, in order to set my research in a broader social, political and economic environment. Since the publication of the Bolton Report on small firms (1971), if not before, there has been a widespread recognition of the role and contribution which small companies make to the economy, and hence of the need to understand – and thereby to help and support – the small business sector. More recently, based on data collected through VAT registrations, the Department of Employment concluded that firms employing fewer than twenty people account for 96 percent of firms in the UK, employing 36 percent of the private sector workforce and producing 21 percent of all UK turnover (Anon. 1990). Furthermore, small manufacturing firms still play a significant part in the UK economy. They provide employment for 50 percent of the workforce and contribute about a third of GNP (Lawlor 1988).

Thus, small manufacturing firms, in spite of the shift in Britain towards the service sector, are still an essential part of the British economy, and in some respects can be said to create the wealth on which the service firms are dependent. Furthermore, in 1987, 94 percent of all local units of UK manufacturing companies employed less than 500 people (Sharp *et al.* 1990).

Studies of production in small firms have been largely quantitative or of the action research variety, concentrating around the implementation of particular systems or techniques without reference to the special circumstances of small firms. The ignorance of quantitative researchers regarding the small-firm situation in the past has been typified by Sausbauer, who more recently has received some strong criticism:

> According to Sausbauer (1979), small businesses represent a microcosmic image of larger enterprises without much of the distortion of size, human interactions, structure, and history of the more complex organisations.
>
> (Riggs and Bracker 1986: 18)

In other words, small firms have been seen as a testing ground for the implementation of techniques designed for large organisations. Sausbauer's perception that small businesses are not *distorted* by size, human interactions, structures and history is incredible, not simply because it shows a complete and total naiveté of the conditions of smaller companies, but also as it proposes the implementation of techniques in any size of organisation without consideration of the psychological or cultural characteristics of those who work within them – surely the most fundamental feature of any organisation. However, although Sausbauer's research can be dismissed as dated, he is not alone, and to some extent typifies a species of (operations) management researchers, many of whom have felt it necessary to turn their attentions to the small company.

Of course small businesses use different methods and techniques from those of large organisations. This is because they are severely constrained through their lack of funds and stability, along with their disadvantaged power relations in dealing with large organisations. Consequently they have less time and fewer physical and human resources. They do not possess the pools of experts and professionals which large companies can afford to employ.

Many small businesses lack the funds needed to hire an industrial engineering specialist. Work systems in these companies usually evolve apart from an overall plan or scientific study. Jobs tend to be pieced together informally and haphazardly, and great operating inefficiencies result.

(Grant 1988: 8)

In relation to production this means that less sophisticated or more company-specific techniques must be implemented:

Small firms are usually quite concerned with monthly cash flow and cannot afford to invest in systems that do not quickly contribute to the profitability of the organisation. Not only is money unavailable, the people needed to develop or operate the new control techniques either do not exist or are too busy with their daily tasks. The typical production manager simply cannot find the time to implement the latest inventory system, regardless of the money such a system could save.

(Gupta 1988: 17)

Thus, firm size evidently influences the way in which production is organised. Large firms assemble disciplined teams that are designed to capture the economies of volume production. Customised goods which are demanded in small batches can be more efficiently supplied by small firms (Oi 1983). Furthermore, small business owners cannot do all things well. On any given day, the owner may play the roles of executive, manager and operator. This makes critical the identification of techniques which require low levels of expertise on the owner's part, yet which enable the business to run smoothly. Thus, the formal systems developed and employed by many large companies may not work well in small businesses (Gupta 1988). However, even if systems and methods are flawless and absolute, what is the use if they cannot be implemented? This is borne out by the fact that so little of the government help directed towards small companies ever reaches them. As Adams and Walbank (1981: 31) explain:

The genuine entrepreneur is a difficult person to help. At present little of the potential technical assistance or financial support appears to be reaching the firms who need it. Provision for support must be 'human engineered' in terms of the users – and in terms of the supporting organisations.

The task of helping small businesses has been addressed from all sorts of directions, with all kinds of motives and emphases. Consequently the small firms literature is both vast and variable. Its audience is similarly diverse, and ranges from academics to small business managers. The first point to make, then, is that with such diametric authors and audiences there is bound to be a degree of diversity in the quality and style of small firms research. In addition, much of the work generalises across all sectors and industries. What is surprising is that firms from different industries with nothing in common but their size should be assumed to be homogeneous. As Scott (1986: 85) explains, 'it is increasingly clear that size itself [and the consequent potential for close face-to-face relationships] is relatively unimportant in the face of other contingencies, especially in the market place'. A further study splits small firms into four sectors including high and low technology manufacturing and service sectors. Whilst the low technology firms followed the rather depressing pattern of low wages and few opportunities for their employees, 'highly specialised and technically advanced firms can offer software engineers and other scientific workers salaries and other aspects of a package which is superior to that offered by larger firms' (Scott *et al.* 1989: 70). This tendency to homogenise small firms produces conceptual shortfalls, as David Goss (1991: 149) notes:

> There are four areas in which the assumption of small business homogeneity can lead to profound inadequacies of understanding. These inadequacies will be referred to as homogenisation effects. The first of these is the encouragement of a tendency towards essentialism: That is to say, the attribution to small businesses in general of some fundamental and ontologically privileged quality, e.g., 'entrepreneurship', 'industrial harmony', 'innovation', etc. Second, the assumption of homogeneity implies the existence of common small business interests and a shared outlook amongst their owners and workers. Third, it creates problems of definition and conceptualisation, particularly in terms of the nature of small business organisational structure. Finally, the assumption of unitary small business sector discourages the examination of small firms in their wider economic and social context.

It is perhaps time for researchers to refocus their approach and also their methods. The question of whether survey- or questionnaire-based research is entirely relevant to the study of a deeply heterogeneous small firm sector must be addressed. A further analysis of the literature should make clear some of its deficiencies, as well as indicating the complexities of the small firms sector.

A major problem in discussing British and American literature together is the issue of size – what is a small firm? The American Small Business Administration has defined a manufacturing firm as small if it employs less than 1,500 people (Finch 1986) or has a turnover of less than $20 million

(Clifford 1973). Having achieved these parameters, a firm is likely to have attained a degree of stability through an established market, a recognisable management structure and a fairly successful product line: 'small' isn't small. As 75 percent of firms in Britain employ fewer than twenty-five people (Stanworth and Curran 1976), such studies must be tempered when applied to British small business research and vice versa, and indeed distinction is now being made in some studies between small and medium-sized businesses, although these may also be differently defined.

Even the British literature on small firms still uses definitions which may be inappropriate. For example, a 'small' manufacturing firm is commonly defined as having less than 200 employees (Bolton 1971) but even this figure is frequently criticised for being too large (Curran and Stanworth 1982). The Companies Act 1981 defined three criteria – turnover of less than £1.4 million; balance sheet total of less than £0.7 million; and average weekly number of employees less than fifty. Two out of three of these measures must be fulfilled in order for a firm to be classed as 'small', and this definition covers all industries. There are countless other definitions concerning British and American small firms (e.g. Appelbaum and Hinds 1984; Robinson 1983; Department of Trade and Industry 1983).

However, these definitions do not account for firms such as subsidiaries, which, although they may employ few workers, have large funds at their disposal and little to lose when risks taken do not pay off. In another case a firm employing 200 people may do so because it utilises a high level of automation. This firm may have a very sophisticated management structure and be a large operation, yet it still comes under the heading of 'small firm'. Thus, it is more useful to employ qualitative definitions of the small firm:

> in economic terms, a small firm is one that has a relatively small share of its market. . . . [I]t is managed by its owners or part owners in a personalised way, and not through the medium of a formalised management structure. . . . [I]t is also independent in the sense that it does not form part of a larger enterprise and that the owner-managers should be free from outside control in taking their principal decisions.
>
> (Bolton 1971: 1)

Setting aside this definitional conundrum, one 'fact' about which much of the literature agrees is that small firms have the potential to create jobs. However, there is strong evidence to suggest that this has more to do with the relative decline of large organisations than with the growth of small ones. Large firms have been encouraged to rationalise and as a result many ancillary departments have been farmed off. Typical of this kind of practice is the management buy-out of, for example, the maintenance or the cleaning departments. However, to a certain extent this has occurred within manufacturing. In any case small firms are then in a position where they compete with other similar firms for the contract to clean, maintain or manufacture for the larger company. One of the prime reasons advanced for large firms 'farming out' some element of production to small firms is to facilitate the riding out of periods of uncertainty and instability. This also begs the question, then, of what kind of jobs small firms are likely to create.

This notion of large firm/small firm relationships has been developed, particularly by Andrew Friedman (1977). He labels this dependent relationship as that of one between core and peripheral firms, with core and periphery being defined by relative monopoly power:

> As workers within a small firm may be viewed as either central or peripheral on the basis of specialised knowledge, relation to authority or power resistance, so firms in an industry may be considered central or peripheral on the basis of their monopoly power. These two dichotomies are connected. Large firms are able to bypass or forestall internal technical reorganisations to some extent when adjusting to changed product demand by increasing or decreasing their co-operative relations with smaller firms. Similarly they are able to bypass disruptive consequences of central worker lay-offs by reducing co-operative relations in times of adversity. This is particularly important when top managers are faced with strong, organised resistance from the majority of their workers. Co-operative relations with smaller firms allow top managers in large firms the luxury of treating a high proportion of their workers as central and to use Responsible Autonomy strategies when dealing with them. Of course, the steady profits which co-operative relations allow top managers in large firms and the security enjoyed by their workers have another side. The flexibility which large firms acquire from their co-operative relations means hardship and insecurity for workers in smaller supplier and distributing firms.
>
> (Friedman 1977: 114)

This theme is further developed in work by Rainnie (1989), Phizacklea (1990) and Johnson (1986). Having one large customer responsible for 50 percent or more of all business is one of the most dangerous yet perhaps one of the most frequent traps that small firms fall into. In this situation the large firm is in a particularly powerful position. Small firm managers cannot dispute prices for fear of losing orders to a competitor and probably thereby losing the company (Hankinson 1987).

The notion of core and periphery workers is linked to post-Fordist ideals of flexibility. Post-Fordism represents a move away from mass production

and consumption towards short-run batch-type production in small or de-
centralised firms (Bagguley 1990). However, such ideals, though similar in
outcome, derive from opposing political perspectives. The so-called man-
agerialist perspective is represented by the work of Atkinson (1984) who
uses the concept of the 'flexible firm'. Atkinson's argument hinges on the
idea of numerical flexibility, meaning a reliance on peripheral workers who
are taken on and laid off as demand dictates. In addition differential rates of
pay are used to encourage functional flexibility by rewarding individual
performance or scarce skills (human resources). Thus, labour becomes a
simple commodity to be bought and sold as required.

Piore and Sabel (1984) represent the 'Institutionalist School'. Their
focus is on the 'crisis' of mass production which has precipitated the
restructuring of large corporations and the development of small specialised companies. These 'new' small companies are organised into regional
agglomerations or federations which function collectively through the
social regulation of competition and co-operation. By creating this new
form of business 'community' Piore and Sabel see the birth of a
'democratically regulated enterprise culture' (Bagguley 1990: 164). This
conception has been criticised as being little more than a 'utopian myth'
(Amin 1989: 13; see also Williams *et al.* 1987).

The entire notion of flexibility has been deconstructed by, among others,
Anna Pollert, who concluded that:

> the 'discovery' of the 'flexible workforce' is part of an ideological
> offensive which celebrates pliability and casualisation, *and makes them
> seem inevitable.* . . . [T]he language of 'flexibility' reveals itself as the
> language of social integration of the 1980s: how to live with insecurity
> and unemployment, and learn to love it.
>
> (1988: 72; original emphasis)

Aside from flexibility, another reason for the privileging of small firms is
their perceived ability to innovate. Many writers attribute the innovation
thesis to some kind of essential 'Entrepreneurial Spirit' and suggest that
entrepreneurs, unlike formally educated and socialised managers, retain
their creativity (Gilder 1984; for criticism, see Goss 1991). Others discuss
the ways in which entrepreneurs should exploit their creativity by, for
example, licensing the manufacturing of a product to others, leaving the
small company more time to invent new products (Anon. 1985). Cannon
(1989) debates the myths and realities of small firm innovation, finding that
the inventiveness tends to lie in the new firm formation. He also found that
further new product development depends very much on strong links
between suppliers and customers, but that nevertheless 'the "problem solving"

orientation of the majority of these firms, allied to ease of communication, was a real asset in managing the improvement and adaption of existing products or processes' (Cannon 1989: 11).

Mason (1973) looked at the cheapest and most cost-effective ways in which to innovate and introduce new technology. He continued by explaining that product modification should be the preferred strategy of small firms in view of their limited resources. However, he concluded by pointing out the small innovatory capacity of the small firm and that the innovativeness of a firm is dependent on its management, and as managers in small firms are more likely to be promoted through their conformity with the views of the owner-manager, then this promotes conformity and lack of flair for innovation. Rothwell (1988) talked about the distribution of innovation between small and large firms, explaining how an initial innovative 'spark' from a large firm is then sub-contracted to smaller firms who develop the technology. As the industry matures and the products become viable or marketable, the technology is reconcentrated, through mergers and take-overs, into the hands of large firms. In this way it is small firms who shoulder the risk of innovation but large firms who reap the rewards. It must be remembered, then, that the majority of small firms are not innovative.

Another key subject to which many writers have contributed is the psychology and sociology of the entrepreneur (Chell *et al.* 1991). This is important to ask two questions: Who is likely to become an entrepreneur? And how do entrepreneurial characteristics effect the growth and structure of the firm? Firstly, the people who are most likely to become entrepreneurs are generally accepted to be particular personality types. For example, Gibb (1988) shows that the propensity of entrepreneurs to initiate a new business is contingent upon:

(i)   the time of life of the entrepreneur (the older person with little prospect of further promotion);
(ii) the social and political context (the 'enterprise culture');
(iii) the types of market (if the preferred market open to the entrepreneur is associated with ease of access);
(iv) the entrepreneur versus the corporatist (the person who is fed up with structure and task orientation in larger firms).

Further, Shapero (1975) argued that most entrepreneurs are 'displaced persons'. For example, they may be very intelligent but uneducated and thus in poor jobs. There is also evidence that people who had achieved high status within the armed forces and then found themselves in uninteresting civilian jobs are likely to start their own businesses. Finally, Shapero uses the notion of 'loci of control' in order to discover the perceived ability of entrepreneurs to control their own destiny. He found that managers who were not entrepreneurs had a higher propensity to externalise control, blaming occurrences on, for example, fate.

Once again, however, homogeneity is assumed. Cooper (1986) found a radical difference in the types of entrepreneurs involved in new firm formation within two different sectors. Founders of new technology-based firms were often in their thirties, had at least one degree (usually in engineering), were single-minded and career-oriented, and leadership- and achievement-motivated. These entrepreneurs also tended to form firms in groups. Traditional entrepreneurs, by comparison, were likely to form firms as single owner-managers and be poorly educated.

Another way of determining the characteristics of entrepreneurs is to examine their expectations. What do entrepreneurs expect to achieve by starting their own companies? Some writers emphasise their desire to achieve outstanding growth and financial rewards (Jarillo 1989), whilst others argue that most entrepreneurs have in common a desire to be their own boss, hence real growth is often stunted as owner-managers struggle to retain control (Bosworth and Jacobs 1989).

The most frequently stated objectives of the new entrepreneur, according to Donckels and Dupont (1987), are: personal independence and achievement, job satisfaction, the manufacture of quality products, and the desire for a secure and stable job. These goals look misleadingly harmonious, but the motives for starting a business fall into two groups: entrepreneurs may feel that they can manufacture an improved product to that of the competition or the firm in which they presently work; or entrepreneurs may be in search of job security or relief from the paperwork and bureaucracy of a large firm. These two kinds of motives have been termed the 'pull' and 'push' effects (Binks and Coyne 1983). Entrepreneurs are either pushed into independence through worries about security or pulled by a strong belief that they can do better on their own. Not surprisingly, it is the latter who consistently perform better, achieving higher growth rates than their reluctant counterparts. This phenomenon perhaps finds its origins in work by Shapero (1975), who talks about positive and negative displacement.

The reason that entrepreneurial characteristics are so important to the study of small firms is bound up with their structure. Small firms generally consist of an operative unit with a single manager controlling most of its actions, and thus the entrepreneur is the central and absolute power in the firm. In this way the personality of the owner-manager governs completely the culture of the firm and thus enhances or inhibits its operation. For example, owner-managers whose initial reason for founding a firm is to be their own boss are unlikely to allow the firm to grow to any significant extent as with firm growth comes the necessity to delegate. This may stunt the career prospects of competent non-owner-managers within the firm, and lead to their resignation from the company. In this way vital skill resources are lost. However, if firms decide to grow then a complete range of skills are required. The danger here is that owners will choose managers whom they understand in terms of both character and expertise, thus decisions will go unchallenged and the skill base of the firm will become concentrated in one area (Brytting 1990; Lowden 1988).

Finally, Chapman (1989) pointed out two important characteristics of small firm entrepreneurs. Firstly, they spend an enormous amount of time at work and as such have very limited contact with their families. Secondly, when small business owners are not actually at work they tend to bring their paperwork home with them. This appeared to be due to the belief that paperwork does not contribute directly to production, and hence profit. This also led to a tendency for paperwork to be ignored. There is also a reliance on 'informal' labour, for instance members of the owner-manager's family, to deal with such 'unproductive' elements of management (Ram 1994).

The problem of management education and training in small firms is similarly a huge one, since lack of training and education hinders development. For example, growth requires considerable financial investment, but obtaining finance is often contingent upon the skills of the entrepreneur. Since new venture success is foremost a function of entrepreneurial knowledge, entrepreneurship education may be one of the most promising economic development mechanisms. Unfortunately it may be one of the most difficult to implement.

Of course the biggest problem facing small business training is lack of time. Training is often something to be introduced 'in the future' when a firm will be more stable and organised. However, if more people in the firm were trained, particularly in management, then better organisation may lead to more time available.

Other barriers to the take-up of training lie in the decision processes of the owner-manager. To continue the theme of limited time, the owner-manager is likely to choose the first satisfactory solution to the immediate problem, without looking for an optimum long-term solution. This process is termed 'satisficing' (Tait 1990). A further aspect of this is that the owner-manager's knowledge of education and training is likely to be limited owing to the probability that he or she has little direct experience of these facilities.

A study by Watkins (1983) indicated a further problem in the attitudes of owner-managers. Managers in small firms are some of the most likely groups of people to become entrepreneurs. In fact, many people join smaller companies simply in order to determine a market for a similar product or to develop the wide-based skills necessary in the initial stages of business start-up. Hence it is understandable that owner-managers are reluctant to develop the skills of those people who are likely to become their future competitors. Watkins also found that one-fifth of all owner-managers in his survey have a fear of developing their managers for this reason.

In addition to training and education, much small firms research has focused on the actual processes of starting a business. The literature on small business start-ups is overwhelmingly concerned with raising finance. Mason (1984/5), in a study of fifty-two new manufacturing firms, concluded that only 16 percent of the case study firms had difficulty raising outside finance. However, many would disagree with this. Peterson and Schulman (1987) pointed out that borrowing becomes easier as firms establish a good financial record, thus initial borrowing may be very difficult. Many respondents began by borrowing from relatives or using personal savings. Bennett (1989) stated that 75 percent of all funding capital is generated by small firm owners, and that when small firms do borrow from banks they pay a higher rate of interest than large firms. This is because smaller sums are more expensive to borrow and because small firms, especially those just starting up, are placed in a high-risk category and are expected to pay accordingly for this risk. Lawrence (1985) discussed the particular problems which engineering companies face in raising finance as bankers do not understand the language of technology, despite the insistence of bank advertising to the contrary.

Finance is not, however, simply a problem at start-up: the most obvious sign of a rapidly growing company is its hunger for money (Cornell and Shapero 1988). Although income rises along with sales, cashflow is nearly always negative because of the constant reinvestment necessary to fund the growth in sales. This is why many writers suggest that a period of growth should always be followed by a period of consolidation (Perry 1985/6). Consolidation should not be simply in terms of tangible (financial) assets, but should also provide an opportunity to accumulate intangible assets such as expertise (by recruiting or retraining). This is particularly important as expertise provides a major competitive advantage to the small firm (Tiler *et al.* 1990).

There is also much discussion about the pattern of small firm growth and much of this centres around the theme of stages in the growth process

(Churchill and Lewis 1983; Steinmetz 1969; Vozikis and Glueck 1980). Growth models have been criticised for assuming that growth is independent of firm size or that the relationship between firm growth and firm size is linear. Growth has been shown to decrease with firm age and firm size, and thus growth can be represented on an exponential curve. In addition, Stanworth and Curran (1986) challenge the very idea of stage models due to their idealistic and positivistic nature and the lack of empirical evidence with which to back them up. They also point out that most firms do not expand at all and that substantial growth is, in fact, exceptional.

Another problem of the literature on growth is the plethora of indicators used to determine the amount of growth itself. Growth is not a unidimensional phenomenon, therefore no single measure can be used to analyse the issue of growth in small firms.

A major paradox of growth is recruitment. Internally-recruited managers may have an intimate knowledge of the company in which they work, but may never have undergone any formal management training. As such, an employee may be intimidated by the prospect of increased responsibility, or simply satisfied in his or her present position. Externally-recruited managers may be competent and well-trained, but the complex methods and rigid structures with which they are familiar may be inappropriate to the smaller firm. Thus, a small firm demands different modes of expertise than a large firm and, in particular, a greater variation of skills. This problem is acute during growth, when managers become necessary, yet not in a full-time capacity. An additional problem of the externally-recruited small firm manager is that of resentment from other staff. When a company is small and under certain stresses it is possible for a sense of camaraderie or 'family' to quickly build up amongst employees. New employees can be seen as imposing on this, or as not having 'earned their passage' in the early days when wages were perhaps lower and long working days were integral to the survival of the firm (Strauss 1974).

Growth alone, it must be remembered, is not necessarily synonymous with success. It imposes considerable costs in terms of developing new resources and creating more appropriate management processes. These costs are often greater the more complex the environment because of the necessity to create a distinctive market or competitive position (Bennett 1989). Indeed, some articles are quick to point out that growth should not actually be the goal of every entrepreneur, as the skills necessary to found a business are not always the skills necessary to run a larger, more structured company (MacMillan 1975). Others point to the dangers of growth, emphasising the personal risks involved, especially since many entrepreneurs sink all their savings into their own business, or even remortgage their houses (Case 1987). However, although growth may lead to failure small business owners are still inevitably inclined to measure their success in terms of it (Berryman 1983).

Indeed failure is another area of prominent small firms research about which there is much discussion. Perhaps the first question which needs to be addressed when tackling this subject is: What exactly is meant by failure? Is this simply the bankruptcy of the firm, or should the definition be so broad as to include the failure of entrepreneurs to achieve their desired goals? To take account of the failure of entrepreneurs to meet their expectations would be a very difficult thing to measure, especially since personal objectives frequently change. A workable definition of failure should include the inability of firms to pay their creditors (and therefore being deemed legally bankrupt), with the possible inclusion of the circumstances where the firm must be sold in order to cover losses (Berryman 1983).

The most frequently quoted failure statistics are probably the Dun & Bradstreet Reports, hailing from the USA. According to Berryman (1983) many people believe that this source reveals a high failure rate, especially amongst small businesses. However, this myth is dispelled by Massel (1978), who claims that mortality rates taken from the Reports were actually 0.43 percent in 1975, which could hardly be said to be high. Further, there was no detail of size given by the Reports other than the size of the liability, which is not conclusive (Wright *et al.* 1983). However, studies in Britain have conceded somewhat higher rates of failure. For example, Keeble (1990) advanced a 50 percent mortality rate after five years, while Storey *et al.* (1987) found that nearly 40 percent of new businesses cease to trade within three years of start-up. Hill (1987) notes that in the period between 1980 and 1982 there were an estimated 363,100 births, but in the same period 343,300 small firms collapsed. Also, Berryman (1983) notes a study which observed a 77 percent survival rate in the first year of operation; 54 percent survival in the second year; 29 percent in the fifth year. Twenty percent of the study-firms were still in existence after ten years.

The reason for this wide discrepancy between American and UK data is probably less an actual difference than a difference of records. This probably originates not only from the American definition of a small firm being much larger than that of a British small firm, but also because there is no distinction drawn between large and small firms in the Dun & Bradstreet Reports, whereas this distinction is made in the British literature, which relies on VAT deregistrations.

No matter what the statistics say, some small businesses do fail, and we must ask the question 'Why?' It seems that an overwhelmingly common theme in small business failure is poor management. This is perhaps unsurprising considering the entrepreneurial characteristics and entrepreneurial education already addressed. Abdelsamad and Kindling (1978) feel that there are twelve managerial weaknesses at the heart of any small business failure: excessive optimism, inadequate board (poor representation of skills on the board of directors), nepotism, inability to delegate, negligence in developing subordinates, inability to recognise what business the firm is in, underestimation of economic effects, doing things that they like, failure to grow with the business, improper selection of associates, unwillingness to make sacrifices, and failure to monitor results and take necessary action. As with studies of growth, there is a tendency among researchers to devise their own models or schema of the causes of failure. As Abdelsamad and Kindling ascribed twelve faults which may cause business mortality, Vozikis and Glueck (1980) classify the problems small firms face under four headings: general management (including dependence on survival of principal manager, neglect of personnel management, lack of planning and misuse of time); operations (lack of experience in periphery activities, inventory mismanagement, wrong location, and heavy operating expenses and overheads); finance (insufficient capital and slow debt collection); and marketing (non-aggressive marketing). There also exist more specific studies which highlight particular aspects of business trouble: Warnes (1987), investigating cashflow, focused on the need for sufficient initial funding and the gap between funding needs and finances available during growth as typical stumbling-blocks. The question of finance is intimately linked with failure in many studies.

There are, of course, much broader external factors which have an influence on the failure rates of small businesses, often hitting particular regions or sectors. Keeble (1990) has noted the explosive birth of small firms in the finance/property/business services sector over the period 1980–88, centred geographically on the South-East of England. In contrast with this, Birley and Westhead (1990) have shown that the highest rates of private business sales in 1983–88 were in exactly this region, perhaps a reflection of the fragility of service sector firms in a time of tightening recession.

Whatever the actual proportion of small firms which do fail and the causes of failure, there is agreement that it is important to predict, and thereby prevent, small business mortality. There is a body of work, therefore, which attempts to devise predictive tools in order to save businesses. Norgard (1987), for example, lists eleven warning signs: overtrading, margin erosion, 'the big project', high gearing, corporate inertia, altered business focus, problem borrowing, undercapitalisation, declining service standards, 'too much money!' and a history of losses.

Of course, not all small businesses fail. Some even exhibit substantial growth, and attain that growth through a diversity of strategies. Meyer and Roberts (1988) note that while product diversity may be an attractive growth strategy for large firms, small firms would do better to build up an internal mass of engineering talent in a focused technological area. In this way the company sells expertise and has a distinctive core technology with which to develop distinctive products. Connell (1985) also sees technical specialisation as a key to growth. Small firms are able to gain entry to a market when barriers are low. As the market expands so too does the need for service and expertise, which the small firm is in a privileged position to provide. To continue the growth strategy, Connell sees increasing market development leading to a switch in research and development costs towards improving the production processes. This inevitably leads to lower operating costs, and thus as the firm increases in size, it is able to compete on price.

A survey by Libatore *et al.* (1990) reviews the use of FMS, CAD/CAM, CIM and CNC. The advantages of such technologies are shorter production lead times, decreased costs and inventories, flexibility to changing customer specifications, consistent quality and improved adherence to tolerances. The survey focused on small family-owned engineering companies. The results showed that 52 percent of firms had no computer-controlled machine tools and that only 6 percent of all machine tools are computer controlled. The larger the company the more likely it was to employ such equipment.

Phizacklea (1990) has stressed that technological innovation only comes about when labour costs are high. She cites the fashion industry as an example, explaining that flexibility is created here by women in small sweatshops making-through garments using a simple sewing machine. More stable lines, however, are manufactured in greenfield medium-sized firms where standard products allow economies of scale to be generated by labour-saving equipment such as CAD/CAM cutting equipment and so on.

So why is technology not being accepted by more small firms? Lawlor (1988) suggests some factors which influence the adoption of technology. Insufficient training does not expose a workforce to new technological developments, thus knowledge of technology is limited. In addition, because many small companies accept any job which is offered to them, they are rendered do-it-all plants where purchase of expensive equipment is likely to solve few of the company's problems. Research by Garsombke and Garsombke (1989) gives a further insight to the problem of implementation. The study looked at the performance of new high-technology firms of which one-third had implemented computerisation. Firms which presently employed no technology saw few barriers to its implementation but were content with their present status. On the other hand, firms using technology saw more barriers to further implementation, including finance, knowledge and staff, despite having experienced success in terms of increased output, increased materials flow, decreased inventory, and increases in sales and profitability.

Finally, a study by Dodgson (1984/5) looked at the impact of new technology on the employees of small firms. The study concluded that the loss of jobs through new technology implementation was minimal, and that deskilling had not occurred. All firms in the study made similar products and had roughly the same batch sizes. Firms were split into three (polyvalent, fragmented and mixed) categories. In the polyvalent firms employees were responsible for operating, setting, part-proving and programming machines. In the fragmented firms employees were responsible for machine operation only. The polyvalent firms were found to have fewer employees, less predictable production, enhanced flexibility, a non-bureaucratic management style and a higher turnover per employee.

In this introduction I have sought merely to discuss what I feel to be some of the most pertinent debates within current small firms research. The aim of this chapter has been to 'set the scene' for the research I have undertaken in order that the characteristics and environment of the small firm are considered while the theme of the book becomes increasingly focused. The next chapter deals with methodological issues in small firms research, and outlines the approach taken by my own empirical enquiry into the working lives of small manufacturing companies.

2 Working the field

Textbooks on methodology can never quite prepare researchers for the actual experience of doing fieldwork. The following anecdote should illustrate this point clearly. The rest of this chapter explores the complex nature of the fieldwork experience in three small manufacturing firms. Wellmaid manufactures wax jackets and employs about seventeen people. It is an all-woman company. Logos Engineering employs about fifty-five people, most of whom are men. It manufactures large pieces of filtration equipment for the oil and gas industry, some of which can take up to a year to build. FranTech manufactures meter test equipment and other electronic subcomponents. Its work is split almost equally between development and sub-contract build work. It employs about fifteen people. Further details of all these firms are given in Chapters 3, 4 and 5.

A FIELDWORK TALE

At the very outset of my research I began to worry that I had not really seen the inside of a small manufacturing firm and so had no idea what kind of questions I would need to ask when I began my fieldwork. If I had been researching by questionnaire, of course, I might *never* have seen the inside of a small business, and might not have worried about this. But I arranged to visit a small electronics company owned by a friend of a colleague. The night before I was due to visit the company my temperature soared to 103 degrees and I went down with 'flu. However, I felt that I could not break the arrangement at such short notice, so I decided to go to the factory anyway. After all, I could cope with a gentle stroll around the shopfloor for an hour or so and then I would be able to return to my sick-bed.

I got to the company at 10am. Eventually Raj, the owner-manager, arrived. We had spent ten minutes touring the factory when he asked me if I could drive. I said that I could, so he asked me if I would drive him to another factory about fifteen miles south. I explained that I was feeling unwell and that I really only expected to see his factory today, to which he said that in that case he would drive. After about two minutes on the road I bitterly regretted my decision to be a passenger, so I shut my eyes and hoped for the best until we reached our destination.

When we arrived my head was spinning and my knees were weak. I was introduced to the engineers at the other company as Raj's 'shadow', after which we all trooped over to the pub to clinch a large deal. Business and lunch over we walked back to the car (to my great relief – at last I could go home). This time I drove. As we pulled out of the car park, Raj turned to me and said, 'I'd just like to pop down to an exhibition in Birmingham – is that okay?' My heart sank, but I didn't have the strength to protest, so off to Birmingham we went.

During the journey down, Raj told me about a crisis which had occurred recently within his company. Another small firm had ordered a very substantial piece of equipment from him, which had required a huge amount of development work. Once the item was supplied the company which placed the order promptly declared itself bankrupt and refused to pay. Through a court action a tiny proportion of the money was reclaimed, but this was outweighed by the court costs, and so Raj's company had nearly folded. By the time we reached Birmingham my sense of injustice was well and truly inflamed. How could this practice be legally tolerated? What a terrible personal tragedy for this man! 'So', Raj continued, 'this company has a display of *our product* here today and I want to get their brochure on it. The trouble is they know me, so you'll have to get it. We'll split up at the door and I'll meet you in an hour. Tell them you're a customer or something . . . .' I couldn't believe it. I was being asked to commit industrial espionage in my first few hours of fieldwork. What did the work I'd read on research ethics have to say about this? I couldn't believe that Raj was asking me to do this, and that he'd planned it from the beginning. On the other hand I felt sorry for him after what the other company had done.

I got the brochure pretending to be a student – from Southampton, interested in researching small firms. I even got an invitation to the factory to come and research them. Then I passed the intelligence to Raj and began the long drive back. I arrived home at 8.30pm exhausted and feverish, and with a very guilty conscience.

THEORY AND PRACTICE

The techniques used to collect the information for this research relied heavily on qualitative methods, that is a combination of participant observation and semi-structured open interviews (documentary evidence, such as company manuals, accounts and reports, was also used where possible). This combination enabled me to see what happens in the companies, and to talk about it with their personnel.

> Although it is widely acknowledged that in the study of entrepreneurship there is a need for grounded data collected by using ethnography, little research using this methodology has in fact been undertaken. This has meant that small firms research has remained positivist, repetitive, quick and risk averse. Consequently, our understanding of entrepreneurship has not advanced as far as it could or should have over the past decade.
>
> (Stockport and Kakabadse 1991: 2)

For some time the emphasis of social science research, particularly in management, has been on statistical methods (Curran 1986). In general, it can be said that quantitative methods provide a wide but shallow emphasis, whereas qualitative methods give a narrower but more detailed focus (Bryman 1988). Surveys are useful for gathering statistical data but they cannot account for notions of process or system, and cannot be reactive. Participant observation, on the other hand, provides an idea of interaction and the interrelationships of social relations in a group, and a sense of process which cannot be obtained in any other way (Frankenburg 1963).

ETHNOGRAPHY IN SMALL FIRMS

That ethnographic studies of small firms are still an exception is surprising given that the small firm may be the ideal arena for ethnographic organisational research (Curran and Burrows 1987). The size of the enterprise and its workforce liberate the ethnographer from interdepartmental wranglings and facilitate the nurturing of close relations with the study-group. A questionnaire aimed at small businesses will, in many cases at least, be answered by the owner-manager, and although formal interviews may still require his or her consent, it is possible through participant observation to investigate away from the entrepreneur's gaze, thus avoiding results based on a single set of perceptions. There is a high level of personal involvement by the owner-manager in the small firm and thus one-sided accounts are likely to appear, especially given the entrepreneur's tendency to externalise failure and internalise success. Participant observation also presents a moving image rather than a static 'snap-shot' view. This permits the temporal examination of processes in a longitudinal context, and a clearer picture of action and reaction to specific events.

One frequent criticism of small firms literature is that it assumes homogeneity in what is in fact a very diverse sector (Scott 1986) – and inevitably research methods such as questionnaires must make this assumption. Thus, participant observation can be much more individually tailored, and change as often as is required to suit the environment under scrutiny – it is also more responsive to sudden switches of emphasis, thereby reflecting the processual nature of operations. In practice this meant that in my fieldwork I was able to use triangulation techniques, which seek to provide a more holistic view of events by catering for a plurality of ideas and perceptions.

Through the use of ethnography it is also possible to see at first hand why some recommendations to small firms, although sensible in theory, cannot work in practice (Curran 1986). Here again survey research cannot present the detailed overview of what Atkin and McArdle (1992) call the 'workaday life' of small companies. The consequence of this is work which identifies best practices for small companies to follow without any notion of the practical constraints on their implementation. This also ties in with management research which tends to be pragmatic and goal/solution-centred without thorough investigation into the nature of the settings in question. This is perhaps a product of the consultancy orientation of some business schools which encourages the quest for quick, off-the-shelf best practice implementation with little regard for tailoring solutions to specific organisations and requirements (Stockport and Kakabadse 1991). This is compounded by a general tendency for management education and consultancy to be centred around the large organisation.

The fact that ethnography remains an under-utilised methodology in the area of small firms research probably also stems at least in part from the kinds of researchers likely to be attracted to such areas of study. Furthermore, since resource allocation in business schools tends to be directed into areas other than research, business studies researchers are less likely to be full time, and consequently more likely to use quantitative methods as these are less time-consuming (Carter *et al.* 1986). For those of us located within business schools the anti-qualitative culture is exasperating at times, as Mintzberg (1979: 583) illustrates:

> What, for example, is wrong with [small] samples? Why should researchers have to apologise for them? Should Piaget apologize for studying his own children, a physicist for splitting only one atom? A doctoral student I know was not allowed to observe managers because of the 'problem' of sample size. He was required to measure what managers did through questionnaires, despite ample evidence that managers

are poor estimators of their own time allocation. Was it better to have less valid data that were statistically significant?

As Stockport and Kakabadse (1991: 9) conclude, while questionnaires can help us gather statistics, '[e]thnography represents the only true way to study *the life* of a small firm' (emphasis added). Nevertheless 'there is still too much labelling of ethnographic work as "unscientific" and thus not to be taken seriously' (Stanley 1990: 622). This line of argument is a common one, which seems to stem from a fundamental misunderstanding of qualitative methods, and a continued acceptance of the centrality of so-called objectivity and 'scientific' procedure in social research (Bryman 1988; Hammersley and Atkinson 1983). However, there is a growing body of research which adopts the viewpoint that 'it is more logical to accept our subjectivity, our emotions and our socially grounded positions than to assume that some of us can rise above them' (Ramazanoglu 1992: 211) and that

> a rejection of the notion of 'objectivity' and a focus on *experience in method* does not mean a rejection of the need to be critical, rigorous and accurate; rather, it can mean making interpretive schemes explicit in the concern to produce good quality knowledge.
>
> (Gelsthorpe 1992: 214; original emphasis)

While accepting that quantitative methods are an important tool for comparing narrow phenomena over a wide sample, and not wanting to totally reject the notion that quantitative methods can be creative, there is a sense in which they can be constricting, through the use of a rigid, predetermined research design. On the other hand, ethnography allows the researcher to drift and reformulate ideas in the research setting, and to explore uncharted ground (Rosen 1991). While at times this may feel like losing one's way, it in fact produces a far more dynamic and processual view of the research setting (Foster 1990). Further, it shows clearly how research itself is processual, and that in this way issues which may not have been thought of at the outset emerge through the fieldwork, and can rise to prominence.

In summary, the characteristics of ethnographic research are: 'seeing through the eyes of the researched'; a reliance on description; the contextualisation of events within the social system under study; an emphasis on process, both in terms of studying process and the study as process; flexibility in doing research – there are no prescribed frames of reference; and the emergence of theory and concepts through description (Bryman 1988). These combine to provide a way to

come to terms with the meaning, not the frequency, of certain . . .
phenomena in the social world. . . . [Q]ualitative methods represent a
mixture of the rational, serendipitous, and intuitive in which the personal
experiences of the organizational researcher are often key events to be
understood and analyzed as data.

(Van Maanen 1979: 520)

Finally, I would challenge the idea that research methodology should be an
either/or choice. I have used a predominantly qualitative approach but have
also used more structured interview questions associated with a quantitative approach, as well as documentary analysis. Without reference to
quantitative studies, proving the value or relevance of this study would be
difficult. Furthermore, some theoretical developments included in this book
are shaped by models from the literature, some of which are based on
quantitative analyses. Therefore I would advocate a kind of methodological
heterodoxy which draws on different methods in order to obtain a wider
view of the research problem.

REFLEXIVITY AND EMOTION

An important component of qualitative research is reflexivity. Being reflexive
about research and recognising the value of autobiographical references are
two important components that make ethnographic methods rich sources of
data (Letherby 1992; Okeley and Callaway 1992), especially when 'we
consider that the objective of [ethnographic] interpretation is "to bring us
into touch with the lives of strangers", [and that] one of those strangers is
inevitably ourself' (Jeffcut 1991: 13). Issues such as the researcher's emotional engagement with and reactions to the research and the researched are
thus important ingredients in an ethnographic 'story', given that 'accounts
of actual and "messy" research are probably more useful than pristine
prescriptions, for they provide valuable insights into a range of real issues
that researchers face in the field and different ways in which they can be
addressed' (Ram 1992: 32). However, the intellectual and emotional strug-
gles of researchers are frequently ignored or at best relegated to a
'methodological appendix'. David Berg (1988: 214) argues against this
practice, stating that 'the emotional as well as the intellectual consequences
of research involvement need to be described and examined because of the
influence they exert on the development of both theory and method'.

The first emotional issues which many researchers face are fear and
anxiety. It is difficult to practise ethnography before entering the field. As
a novice researcher this meant for me that I was never really sure whether I

was 'doing it right' or not. One of my prevailing fears was of incompetence. Furthermore, I never overcame this fear, and I would feel anxious before any new period of fieldwork. Perhaps 'ethnographer's bladder' (rushing to the toilet to take field notes) should be joined by the 'ethnographer's bowel' (rushing to the toilet to *go to the toilet*)!

Another aspect of this anxiety was my concern about being liked. As Berg (1988) comments, the way research relationships are managed can threaten the research itself, but it goes deeper than this. Being disliked in a work setting could lead to very unpleasant and stressful fieldwork experiences as well as restricted information. As doing fieldwork is such an unsettling experience I found that I needed to make good relationships with people in order to defuse some of the nerves. Thus, during my visits to companies I expended much energy on being 'nice' to people, hoping that they would reciprocate. As Rosen (1991) says, ethnographic fieldwork calls upon the personal and interpersonal resources which we employ in our everyday lives. Our own apprehensions and insecurities may indeed heighten our wanting to be liked in the field, making us amplify our social skills – perhaps being 'over-nice' to people.

A further problem associated with this is the dilemma of whether or not to disagree with or challenge people. During fieldwork there are inevitably times when researchers face sexist, racist or heterosexist remarks. To challenge them can put not only access to, but also my relationships within the field in jeopardy. The rather pathetic strategy with which I learned to deal with these issues was to look sullenly at my shoes (Holliday 1992b). I never actually gained the courage to deal with these issues in a confrontational manner. This feeling of uneasy powerlessness is commonly felt by researchers faced with others' disagreeable opinions:

> By adopting a non-judgmental interviewing mode [the researcher] had to listen, and not respond, to offensive and occasionally sexist remarks; the traditional interviewing stance made her powerless. Our silences and failure to confront these issues made us feel uneasy at times. We had to absorb comments about 'fat' women, 'neurotic' women, unintelligent women, women who were 'a good lay' and so on.
>
> (McKee and O'Brien 1983: 158)

Carol Smart (1984) also found that she was unsure about how to deal with material which she found objectionable, while her interviewees just assumed that she would agree. But her silence, she felt, implied consent and may thus have reinforced views that she found offensive. However, the alternative of challenging these views may sometimes have unforeseen and undesired consequences:

I had also decided [during the course of my fieldwork] that I would find some way to challenge overtly sexist language while remaining conscious of the dubious grounds on which ethnographers can assume the role of 'thought police'. The ambiguities of this stance, however, became evident early in the fieldwork . . . and one early incident led me to tread warily. The upshot of this was that a mildly quizzical comment on a sexist observation set off a brief chain which culminated with a woman manager being hugged and kissed, indeed molested, by a male colleague.

(Filby 1991: 12)

A final but equally large anxiety is over-confidentiality. Within the small firm setting news travels fast. I was often asked what one person said about another. This was more difficult to deal with the closer I was to the respondent as the pressure to tell became even stronger. One example of this problem occurred in my first case study. An employee confided in me that she was leaving the company to take up a better-paid position in a larger factory, and also that after she received her wages at lunchtime she would not be returning to work. Later in the day one of the partners approached me and asked me if the employee concerned was coming back and whether she had got another job. I lied, saying that she had not discussed this with me. Although I felt that it was unfair of the partner to ask me this, I felt guilty that I had deliberately lied to her rather than stating that I could not possibly divulge such information. Ethnographers have to constantly make judgements about when to tell the truth, again since they are acutely aware of their positioning in the research setting (Burgess 1984; Stockport and Kakabadse 1991). All these issues are inevitably made more difficult by exhaustion which is compounded by doing two jobs simultaneously, that is the fieldwork and the actual tasks performed in the process of participation.

FRIENDSHIP

Much of what I have talked about so far seems rather gloomy but there were also many intrinsic satisfactions of conducting the research, one being the friendships which I made. It is worthwhile here to discuss why such 'friendships' evolved. It is easily possible to conduct research without cultivating friendships. However, in every company there were women, and in some cases men, with whom I became friendly, and these people frequently became my key respondents, although I have lost touch with them now. In this case these 'friends' were context-specific. Perhaps I cultivated such relationships in order to ease my transition into the companies and to make my daily life in them more comfortable. Becoming 'friends' with someone to a certain extent resolves the ambiguous and precarious relationship of researcher to key informant and replaces it with something more familiar and less threatening. It must be said that the people in the companies with whom I became friendly are not like my friends outside of the research, they resemble more those colleagues with whom I am friendly within my university.

In each company there was one person with whom I became more friendly than my other co-workers. At the first company the pattern cutter soon became my 'friend'. The work was very boring, so we occupied ourselves with chatting about aspects of our lives both inside and outside of work. In this way the frustration that she felt with work (and the causes of this) became obvious to me. Conversation is something which is seldom mentioned specifically as a data source (Johnson and Aries 1983), yet I found it one of the most valuable aspects of the ethnography. However, a problem here is research ethics. Can conversations be used as 'data' in an unproblematic way? Can it simply be assumed that informants do not discuss issues which they would not wish a researcher to report, or are researchers once again to use their intuition to decide what they can and cannot use? Mike Filby (1991) found that his use of a field notebook made it clear to his co-workers when he was in 'researcher mode', something which they then used tactically, announcing 'Write that down, Mike' at strategic moments in conversations. The deeper one becomes embedded within the research context, the more complex these issues become, as one's identities become blurred.

ACCESS AND FIELD ROLES

Access to small companies inevitably involves some kind of bargain. This is frequently struck using the researcher's 'bargaining cards'. These can be skills or knowledge brought to the study setting – work experience, professional contacts and so on. As Gary Stockport found out, the organisations in his study were more interested in the researcher than the research, in terms of what they could get out of him (Stockport and Kakabadse 1991). Monder Ram (1992) adds to this by documenting his experiences of helping with social security queries, housing issues, passport problems, advising on higher education and even tying turbans while in the field. My principal bargaining card was more straightforward: I was allowed access to study and interview in return for my labour. On the going rate in my case study firms this meant that it cost me approximately £2,500 to buy my interviews and ethnographic data!

No amount of reading and 'desk research' can prepare you for entering the field for the first time. When I arrived at the factory where I began my fieldwork I realised I had no idea about what I would do or how I would explain myself. I met with the partners and started to explain the concept of ethnography to them. They confirmed my worst nightmare by asking: 'Yes, but what will you actually do?' I was at a complete loss. However, this was soon to be resolved when one of the partners suggested 'Would you like to do some pattern cutting?' I leapt at the idea, and so that is what I did for seven weeks whilst undertaking fieldwork in this small company.

This experience produced its own data, of course, and proved to me through experience the notion that

> people in the field will also seek to place or locate the ethnographer within their experience. This is necessary, of course, for them to know how to deal with him or her . . . [and] there may be some mismatch between their expectations of the researcher and his or her intentions . . . . They will try to gauge how far he or she can be trusted, what he or she might be able to offer as an acquaintance or friend, and perhaps how easily he or she could be manipulated or exploited.
>
> (Hammersley and Atkinson 1983: 77–78)

Being an ethnographer calls for a measured amount of performativity, as I was to discover time and again in the field. And of course this impression management is constantly evolving, since 'researchers using the ethnographic approach must appreciate that they are constantly interacting with different types of individuals. Consequently, their strategy for dealing with each person must vary' (Stockport and Kakabadse 1991: 4). The process of managing one's identity as a researcher – and the more complex schizophrenic identity of researcher-cum-employee – is itself very stressful, involving continual renegotiation. Obviously there is a mismatch between such experiences and attempts to devise models of ethnographic field roles (e.g. Adler and Adler 1987).

Initial entry to the field can involve 'learning the job' to be done during the period of fieldwork. Thus, it is possible to be both insider and outsider simultaneously – insider as a new recruit and outsider as a not yet fully fledged member of the organisation. The initial focus of fieldwork is concentrated around learning how to do the task, leaving little time for reflection. Later, when the job is 'learnt' and a position within the firm consolidated, it is possible to take a more detached view of the study setting. Thus, contrary to popular processual models of field relations, I found that my cultural separation from the setting increased rather than decreased over time.

A dimension of impression or identity management is not only that this changes for each individual with whom the researcher comes into contact, but also that it is 'set' to a certain extent through access to the setting. Thus, through my entry to the different companies I was 'given' different roles, which in themselves provided data. For example, at Wellmaid I was a pattern cutter. This meant that I was given a so-called skilled job to do with no prior experience. At FranTech I was given a variety of jobs, from typing and answering the telephone to 'managerial' tasks such as auditing the production schedule and writing procedures for the BS5750. This seemed to have been due to the understaffing at all levels. Furthermore, I was constantly moved around from one job to another, and in this sense empathised with the other women in the company to whom this happened constantly, much to their frustration. At Logos I was given a kind of consultancy role. This was the only company where I did not fit into the existing job structure. I was taken on to write job descriptions, and procedures and work instructions for the BS5750. This led me to believe that Logos had fewer and less intense personnel shortages than the other companies, since I was not absorbed into the existing workforce as I had been in the other two companies. Another aspect of the roles given to me by the companies was a direct effect on the degree of participation versus observation. At the smaller companies there was much emphasis on participation, whereas at Logos I was allowed more observation time. This was because the larger company's owners were interested in the findings of the research whereas the other two companies did not really understand its purpose. Further, there were certain jobs that I wasn't allowed to do at Logos because they were 'beneath me'. Thus, at Logos I was given a 'professional' role by virtue of my qualifications. This was not matched at the other firms, who had no clear understanding of what academic work is about.

Thus, the fieldwork role is to some extent determined by the expectations of those who manage the study settings. It is further set by gender, and thus by respondents' expectations of women's behaviour or status. But the fieldwork role also varies depending on the behaviour of respondents. This adds up to an incredibly complex array of field roles and arduous impression management. What does one do when faced with a group of respondents in the canteen, for example? Which role should be adopted? And how far can roles be taken?

It is often assumed that participant observation is simply a set of practices not affected by the context in which it is carried out. Furthermore, the context may not simply be linked to the study setting but also to the discipline background from which researchers come. For example, ethnographic accounts from anthropology can be naturalistic studies which simply describe the research setting as the observer perceives it. In sociology there is usually more emphasis on explaining and theorising the situation, whereas a management researcher may develop a kind of action research, identifying and attempting to remedy problems as and when they are discovered. I would argue that the nature of small companies forces an interdisciplinary approach. In small firms, production problems cannot be isolated from financial ones, or from the company's culture, or from external contingencies such as labour market conditions and so on.

GENDER AND FIELDWORK

It has been said that women researchers are seen as less threatening by respondents and therefore that they are sometimes able to gain greater access to fieldwork settings.

> The researcher cannot escape the implications of gender: no position of genderless neutrality can be achieved. . . . Common cultural stereotypes of females can work to their advantage in some respects. In so far as women are seen as unthreatening, then they may gain access to settings and information with relative ease. By the same token, however, their gender may limit women's access to particular domains. . . . Male researchers may find it equally difficult to gain access to the world of women, especially in cultures where there is a strong division between the sexes. . . . In male-dominated settings, for instance, women may come up against the male 'fraternity', from which they are excluded; women may also find themselves the object of 'hustling' from male hosts; they may be cast in the role of 'go-fer' runner of errands, or may be adopted as a sort of mascot. . . . In some circumstances it may be easier for females to present themselves as socially acceptable incompetents, in many ways the most favourable role for a participant observer to adopt in the early stages of fieldwork.
>
> (Hammersley and Atkinson 1983: 84–85)

My initial access to the case study firms was much easier than I had anticipated, but how much of this was attributable to gender is difficult to say. However, regarding continuing access my gender sometimes presented further problems. In each company I was assigned to a woman not necessarily connected with the production process. The result of this is that I actually had to work quite hard to ensure that I found out about the production processes in the second two cases. The converse advantage of my position was that I was subsequently able to obtain a wider picture of production through being positioned within its administration and not simply on the shopfloor. This gave me access to information such as the cause of hold-ups or other problems which people on the shopfloor seldom knew.

However, working hard to obtain production data can frequently mean battling against sexist attitudes in companies. For example, in one firm when I asked to interview the production supervisor he declined, saying 'I can't talk to you about production, I'll talk to Peter [another employee], but not to you'. When I asked him why, he explained 'There is a difference between you and Peter; maybe not much but there is a difference'. What I understood from this was that he would not talk to women about production. At another firm I asked the engineering director if he would talk to me about production scheduling. He replied, in a very off-hand manner, 'It's all in my head, duck'. This was after I had plucked up the courage to speak to him as he had completely ignored me since my arrival at the company. At one point I was forced to ask him whether he thought I should move to another office, to which he replied tersely 'I don't care what you do'. On other occasions he deliberately attempted to belittle me in front of other employees. A breakthrough occurred when I was admiring his vintage car. Seeing me taking so much interest he conceded to tell me that he had restored it himself. I replied by telling him about my similar fascination with restoring cars, although they had not been vintage in quite the same sense. This was a turning point. We continued to chat for about ten minutes, and then he said 'Why don't we do that interview tomorrow and get it over with?'

So, while women may be able to gain access through being 'unthreatening' they may be blocked and have to negotiate a status as 'honorary male', for example by forcing greater acknowledgement of other aspects of themselves, such as technical knowledge or skills (McKeganey and Bloor 1991). This may not always be possible, though, as there are many constraints and pitfalls associated with culturally-specific notions of acceptable gender roles. Transgressing these can inhibit access and jeopardise the research.

Lastly there is the issue of male–female power dynamics. I felt more comfortable interviewing women (most of the time) than men, thus I always tried to interview women first, as a kind of ice-breaker. However, no matter how confident I was feeling, conducting interviews with powerful men was very intimidating. Interestingly these men were not always powerful by virtue of their structural power within the organisation, but rather in terms of their aggressive or sexual power. Going into a room alone with a man would prompt innuendoes not only from co-workers but sometimes from the men themselves. Perhaps on their part this was defensive, stemming from their discomfort with the interview situation. This did not, however, do anything to make me feel at ease. But even when power was simply structural I tended to be more compliant and less inquiring with powerful men. I also avoided challenging some of their beliefs or presenting them with questions or information which they would have found disagreeable. Therefore, gender and sexuality have a specific influence on the nature of the information gathered (see also Filby 1991). Sexuality and gender played a part not only in who I interviewed but also the nature of the interviews conducted, and thus the character of the information gathered.

Overall, I found my fieldwork experiences very different from my expectations. I had not expected it to be so arduous or confusing. I feel that this is in part a fault of the literature for not presenting realistic accounts of the fieldwork process. For this reason I have attempted to provide some insights into the chaotic nature of my experiences. In the chapters which follow I present the outcome of my research experiences. This is written in form of case studies and is based on ethnographic, interview and documentary data, from which emergent themes are then theorised.

3   Wellmaid Clothing – all sewn up?

INTRODUCTION

Wellmaid Clothing is a small clothing manufacturer making wax jackets of the sort sold in shooting and fishing shops. The company is managed by its owners who are the three partners – Pearl, Rita and Sue. The firm trades as a limited company although the three partners own all the shares between them. Two of the partners are sisters, whilst the third is a friend. They met at a larger company where they all previously worked making similar jackets. There, Pearl was training manager, Rita works manager and Sue sales manager. Wellmaid was founded in 1986 and became a limited company the following year. At that time the company had no employees. It now has seven full-time employees who work from 8.00am until 4.30pm, five part-time employees (9.00am–3.00pm), and about four outworkers who are called on in busier times. The company has a turnover of £240,000. The order book is usually full, and during very busy periods orders are turned down.

Wellmaid has found a comfortable market niche between the high quality manufacturers such as Barbour and Belstaff, and the low quality jackets that are sold on market stalls. The quality of the material which Wellmaid uses is comparable to that of Belstaff, and indeed Wellmaid buys its fabric from the same supplier. There are only three suppliers for waxed cotton in the country. However, Wellmaid is able to undercut the big manufacturers by making less intricate jackets and selling them at a lower price. Wellmaid jackets are often stocked in shops as a cheaper alternative to the 'famous names'. The company's two largest customers are an agent who takes care of most of their exporting and the owner of a gentlemen's outfitters who also runs a stall at major game fairs. However, no significant proportion of the company's business goes to any one customer, and it has 130 customers in total. Wellmaid exports to Turkey, Italy, Spain,

Scandinavia, Canada, America, Eire, France and Germany. Apart from price they also compete on delivery to a certain extent, as the larger companies who do longer production runs are unable to supply all their styles at every time of the year. Wellmaid quotes a delivery lead time of two weeks although this has been known to rise to ten weeks leading up to the busiest period at Christmas.

The range of products that the company makes includes jackets in about five children's sizes and six adult sizes. The four principal types of coats are blousons, bodywarmers, jacket length (four styles) or full coat length (two styles). Most of the styles are variations on each other rather than being fundamentally different, and as such within the three different lengths many of the pieces are the same. There are usually four different colours available – brown, green, blue and burgundy – although other colours are sometimes used for special orders or experimental sample coats. Other alterations are also made to coats for a particular customer. For example, coats sold to Italy are three inches shorter than those sold domestically as the Italians prefer the cut of a shorter jacket.

LAYOUT

The layout of the factory is shown in Figure 3.1. Immediately to the right of the main entrance is the office space, divided from the rest of the factory by a row of filing cabinets. This incorporates a desk, telephone and filing space. Next to this is the area used for studding, where the two studding machines are located. The next space is for finishing and packing. It is lined with tables. These areas are at the right of the main thoroughfare which leads directly into the cutting room. The cutting room's main feature is a huge table upon which all the pattern cutting takes place and underneath which all the fabric is stored on rolls. The cardboard templates for all of the different patterns hang on hooks on two walls around the room. This room is separated from the others nearer the door by another large table upon which all the quilted lining material is stacked in huge rolls. Underneath, all the scraps of material which may be used at a later date are boxed.

The other wall is mainly taken up by windows which are covered with sun-bleached drapes when the sun shines in order to prevent the waxed fabric from fading. At the far end of the room is a door which leads to the sewing room. This is where the machinists work and is mainly taken up by machines in use with others, not in use, stacked together at the edges of the room. At the end nearest to the door there are two long rails where semi-finished jackets are hung.

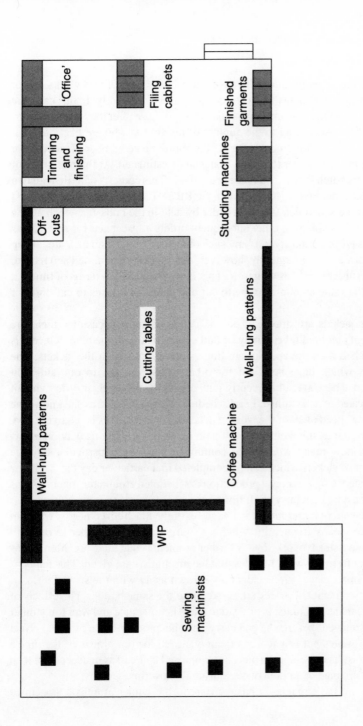

Figure 3.1 Layout of Wellmaid Clothing

SCHEDULING

Orders are taken by Sue, who quotes a delivery time of two weeks except at Christmas when this lead time can increase significantly. In this case Sue phones all of the customers personally to apologise after they have received their order. According to the number of machinists who are likely to be at work over the following two weeks the approximate number of jackets that can be produced over that time span can be estimated. At the beginning of each new batch Rita consults the order book. This consists of a file with two divisions, marked URGENT and CURRENT. Upon choosing the next order to be scheduled (the next order by date in the book for which all the material is available), other subsequent orders are scanned for any jackets of the same size and style. If any such orders are found then they are laid up at the same time. Frequently, however, other jackets are missed and have to be cut subsequently as a one-off. This is very wasteful in terms of time – it takes the same amount of time to cut one jacket as it takes to cut thirty or more.

The jackets are drawn in one at a time on most occasions, therefore different coloured fabrics may be laid up one on top of the other. Once this is finished then the appropriate linings are cut to match the jackets. The jackets which have been cut for other orders are put to one side and labelled. These are subsequently joined with the rest of their order when it is allocated to a machinist. Pearl schedules the machinists, as she knows the working speed of all of the women in her department. This is relatively easy to work out as the women are all paid on piece rate. In this way once it is known how many women are coming to work on a particular day the number of jackets which can be completed in a particular day can easily be calculated. Consequently, production is scheduled around the machinists as they must be kept busy at all times.

The pattern cutter must cater exactly for the machinists' needs, which in practice means frequently switching from one job to another in order to maintain a steady workflow. A further problem is that there are often pieces missing from the work bundles that the machinists are given. This happens when small pieces are accidentally thrown away with the scrap fabric, or when two identical pieces are packed into the same bundle. The effects of this are that a machinist is obliged to leave her machine and wait for another piece to be cut before she can carry on. This practice has a minimal effect on lost wages but is a source of annoyance to the machinists. If the time a machinist has to wait for a piece is recognised by Pearl as unacceptable then wages are paid at an hourly rate during the lost time.

During the company's busiest time in the winter months a system of outworkers, casual labour and overtime is used. Similarly, during the summer months the employees are sometimes put onto 'short time'. One machinist told of overtime hours starting at 5.00am and finishing at 11.00pm. She explained to me that she would not be prepared to do this again as the owners did not fetch the women anything to eat when they went for their tea, so they worked from lunchtime till 11.00pm without food. This has created a lasting grudge about poor treatment of employees.

Ideally, jackets should be made for stock during slack periods, however the company cannot afford to have revenue tied up in finished goods inventory. This is contradictory as it costs the company far more to pay overtime than to process stock, but it is a question of cashflow rather than cost. Problems with cashflow are accentuated by many of Wellmaid's customers paying late. Sue introduced a cash discount for invoices settled within thirty days, which was abused by customers taking the discount without settling within the agreed time.

PROCESS

The production process begins with the arrival at the factory of the waxed cotton fabric. It is then stored underneath the cutting table. Once the order is identified by Rita from the order book, it is written down on a piece of paper and given to Anna, the pattern cutter. Anna resents this as she feels that it is an infringement on her autonomy – she would rather consult the order book herself. There are also times when Rita is not immediately available to write down the next batch in which case the workflow is interrupted until one of the other directors is available to schedule it. Once the batch has been given to the pattern cutter the templates for the jacket are sought out from the many cardboard templates hanging around the walls of the cutting room. As some patterns share identical pieces, collars and channels are kept separately. Other shared pieces are kept on other patterns. In this way it is sometimes necessary to find pieces for one pattern from three different sources instead of cutting a few extra cardboard pieces and having a complete pattern on each hook. This practice also relies on a large degree of specialist knowledge on the part of operators.

Once the pattern is located the cloth is laid out and the pattern is drawn onto it, making sure that the pieces run along the bias of the material. This is done ensuring that the minimum amount of cloth is used for each 'lay'. There are standard ways of laying most of the patterns out although this is sometimes impossible due to material being of different widths or having continuous faults running through it. In the case of non-standard fabric or for some of the more complex jackets where the layout cannot be memorised, the layout of the pattern has to be reinvented each time it is cut. None of these layouts is recorded in any formal fashion. Once the layout has been drawn in then the 'marker' is cut from the rest of the roll. The marker is then laid on top of the required number of fabric layers and used as a template for cutting.

Depending upon how many jackets are laid up at one time the patterns are then cut out using scissors or an electric cutting tool. Generally the jackets can be cut by hand if there are less than five lays in a batch. Batch size ranges from one to sixty of each size in a particular style. Rita and Sue are the only people in the factory who can use the electric knife, therefore if they are not available the lays cannot be cut. If there are many batches in one day where more than five jackets are to be cut then the lays are folded over and left on the table. After two to three hours the table may be full of batches waiting to be cut and therefore work stops until Rita can be persuaded to cut them (Rita frequently becomes involved in other activities which she is reluctant to leave). Once the jackets are cut and the pockets or arm tops are studded with eyelets for ventilation, they are folded together with all the pieces required for production and wrapped together inside the larger pieces.

After each batch of outer jackets is finished the linings for that batch are usually cut. The linings are made from tartan cotton and acrylic and are laid up and cut in the same way as the outer jackets. As the acrylic is thinner than the other fabrics used then this can usually be cut with scissors. The linings are bundled up in the same way and are passed, with the outers, into the machining room.

Once in the machining room the jacket pieces may be distributed immediately amongst the machinists. If the order is not urgent then they are put in boxes and labelled with the style, size and colour of jacket which they are to make up. If there is an 'extra' jacket in the batch then this is put on a shelf with other pieces of the same size/style for future use in a small order. The jacket linings are made up by one woman and sewn into the jacket by another, who also makes up the outer coat. The process of attaching the lining to the outer jacket is called 'bagging out'. Once the linings are completed they are hung on coat hangers in order of size and style.

All the machinists are paid on piece rate and the rates vary from coat to coat. 'Good work' describes coats with many intricacies as the rate is worked out according to the number of machining operations carried out on a particular jacket. The rate for each operation is usually set from the rate for other similar jobs and the time is set by timing Pearl, one of the partners, who is a very experienced machinist and as a partner trusted to set a 'fair' (from the partners' point of view) rate for the operation. However, the rate is to some extent negotiable, and if there are many complaints about the same operation then another machinist is sometimes timed and the money put up accordingly. The partners have been conned before now, however, as Pearl explained:

> We got took for a ride over one coat before by one girl. She kept saying 'It's not enough, it's not enough', and she was the only one on them, and then the minute she finished doing them, she left and then the other girls were earning very good money on them, so we had to slowly bring them down over the years. We do try and be fair, really, about it.

Each woman sews a paper label with her number on it into the lining of the coat she has just finished and also records the coat in a personal record book. Sometimes when a coat is found to be faulty there is no label in it and it can take some time to trace the machinist who made it, if this can be achieved at all. The machinist is supposed to correct her own faults. When a fault is discovered then, rather than Pearl pointing it out she often asks Rita to take it back. In this way Pearl avoids dealing with discipline and Rita is seen as a 'nit-picker' by the machinists. On one occasion I saw Sue find a fault that Rita claimed she could not see. It was Rita who took the jacket back. However, on more than one occasion I saw Pearl repairing a faulty jacket when its machinist could not be traced.

After a machining time of about three-quarters of an hour (which makes the overall production time for each jacket about one woman-hour) the machined coats are finally collected by the 'trimmers', who finish off the jackets by snipping off the last remaining threads of cotton, shining up the jackets with spray wax, putting on the press studs and packing the coats into plastic bags, and subsequently boxes. The trimming operation incorporates the final quality check before dispatch.

The company is very flexible as far as new product introduction is concerned. New products are almost always introduced as a direct result of a customer request. These are usually variations on coats already produced by the company or a competitor. If a coat similar to one produced by another firm is required then the customer may bring in the coat to be dissected by Wellmaid in order to reproduce the pattern. In most other cases a prototype is made up from existing templates. Due to this relatively simple design procedure and the inherent flexibility of the sewing machine coupled with the make-through system a new prototype can be easily produced within two weeks.

QUALITY

The quality system has three stages. The first check is when the fabric enters the factory. The most important aspect of this is checking the waxed cotton as this is the most visible part of the coat. This is also the fabric which tends to have the most quality problems due to the fact that it is a natural material and therefore inevitably has blemishes and non-uniformity in the weave. In theory the waxed cotton is laid on the table and partially unrolled to check for cotton lines and colour faults as soon as it enters the factory. The fabric is also scrunched up and then re-flattened to test the quality of the wax. If this leaves white lines on the fabric it is too dry, so the coats will mark very easily and lack the shine of standard waxed cotton. In practice this process hardly ever happens until the fabric is brought onto the table ready to be laid up. The consequences of this are a stock-out, and if more fabric cannot be delivered quickly then orders are held up and the firm fails to meet its delivery dates. Alternatively, if there is a continuous fault in the roll of fabric and no more can be sourced quickly then the faulty material is used and the pattern is cut around the fault. This process is extremely wasteful especially since the waxed cotton costs about £5 per square metre.

The next quality check is as the cloth is laid up. As each layer is placed on the table it is checked for cotton flaws and so on, including smaller marks. If any are found then the fabric can sometimes be moved around until the fault rests in a blank space and jacket pieces are cut around it. If a fault is found then it is circled with white chalk so that it is more easily seen at the next checking point.

Once the patterns have been cut the pieces are checked individually. This is done by taking each piece at a time and inspecting it. If a fault is spotted, then depending on the severity of the fault it is either automatically failed or shown to Rita for a second opinion. If it is failed the piece must be re-cut. Here again there is a difference between the theory and the practice of the system. In theory the big pieces should always be checked first in order that any small faulty pieces can be re-cut from the larger rejects. However, this system is rarely used and in practice it is the first pieces cut (the pieces which have been drawn in nearest to the edge of the material) that are inspected first. There is also a 'culture' in the cutting room which favours overlooking faults as much as possible, perhaps because re-cutting is a boring task. The consequences of this are that the faults travel much further through the system than is necessary. When I undertook the inspection task I was given the nickname 'Hawkeye' because at first I failed to overlook any faults.

The next stage of checking is performed by the machinists. They scan each piece for cotton faults before they sew it into the main body of the jacket. However, as the machinists are all paid on piece rate (unless there is a hold-up or too little work) they do not devote much time to checking and many faults slip through. Further, it is tempting to ignore the faults they find as stopping work to find a new piece costs them money.

Finally, the finished jackets are thoroughly inspected at the trimming stage before they are packed and dispatched. Here the checkers look for fabric faults, stitching errors and 'shading' (different shades of fabric in the same coat). If there is a stitching fault the machinists have to put it right in their own time, unpaid. Otherwise faults are put right on hourly rate. Even at this stage many faults are put right by unpicking damaged pieces and re-sewing them. Those jackets that cannot be repaired are sold as seconds directly to the public. Even coats which are sold as seconds are of a high standard.

INVENTORY CONTROL

The company uses about a dozen suppliers in total. There are no formal agreements between Wellmaid and its suppliers, only 'mutual trust'. Sue knows that she could get cheaper studs, for example, but she explained: 'If I am happy with a company I will never move from them, if I think their attitude and their service is probably better than anywhere else'. She goes on to say about one supplier: 'I like the company, I've been with them from the word go, and they've trusted us. I like the people there and I get good service and I like the product as well, so I won't change'.

A breakdown of Wellmaid's product cost is: labour 26 percent, materials 47 percent and overheads and profits 27 percent. The company uses a profit margin of between 75 percent and 100 percent depending upon the product and the customer. As materials represent such a large percentage of total costs it is imperative that they are controlled properly.

Delivery of waxed cotton and lining material takes place every two to three weeks. There is no regular agreement, the company simply works out from its orders the amount of fabric required and then phones through an order for that amount. The company only changes suppliers if the quality of the fabric declines. There are only three suppliers of waxed cotton in Britain however, and all the material is finished (waxed) at the same place. The required amount of waxed cotton and lining material usually arrives in batches of about ten and six rolls respectively. The rolls of waxed cotton are fifty metres long and from this about thirty jackets can be cut. Once the waxed cotton and lining arrives at the factory it is placed underneath the cutting table wrapped in a plastic bag. In this way inventory control is visual. An order arrives, the whole rolls underneath the table are counted and subtracted from the number of rolls required to fulfil the order, and any remaining rolls are then ordered if necessary. This system works well unless the material is faulty in which case either more material than usual is used in order to cut around the faults, or alternatively the rolls have to be sent back, leaving the company short of fabric. Lining materials for coats are dealt with in exactly the same way as is the quilted lining fabric for the bodywarmers.

Visual inspection works adequately as long as the quality of incoming materials is checked. Although no real problems arise with the control of whole rolls of material, the control of part rolls is chaotic. The main reason for this is that the fabrics are all in different shades. Faults in the material which are spotted immediately can be re-cut whilst the appropriate roll is still on the table. However, when faults are missed in the initial inspection and only spotted by the machinists as they make up the garment, especially if these garments are being made from work-in-progress inventory, then the roll from which these pieces are cut is replaced under the table. The system here is that a label showing the size and style of the garments cut from the roll is pushed down the end of the cardboard tube at the centre of the roll. However, this system is ineffective for two reasons. Firstly, there are about thirty to forty rolls of material stored underneath the table, which means much searching for the labels. Secondly, because this practice is so ineffectual the label is frequently seen as a waste of time. Thus the label system is not usually implemented, meaning that the piece for re-cut must be visually matched against the stored rolls of material. This practice is extremely time-consuming and requires great skill.

When the waxed cotton offcuts from the patterns include pieces which are large enough to cut other coat pieces from then they are kept in a large box at the corner of the room. This is perhaps the worst aspect of the inventory system. The only pieces of cloth which are visible are those at the top of the box. None of the pieces are marked or labelled in any way and thus the process of matching once again relies on visual inspection. Finally, the material in this box is folded which introduces obvious discoloured lines to the waxed fabric, rendering much of it unusable.

Stocks of fabric consist of waxed cotton in five different colours, 'super-wax' (silicon-coated cotton) in two colours, tartan in two colours, Dress Gordon cotton in one colour, four-ounce and eight-ounce acrylic (each in two colours), and quilted Dress Gordon lining in two colours. Other raw materials stock includes press studs, eyelets for ventilation under coat arms and for drainage for pockets, zips of different sizes for pockets and fronts, cotton and sewing machine needles. All of the stock levels are assessed visually except for an annual stocktake each May.

Apart from these stocks work-in-progress inventory also exists. This consists of part-finished jackets. The first level of this is after the cutting process. The pieces required to make each individual outer jacket for a specific order are bundled together and placed in boxes where they wait for up to a week before being sewn up and bagged out. The linings are put together in bundles of three. These rarely wait before being sewn up and if they do it is in a pile on the floor next to the 'lining girl'. Once these are sewn together they are hung on rails where they wait until the other machinists are ready to bag out their outer jackets. There are also shelves where 'spare' jackets are kept. These are jacket pieces which have been cut but do not form part of an order. The purpose of this is to cut an extra jacket with a large lay of the more popular jackets (as this takes no extra time), then if a subsequent order arrives requiring one of a particular size/style this can be retrieved from the shelf and sewn up to meet the order. This system is also controlled visually. Finally, coats which are finished except for trimming are hung on hooks next to the individual machines, where they remain until they are fetched for their final inspection and trim.

Finished goods stock is practically non-existent for nine months of the year. On the whole, an order which is completed on a particular day is dispatched that day or the next. The only significant number of jackets that are stored in boxes in the attic are the seconds. These are sold annually in a special factory sale that is open to both usual customers and the general public. Soon the company will be opening a small shop at weekends in order to sell-off seconds. For the first time this June the company hopes to produce for stock in order to buffer against the huge demand of the winter months. The stock will consist of the items that take the most time to produce. These are the bodywarmers and the long coats with trims. Attaching the trim to a coat is very time-consuming and can only be done by a few machinists who have sufficient skill to accomplish this neatly. Preference is still with stocking waistcoats, however, as these require relatively small amounts of cloth. The company can therefore afford to stock more of them. Potential for stocking any finished goods is severely limited by cashflow as any stocked items represent tied revenue.

EQUIPMENT/TECHNOLOGY

The level of technology within the factory is very low as Wellmaid is ostensibly a traditional manufacturer. The predominant technology is the sewing machine. Nine of the company's sewing machines are hired at a cost of £3.95 per week and the remaining four machines have been purchased. To buy, industrial sewing machines cost between £450 and £600. The three studding machines are also hired as is the electric fabric cutter. This has been a deliberate policy of low investment although the company is considering purchasing some sewing machines in the near future to replace some of the older rented machines. Another advantage of hiring agreements is that all the maintenance is carried out by the lessor. This means that in the case of a breakdown a repairer can almost always be called out within twenty-four hours. Further, routine maintenance is carried out at regular intervals.

As far as introducing new technology is concerned the company does possess and frequently uses a fax machine and has purchased a computer for use with IT packages for invoicing statements and commission, and later on they hope to introduce a computerised purchase ledger. None of these has been implemented to date, however. Indeed Sue, who is responsible for the introduction of new technology, has conflicting opinions about its use:

> We have got a computer and we will be going computerised, only on invoicing statements, commission, that's all, and then I will introduce purchase ledger, I'll introduce everything on and do it in stages. But I have got a computer. I don't think it's vital, no, because you have to look at the cost of it. Being so small, people keep saying to me you must go computerised, why don't you put your sales ledger on computer? Well, I think if I was computerised totally I would spend a lot of time on there, I would spend a lot of hours a day on there, you know, so I can't see that being cost-effective really. You have to put all the information on to start off with. It would take me a couple of weeks to get everything on there, all the different products and coding, so no, I don't think it's vital.

RECRUITING AND TRAINING

The women who work at the factory are almost always recruited from two sources, the other local, but larger, wax jacket manufacturer or a nearby manufacturer of jeans. Recruiting is sometimes done by placing an advert in the local paper or in the JobCentre, but more usually workers are told to ask around their friends and former colleagues, and most new recruits hear about the job by word of mouth. Thus, on the whole, new recruits are trained machinists. However, there are enormous problems with recruiting and the company often has unfilled vacancies. Rita feels that recruiting is difficult for two reasons. Firstly, there is a high concentration of factories in the areas, as she explained, 'All the surrounding area's got factories. It seems to be a machinist's paradise around here. You can go from one job to the next'. Secondly, she feels that her potential employees have a parochial attitude: 'And if you ask them to travel it's like asking them to come to the ends of the earth to travel just a few hundred yards!'

Many of the machinists complained about the money as an important factor in their discontent. The training wage for new machinists is £2 per hour.

Recruiting is very important at Wellmaid as there is a high turnover of new employees. There is a pattern of employment in that there is a hard core of employees who have been with the company virtually since its inception who seem fairly contented and happy with the work. Then there are the newer recruits, almost all of whom talk of leaving, and indeed many of them do leave. During the six-week period of the fieldwork in the company two employees left and two were taken on. The reason given by the 'transient' employees for their discontent was usually money, although some mentioned the make-through system as a problem. The majority of the 'transient' employees had also been recruited from companies where single machining operations were performed by each machinist. Of course the two aspects are linked so if a machinist is not used to a make-through system then her speed is reduced and as all machinists are on piece rate her wages are consequently low.

None of this is helped by the training system. This is described by Sue:

> They do get Pearl to train them, but they tend to train each other. It's alright Pearl showing them her way, but the girls get their way too. They do tend to sit by different girls that are on them. Most of them are pretty well-trained before they arrive. We have tried taking absolute beginners, and I don't think we've ever finished anyone – they've finished them-selves.

This system does not then appear to be extremely successful. Vera, one of the machinists who has been with the company for over four years, explains the situation best:

> Not a lot of people know how to do the full job and they've always been used to doing very small parts, and they don't like it when they've got to come and do big parts. Then they don't get trained properly. They're left on their own to get on with it which is wrong because some of them haven't done this kind of work before and you don't know what you're going into and you set off wrong, you don't know what you're doing and no one shows you where you're going wrong. It's not good, it could be a lot better. But that's the main reason that they don't stop.

So the problem is that people who have never used a make-through system are rushed without adequate training into making up whole jackets. They are put on a training wage of £2 per hour and discouraged from asking too many questions. Then their work is scrutinised by all three directors. Thus, a new machinist's probationary period is also used by the directors to assert their authority. At the same time, they are being continually pushed to increase their speed. Not surprisingly, new employees quickly become demoralised and demotivated and most leave within their first six weeks. The following two quotes are from people who do exactly the same job; the former has been with the company for about four years and the latter, six months:

> Some of the girls, they do parts here, but a lot of them know how to do the make-through and that's a good thing. I'd find that if I was sitting in a factory just doing bottoms of trousers day in day out all my life I'd feel like I should become a cabbage, useless to anybody. At least here we've got a trade that we know . . . so I could cope with doing this.

> You have to really slave your guts out to get any money in there. It's supposed to be timed. I don't really know how they work it out cos I've never ever seen anybody timed. See, every jacket has obviously got to have a different time as there's more work in some jackets than others. Plus the thing that I didn't like up in there is that you do collar and outer or what they call bagging out . . . where as Westcoats will do one job and one job only so you get timed, and you're picking money up cos you're only doing one job and you just race at it. It's a lot harder here. That's what put me off.

Training in the other areas of pattern cutting and trimming is also very limited. In these departments, however, the effects are less obvious. This appears to be because employees in these departments have less autonomy, as the ratio of employees to owners is far less than in sewing. In the cutting room Anna is theoretically responsible for Lisa, the YTS trainee. It is her job to draw in, lay up, cut out, inspect and put into bundles the coats ready for machining. There are standard ways of laying out the patterns on the cloth, thus the job soon becomes mundane as all the layouts are memorised. The jobs which Anna would like to do are the scheduling and cutting big lays with the electric cutter. She has been waiting to be trained to use the cutter since she was promised that this would happen two years ago. Further Rita will not allow her to schedule her own work and also frequently gives Lisa alternative instructions to those already given her by Anna. Therefore, although there is a low level of training in this department this does not have an effect as very little responsibility is delegated. This is especially strange as Rita often talks about 'grooming' Anna to take over her job as the company grows.

In the trimming department only one of the two women is actually trained to put on the studs although they have both been in the job for over a year. Here, too, it is the owner who does a final check on everything that leaves the factory. When asked about training for her job one of the women in this section explained:

> They tell you a few things, what to look for and things like that. Not really any training. Maybe just for a week really, you know if you want to ask any questions. If you're not sure about anything you just ask. Sue has the last word.

A final problem with training is wastage. Training entails both the cost of materials usage in faulty products, plus the cost of unproductive labour. This level of expense is proportionally very great for a company such as Wellmaid, especially since their material costs are high.

One of the biggest problems that the company faces is in human resources management. The company is always short of machinists for reasons outlined above, but the machinists which the firm employs are frequently absent. In fact there is an extremely high level of absenteeism amongst all employees at the company. This is especially strange as there is no company sick pay. During the six-week fieldwork period there was no day when every employee was at work. This was particularly apparent in the passing or final quality inspection area where two young women were employed. In many cases it appeared that if one woman was present then the other was absent. One of them complained about the unstable workflow, explaining that sometimes there was little to do and subsequently they were being pushed to work hard to get through a large quantity of jackets. However, her outstanding complaint was that the work was very boring:

> To tell you the truth I find the job very boring. As far as I'm concerned a monkey could stand where I stand and do the job that I do. You know I flex my arm. I'm the kind of person that wants something to tax my brain a bit more. Where to me anybody could look over a coat and see that the stitching's too close to the edge or if this needs doing or that needs doing.

A problem here is that there are no other jobs on a similar skill level that these employees can be rotated onto. In a larger factory the very boring jobs are often only performed for one or two days per week and employees are then rotated onto other jobs. This is not possible at Wellmaid due to the small number of operations involved in the production process.

The machinists are also prone to absenteeism. This is more difficult to explain as some of the women who were absent found a degree of satisfaction in their jobs. Some women did have time off due to family illness and so on. However, one woman who was young, quiet, single and the company's most productive machinist was often absent, while other young women who enjoyed active social lives were absent with hangovers. The traditional stereotype of women working for pin money and thus not being as committed or reliable is therefore broken down as both women with and without partners were absent. Further both transient and core workers took time off. There appears to be a strong 'culture of absenteeism' within the firm. The company is trying to resolve this by introducing a quarterly bonus for those who have taken no time off.

There is little or no disciplinary action taken against women who are absent; perhaps this is because trained machinists are so valuable that they must not be dismissed or even upset. However, there was one morning when the pattern cutter was (uncharacteristically) absent and Rita telephoned her and told her to come in at once. This kind of treatment was rare with other employees and was perhaps due to her close relationship with the partners (she was the only employee to describe the firm as a family, emphasising her daughter-to-mother relationship with the partners) and her strong sense of loyalty to the firm. In this instance at least, absenteeism appears inversely linked to loyalty.

CULTURE AND CONTROL

The first aspect of control is evident in recruiting. The selection process aims to recruit women with a particular character or personality and there is much emphasis by the partners on fitting in. Sue explained that 'It's just attitude really. Just attitude, and personality a little bit, because it is such a small area, and they would have to fit in with everyone else'.

However, others in the factory believed that is not really the case as the partners must take whoever they can in order to keep up staff numbers. The second stage of initiation to the control system is that when a new employee starts, her work is inspected by all three partners at regular intervals. This process is very intimidating for the new employee. However, after this initial period control becomes much more haphazard and lax. There is evidence to suggest that one control mechanism is emotional extortion. One woman explained what happened when she attempted to leave to work at a bigger company:

Twice, they haven't stopped me but they gave me a headache about it.

Things like 'They'll be horrible to you, not like here, they won't treat you like I do, you'll miss it, everybody loves you, you're like a daughter to everybody. It's a dead-end job, you don't need any brains', etc. Do you want me to go on? It screws your head up and it makes you confused and you don't know where you're going. And then there's promises, they make you promises. It's bullshit! IT'S BULLSHIT, quote!

Several characteristics of the company's control mechanisms led me to believe that it is essentially governed by a 'family' culture. Firstly, new employees are informed early on of its familistic attributes by Rita. Secondly, a common incident is that when one of the employees does something 'against the rules' Rita is apt to say 'Don't let Sue catch you doing that!' This seems ironic as Sue is perhaps the least likely of the partners to play the stern boss, and tends to avoid disciplinary problems wherever possible. However, Rita uses the threat to signify her disapproval whilst deflecting the act of punishment onto Sue – all the time maintaining actual control through hypothetical intimidation. This aspect gives further weight to the family analogy of control as it echoes the threat 'wait until your father gets home!' (in practice the father is never called upon for reprieval).

Two of the bosses are in fact sisters and this adds to the feeling of a family, albeit one in which there is considerable tension. Interestingly it is the third partner who controls the paperwork and deals with all of the suppliers and customers. Thus, the interface and external workings of the company are a mystery to the other two partners who are left frustrated and even suspicious by their lack of knowledge. This appears to give further credence to the notion of Sue as 'father' especially since it replicates the public/private split found in gender roles within the family. Consequently one employee was able to clearly identify Rita as the mother of the firm:

I'd say in our department – Rita [is the mother], in ours, the one who looks over everybody, and in there, yeah, I'd say Rita out of all of them. She always asks if there's anything wrong, she sorts problems out, and the girls really go to her.

Further, the partners also have different views of the company's culture. Sue tends to see this in terms of the company's image – externally:

I want them to feel secure, and proud of being part of a team . . . rather than being an employee. They do tend to know a lot of the customers . . . I don't know if that's right or wrong. You hear them talking about the customers by their first name as if . . . but that's probably nice, because at a much larger company they're just doing this number of coats . . .

they don't know where they're going. I mean here they know if it's going out to Italy, they know if it's going to Turkey. You know . . . I just want them to feel a bit of pride, and part of a team.

Rita's view represents a more internal or 'atmosphere' view:

I don't know, I just like us being friends, but not over-friendly because you can't run a factory being a family, you know, it's got to be . . . they've got to be there, but not in a way where they're frightened to ask you anything. I just wish they'd come to work. I mean this situation with the machinists at the moment, there's nothing we can do about it.

Pearl is probably most involved with the employees as a peer. She always works as a machinist in the same room, using the same equipment as the other women. She even stays in the same room with the employees as they eat their lunch, something which Rita feels that she is unable to do as the employees may want to 'have a moan behind the boss's back'. Thus Pearl's view of the firm's culture is that:

It's like anywhere else, we're women and some days you get fed up and some days we're on top of the world, if you get a few of you that's fed up then you can get really down, then you can start laughing and it's all sort of gone. But I think a lot of that comes with being a woman anyway, you do get more ups and downs with women anyway than . . . I think the main thing is that they're all happy. I think that is one thing with being small, when they have got something to moan about they can say something.

In summary, Sue's view of the company and its employees is substantially different from Pearl's and Rita's. She is the only partner who sees the employees as a separate entity from herself. Both Rita and Pearl when questioned about their employees' view of the company talked about their relationships with their employees rather than their employees as separate from themselves. These attitudes undoubtedly make power relationships more complex and personal in small companies.

An even more surprising aspect of power and control relationships within the company were the feelings of exploitation felt by members of the firm. In interviews these feelings were very much in evidence and were not limited to employees or indeed felt by all employees, but were also felt by the managers. Some of the employees talked about the long hours that they had put into the company during busy periods but explained that they would not be prepared to do this again as they had not been given thanks for this. One of the passers in the finishing department explained:

There's no [trade] union. There's not a lot you can do here really. You've got a lot of advantages with a large company, where they've got sick pay and that; here you're on your own really. You work and then you get a wage at the end of the week and that's it. There's nothing else involved.

However, another employee, Vera (a machinist) illustrated the lack of regulation:

What I like is, as I say, it's all friendly. You get on well with everybody. And you can do what you want more or less, up to a point. I mean we do have rules but not like what the big places have.

Pearl spoke of an event where they were 'taken for a ride' by a particular machinist over an operation that was over-priced. She also feels very let down by absentees:

They have a few days off, think they like it, think 'Ooh I don't want to go back now for a while' so they stop off longer – a few genuine cases, some are – I think there are ones who just get helped along a little bit. But . . . it's very awkward, very awkward . . . I mean we won't make any money, with girls being out, but it's all you can do when you're really whatsaname, y'know. . . .

Rita's complaint also concerns absenteeism. This is undoubtedly the area where the partners feel most let down:

Now I never was like this, I never lost time. I had three children, I used to have to have to get a minder or someone to come in . . . I used to think more of being an employee than people do today. As far as girls go, I think these are great. You can talk to them. I mean, just think, they're all the same temperament, they're all the same. You know sometimes we think we should we have a bit of a row in here to make it a bit different . . . take Doreen, she was a willing soul, but she was useless on a machine. She was so willing to work, and work all the hours you'd give her . . . you can't win, can you?

Sue's complaint related to a particular event but continues along the same theme:

But we've only ever had one that's left bad really, and I'd written her a letter anyway and she responded to that with her notice; well we decided anyway that I would do that letter, and if it did mean her notice then that would be it. You can only stand so much from people. And some of them tend to treat you . . . they get away with a lot more here than they do at a big company, you know, they come in late, if they want time off they can have time off, if they have to go at three o'clock or two o'clock to the dentist, there's never any question, they go. Wherever I've worked before you've been frightened to ask. You wouldn't ask. You'd book it outside working time. We're very lenient with them here to the point where you just have to draw that fine line between management and employee. And some of them tend to cross that line, and this particular girl did and so I wrote to her.

It is possible that all these feelings of ambiguity and indignation arise from unclear work roles. Nobody in the firm has a job description and no one appears to know exactly who they are responsible to or for. The roles of the partners are also ambivalent, preferring sometimes to be friend and colleague, at other times parent and sometimes manager. Without defined roles or contracts people are left guessing in a purely social context which role they should undertake on any occasion.

STRATEGIC OPERATIONS

The firm is split into three functional areas. These are sewing, cutting and paperwork. One partner is responsible for each area. Other areas, such as training, recruiting and control are supervised jointly or by the partner who is available for the particular task at a convenient time. Managerial meetings are conducted every lunch time and after the employees have left, when the partners huddle together and talk in a whisper about sensitive issues. In theory, with this level of contact communications ought to be very good, but in practice they are not. It has already been stated that there is a good deal of tension between two of the partners who are sisters and third partner. This is almost entirely due to the third partner's secrecy about company accounts and external relations. For example, in many cases customers did not know that the company was a partnership and thus perceived Rita and Pearl as employees in the company. Sue rarely tried to rectify this misconception. The extent of the two sisters' limited knowledge of their suppliers and customers became evident in the interviews. When a question was asked about either of these areas or about finance I was referred to Sue to the extent where neither of the other two partners knew the cost breakdown of their products.

Decisions are never made on the basis of formal rules or procedures. Sue explained that decisions have to be made on initiative as 'every situation is different'. Pearl explained that there are a few ground rules for dealing with who makes a particular decision:

We just talk about them really, if it's a really important thing then the three of us talk about them. If it's something to do with the girls then you might as well just do it off your own head, you know if it's something in your own department, but if it's something really important that warranted all three of us then we all talk about it. You do it if you know it's solely yours or if you know that it wouldn't make any difference to the other partners.

However, Rita obviously feels that it is not as simple as this and feels excluded from important decisions:

We haven't got any rules. That's what I'm saying. We need more talk and co-operation and things like that. Decisions are made without being talked about . . . decisions are made without you knowing. Do you understand what I mean? I knew you did – you've been with us too long! You'll be glad to finish here. I mean you've seen that, over the weeks you've been here, what I'm talking about. Communication isn't as good as I thought it'd be, and I hope it gets better. It's got to get better.

Similar ambiguities and misconceptions exist in the area of communications with employees. All of the partners agree that they are approachable and open to criticism and complaints. Although there is no union in operation within the firm Sue feels that the employees have a spokesperson in Vera:

They don't have a [trade] union, but it wouldn't bother me at all. I mean they've got a spokesperson in Vera . . . but I think Vera probably because she's known Rita for so long. . . . I think she worked with Rita when Rita was just a machinist, you see, and I think she respects Rita, the way she built herself up through [a competitor] into management. But then she's not frightened to say if there's something wrong, or if she thinks there's something wrong – and it just gets sorted out, which is a good thing. It's better that than someone sitting there thinking 'Right, I'm going to leave on Friday' you've got to sort it out. If you can't sort it out, then they can go.

Pearl echoed these sentiments when she was asked if there had ever been any industrial disputes:

No, because girls, if they're not satisfied, they would say. I mean when we've ever said anything that they haven't been happy about, we've talked about it and it's come out but it's never come to the point where they've got nasty about it.

However, although some of the women felt that they were able to complain about some aspects of the company, such as the pay for a particular operation and so on, there were other things which they found very irritating about which they did not complain. For example, when the women arrive at the factory in the morning the doors are rarely open. The machinists in particular like to set up their machines and organise their work before they actually start, thus not being able to enter the factory even when they have arrived early is a source of discontent, particularly as they have to sit on the stairs outside the doors and wait. Many of the machinists complained to me about this but nobody would mention it to the partners. This and other similar incidents suggest that communication is not as good as it is thought to be by the owners.

The aims and objectives of the company also appear somewhat confused. On the whole the company's aims are survival and steady expansion. This of course is what it has achieved so far. However, the reasons why the partners feel that the company should grow are not apparent. There is no formal statement of objectives or business plan. Further, all implicit plans are fairly short term. Rita explained her view:

> It's got to get bigger, it's got to expand, hasn't it? I mean, we owe ourselves that. It's going to get better . . . it's got to. But not much. You've got to do it gradually, haven't you. Cos, I mean you could employ another twenty tomorrow, and then they'd be out of a job. We'd go down, wouldn't we? You've got to do it gradually. It's nice, you know, taking people on, but we can't afford to pay these people's wages. It all depends on orders and all, doesn't it?

Pearl's view of the firm's objectives is equally confused and short term. When she was asked if the company had a statement of objectives she replied:

> Well, a lot depends on your orders, what orders they are. I mean some people like big orders from one firm, but if you want to put all your eggs in one basket and they dump you then your name's no good anywhere else. So you have to keep everybody happy if you can. I don't know really to tell you the truth, you hope for the best, don't you? You've got to hope you grow, it's just at what speed, especially the way the country is now. Cos there's a few problems in the country aren't there at the moment? We've been lucky this year cos we've done more this year at this time than what we normally do. About February and March it goes ever so slack as a rule.

Sue has a clearer idea of what the company needs to achieve but this is basically short term and only seen in terms of a budgeted output and profit:

> The growth has been so small and so slow, because of the lack of investment if you like, that we can only look forward so far, I mean we can only really look forward to the next six months' accounts. I break the year up into the six months and we know what we want to be doing then, workwise, but no, no plans for sort of three years, four years down the road.

Further there is a reluctance on Rita's part to step back or bring in somebody else to manage:

> I think in time we'd do that really but it would take a long long time before we were ready to do that, and anyway if you haven't got it right yourselves what hope has somebody else got?

This may prevent the firm from growing past the point where the present owners are unable to maintain direct control.

SUMMARY

The layout is governed by accommodation. Limited factory space has led to a poor layout design and sometimes cramped working conditions. It has also resulted in a loss of privacy for the owners due to their lack of office space. Poor scheduling is due to lack of knowledge of simple scheduling techniques and lack of time to develop a system. The consequences of this are increased overtime and therefore increased costs and also dissatisfaction of employees through interrupted workflow and pressure to do overtime.

The process design has faults which have not been rectified due to limited time. Processual inertia (doing it this way because it has always been done this way) is also evident. Missing coat pieces interrupt the flow of work and employees are not given sufficient autonomy to control their own work. Pattern templates are stored in an idiosyncratic way which requires a high degree of job knowledge in order to access all parts easily. There is no communication mechanism whereby employees can improve process quality.

The Quality system is *ad hoc*. The most important point here must be the contradiction of encouraging machinists to look for faults whilst on piece rate, with no consequences for their missing them. Further, the culture of ignoring faults in the cutting department allows faulty coat pieces to travel considerably further through the system than they should, ultimately producing substantially more re-work and second quality jackets than should be necessary. However, other reasons for this will be suggested later.

The company is unable to keep sufficient finished goods stock as it cannot afford to have money tied up in inventory. In the long run this incurs increased cost as this must be compensated for by overtime. Poor control of raw materials leads to stock-outs, caused by late quality checks, and increased scrap due to mistreatment of fabric pieces. However, providing the quality of all incoming goods is checked then the system of inspection of whole rolls works well. This is made possible by good relations with suppliers and flexible delivery arrangements. There are no economies of scale to be gained by more regular arrangements.

The low level of technology within the firm reflects the traditional nature of the business. The hire of machinery is inexpensive and regular maintenance by the lessors sustains it as a viable alternative to purchase. The computerisation of company records will probably be an advantage if the time can be found to enter all of the necessary data.

Recruiting is haphazard and performed in an informal way by inexperienced interviewers, and is frequently done by word of mouth. This could be one reason for the so-called transient workforce. This is not helped by the extreme shortage of trained machinists and the large concentration of the sewing industry in the West Midlands area. Training is based on 'sit by Brenda' techniques and is inadequate given the level of skill required for some of the work. This leads to feelings of dissatisfaction amongst some (especially transient) employees. Training is also costly in terms of unproductive labour and materials wastage. Training schemes offered to small businesses by the government do not (at the moment) apply to training of employees. Finally, absenteeism is rife. This may be caused by boring work due to the firm's inability to use techniques such as job rotation owing to the small numbers of employees at each skill level. There is also a culture of absenteeism which may or may not be redressed by the introduction of the bonus scheme proposed by the company for employees who are present for a whole quarter-year. This problem could also be due to the low wages that the company offers. Therefore missing a day's work may provide more benefits than costs.

Management control is organised on a familial basis. Formal control is only evident during the initial introduction of a new employee into the firm, and during recruiting. The owners at times have to negotiate their authority with employees. Discipline and authority are difficult to impose in an all-woman firm where the stress is often placed on empathy, understanding and consideration. However, despite this, little loyalty to the firm is shown by employees and impressions of exploitation are felt by both employees and owners.

The functional areas into which the firm is split are not those traditionally taught in management education, and indeed are specific to the firm. Communications, both between the partners and between them and the employees, are poor even though the partners work alongside, and are in constant contact with, each other and their employees. Strategic aims are not explicit, and are confused and short term.

A final general point was that, throughout the interviews and observation, relationships were always given precedence over tasks. Most of the respondents also mentioned the all-woman firm without prompting. The fact that the company only employed women was seen as favourable for reasons as diverse as being 'trusted by my husband to come to work', to 'nobody swearing', to 'not having to watch what you say'. Whether or not the owners attained lower status, or were attributed less authority because they were women, is difficult to say.

4 Logos Ltd – engineered for success

INTRODUCTION

Logos Engineering employs about fifty people. It has experienced sustained and substantial growth from an initial turnover in 1978 of £228,000 to £3 million in 1991. According to the finance director, further growth of a similar magnitude is not inconceivable within the next decade. The company manufactures process equipment for the oil, water and chemical industries.

Logos started as a subsidiary of a business owned by the father of its current finance director, James Grosvenor. James Grosvenor's father retired in 1978, but Ian Glover, the current sales director, had been running Logos since 1974. At that time the Logos subsidiary employed about six people. James Grosvenor was then working in Belgium, but had stayed in contact with Ian. James's father sold the parent company to a Danish firm. Ian went to Belgium and convinced James to take over Logos. The two partners then contacted Bob Pike and asked him to come in with them in order to provide the technical expertise. Bob had previously worked with Logos's holding company until 1968. As Logos's directors, these three operate an equal partnership, although their actual shareholdings are different.

The formation of Logos coincided with the recession and cutbacks in the oil industry in early 1980s, and therefore business was very unstable during the first few years. In 1986 the directors decided to move the company away from being dependent on sub-contract work and towards more skilled and specialised fabrication. They developed a better quality profile and became a well-recognised name in their field.

A nearby company wanted to get rid of its process technology, so Logos purchased this to start developing its production. This, and the development of licences in the area, was part of a conscious strategy to get away from a dependency on the oil business. Logos wants to become a purely product-based company rather than partially service-based. As such the development of process technology facilitates a move to a more stand-ardised product range, along with a vastly increased potential for the sale of spare and replacement parts.

Other significant events in the company's history include moving prem-ises from an old factory on two floors to a new purpose-built factory in the summer of 1988, and obtaining a BS5750 quality certificate. The major problems which Logos encounters are associated with its jobbing produc-tion methods: no contract is ever the same and therefore high investment and substantial design are required for each new project. In addition, Logos has been wrestling for six months with a plasma welder which is only just beginning to work. It is difficult for a company of this size to sustain this lack of return on investment. Gradual but steady computerisation is also a goal of the company.

LAYOUT

The layout of the factory is shown in Figure 4.1. The factory incorporates a reception area, boardroom and secretarial office area near the main entrance. To the right of this are the offices of the finance and sales directors and opposite them the finance office. To the right of the reception area is the main office. The third (engineering) director has his desk here. This office is also inhabited by four project engineers, the document control and quality assurance managers, the buyer, planning engineer and technical clerk, the sales staff and estimating engineers.

At the far end of this office is the design/drawing office. Although this functions as a department of Logos it is actually a separate company and as far as payment is concerned acts as a separate unit to which designs are sub-contracted. Thus the design office is paid for its services by the job and its management is subsequently responsible for hiring, firing and paying its own employees.

To the side of the office area is the shopfloor and stores area. The shopfloor is divided into areas for work on carbon steels stainless steels, and for testing. At the front of the shopfloor is a cutting area which is also divided into two areas for the different types of steel used. An oxyacetylene cutter is used for carbon steels and a plasma cutter for stainless steels. All welding locations are situated to the rear of the workshop and are sur-rounded by portable screens. There are two large hydraulic winches running either side of the centre of the workshop, which are used to move units around the factory and for any heavy lifting of components.

When Logos first moved to its new premises the existing factory space

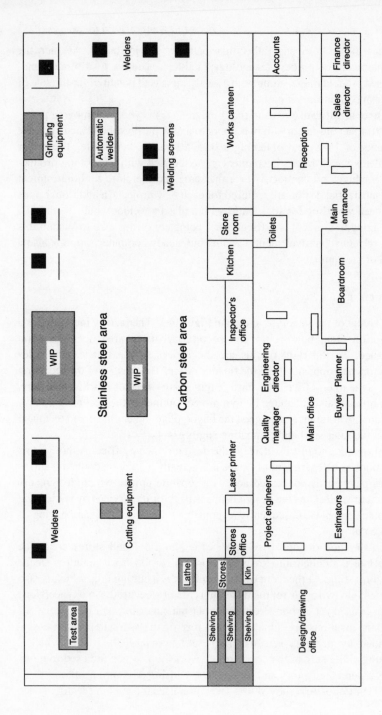

Figure 4.1 Layout of Logos Ltd

consisted of three workshops. This had to be altered to a large workshop and office space. Several late evening meetings were held with all senior staff who had contact with the production department in order to determine the layout. The provisional plans were drawn up by the directors and given to other staff for their suggestions. The comments returned were that the layout of the shopfloor designed by the engineering director was inadequate owing to the considerable waste of space involved. This suggestion was overruled. The consequences of this are that about 70 percent of all shop-floor personnel work in a small area in the back of the workshop whilst much of the space remains empty. Further, it was suggested that the welding equipment be made portable, using a number of power points situated around the workshop. This too was overruled. Many of the welding rigs were wired directly into the mains and thus if a need arises to move them an electrician must be contracted. This is compounded by the extrac-tion ducting which is also fixed to the perimeter of the workshop, and so cannot be moved to welding sites. Large items must thus be moved from one welding station to another.

SCHEDULING

When an order is placed with the company, the design office begins work on the design/drawings as instructed by the technical director. Mike, the quality manager, explained this process:

> Basically Bob is the puppeteer, he pulls everyone's strings . . . in con-junction with Geoff Deane in the design office. . . . They do have a schedule of some sort; they've got a start date and an end date for the contract, and what Bob does, he reviews the contract date, looks at, and gets a general feel for the job. Generally if it's a pressure vessel there's a week-and-a-half's design work, if it's a package there could be up to ten weeks' design, so if you like it's a constant . . . in his mind . . . ebbing . . . of this job coming to the front or being considered and then being put into the back of his mind but never being forgotten, and he just generally communicates with the design office and tries to give them priorities. Then Geoff Deane, the design office manager, tries to schedule in his work book and he will say 'This aspect of the package', say the design calculations, 'will be done by Mr Smith and he will do it by this date', and when it's complete he crosses it out of his work book. Now there's a constant battle going on because at times there's far too much work for the design office to do and you've got an overload situation and then you get the heated rows between Bob and Geoff. Geoff will come back and

say 'Okay, which job do you want me to do?' and I basically haven't got the people to do it. Now that aspect of planning, the man-hours available and scheduling, is non-existent.

As soon as the drawings are finished they are passed to the planning engineer who transfers the drawing information on to a requisition and cutting list. The requisition is then passed to the senior buyer who begins ordering immediately. There are some items on the requisition which the buyer knows through experience should be ordered at a later date (such as nameplates) and these are held back until such a time as the purchaser feels that they are needed.

Job scheduling is done by the technical director who carries out the function of production control, loads the shopfloor and issues work directives. He receives the manufacturing document pack from the planning department which is placed in a pending file from which jobs are issued to the factory. Production is continually monitored by the technical director. He chairs regular production meetings where orders are discussed with the financial director, quality manager, buyer, planning engineer, inspector and a lead hand. From this production meeting minutes are produced. The technical director, having been informed of all priorities by those present at the production meeting and from sales, then advises the priorities of operations to the lead hands and fabricators to ensure that work proceeds in the correct priority. The technical director acts as both production manager and supervisor to ensure that work is completed to schedule. For example, he plans out jobs months in advance, mostly intuitively. Through his role as supervisor he has a good knowledge of the working speed of all of his employees and thus allocates jobs according to individual speed and accuracy. This job is further complicated by the fact that only welders with the required coding (those who have passed a test to say that they are qualified to weld a particular material) can weld certain items. The coding of each welder is known to the technical director which allows him to allocate jobs to the relevant personnel.

It was extremely difficult for me to find out how scheduling worked at Logos. The technical director tried to palm me off several times by saying 'It's all in my head' or 'I do it from experience'. I finally got him to admit that bar graphs were used to help with the calculations. This scheduling system is not always accepted as adequate by some employees. Mike recalled a particular occurrence which he attributed to the growing size of the company and Bob's increasing difficulty in managing all of his functions:

There is no consideration given to [scheduling] at all really and it's similar in production. The job hits the shopfloor, and there is no consideration to how many men are on the shopfloor in work, there's no consideration given to holidays, it's basically a feel for the job again. A classic example of it was that we had a job in [19]89, we had something in the region of two and a half thousand welds to do on pipes, and on average a welder was doing something like three welds a day. We had nine welders so that was twenty-seven welds a day. At the rate we were doing them it would have taken us 100 days and that is five months, but we didn't have that time to weld it. We had something like eleven weeks, and it was only six or seven weeks into production that it was put to Bob 'Look, do you realise we've got all this many welds and you need this many man-hours to do them?' and it didn't register with him until late on in the contract that the man-hours required and the man-hours available didn't add up, so we had to sub-contract the work. But that only compounded the problem because we then had to start looking for somebody who could actually weld these things, and it was Duplex stainless steel so they had to be 100 percent X-rayed, they had to be controlled by our inspection so it just added more work onto another department then, the inspection department. So the production control or the production scheduling, the control's alright, that's really Bob telling people what to do, but the scheduling is not addressed.

When materials become available in the stores the new work is issued to a fabricator who then becomes responsible for its manufacture up to final inspection. Welders or other in-house operatives who are chosen by the technical director to work on the particular job receive their instructions from the fabricator. Each individual fabricator is therefore responsible for ensuring that all work progresses on time. Penalty clauses running to thousands of pounds a day ensure that practically all jobs are completed on time. However, it is commonly felt that false deadlines are set by the directors in order to create a perpetual sense of urgency on the shopfloor. Trevor, the inspector explained:

Every job we do here, they fit in that urgency thing. It comes with the upbringing of these sort of directors, you know they've been tutored into a feeling of urgency behind every job, I think this is always done. You'll have the third week in October what's got to go out, and you know full well it's impossible to do that, but that is left there purposely to create that drive. Well this is typical of small private industry, they've got to make money to live on and all make as much as they can, and this is what drives small industries. I mean you go to British Steel, or you go to a pit or something like that and it's a different way of life, it flows through at just a plod, never with a sense of urgency. . . . Small engineering plants are notorious for this way of life. That's why they all die at fifty-nine! Blown out, you know.

PROCESS

The directors review all enquiries from potential customers prior to the applications engineers and decide if they should put forward a quote or decline the enquiry. This information is then passed by sales to an applications engineer who is responsible for the basic design of the package. Applications engineers assess whether the enquiry falls within the company's normal scope of supply and they also assess the more vague enquiries such as 'A water filter which produces ten thousand gallons of pure water per day from a well'. The design at this stage is simply a matter of calculating the size of the vessels necessary to carry the specified pressure and flow rate and the configuration of packages. Once this has been accomplished then the information is passed to the design engineer who uses a computer to calculate the thicknesses of the vessels needed to withstand the required working conditions. This information is then passed back to an estimation/proposals engineer who calculates the costs involved in each job and puts together a formal quote with the help of the applications engineers. The quote is a very important document as the company is then bound by the price that it shows. This document is also used as a sales device in that it is produced to a very high standard in order to overshadow the quotes produced by other companies. Once the customer accepts the quote and places its order, the contract review procedure comes into play. The purpose of this is to ensure proper order clarification, reconciliation and acknowledgement. It also ensures that all technical changes made to the design throughout production are properly reconciled and documented by the project engineers. When the order is taken a job file is initiated and the order is acknowledged by the document control manager, then the quote and specifications are passed to the design department.

The draughtsperson designs the layout of the vessels and packages and produces large-scale drawings, either on computer or (more commonly) by hand. This shows the dimensions and specifications necessary for fabrication, as controlled by the design and drawing control procedure. The preparation engineer puts together a cutting list for the cutter and a requisition order for the senior buyer, both taken directly from the drawings. Any items which are not in stock (which in this company will be most) are ordered in by the senior buyer at lowest cost. The technical director and the project engineers ensure that materials are ordered at the appropriate times. Further drawings are then compiled detailing individual component parts, and these are given to fabricators who are then responsible for tacking up the sub-assemblies.

All items are ordered from approved vendors who are chosen and assessed under the 'vendor selection and review' procedure. In practice this means that existing vendors are monitored on their quality and delivery performance and new vendors must complete a questionnaire about their quality. Further, inspections are made by the senior buyer and the quality manager of vendors' premises and processes, although at present time constraints mean that less than five visits are made each year from a vendor list of hundreds. If a company fails to fill in the quality assessment form during a set period they are removed from the vendor list. However, vendors are reviewed on an annual basis and have six months to fill in the quality questionnaire. Thus a company who fails to return a questionnaire could still be on the vendor list for up to one year. Furthermore, if there is some delay in the delivery time for an item from an approved vendor, or the company is under pressure to complete a job cheaply, then Logos may source the item from another supplier.

When items are delivered they are subject to the 'goods inwards inspection' procedure. The stores supervisor immediately checks goods for quantity, damage and identification upon their arrival. This inspection is done by a sampling system unless non-conforming materials are discovered, in which case a 100 percent inspection is carried out. Certification of the goods is passed to the technical clerk who passes this back to the stores supervisor if all paperwork conforms to specification. Only then can goods be released from the stores into production.

The design office, project engineers and quality manager issue drawings, design revisions, quality plans, weld procedures and specifications to the planning engineer who puts together a cutting list detailing material specification, quantities, sizes, machining requirements, material source, non-destructible testing and general inspection requirements. This is covered by the 'compilation and use of the manufacturing document pack' and 'welder and welding control' procedures.

Once the cutting list is issued the cutter checks each item to see whether it is in stores. If items are already in stock, or if they are ordered into the stores and the certification has been passed, they are released for cutting. The cutter numbers each item, recording this cast number on the cutting list for future identification. The steel plate is cut to the plan worked out by the planning engineer in order to minimise the amount of steel plate used. The cutter then cuts all pipework detailed on the cutting list, starting with the longest pieces, again in order to keep scrap to a minimum. Offcuts are booked back into the stores.

The fabricators take each sub-assembly from the cutter or from the stores according to their drawings. These are then tacked together following laid-down weld procedures, noting the cast numbers on a job card. They are also responsible for assembling flanged pipework onto a frame upon which all vessels are mounted. Steel plates which are to be made into vessels are rolled between three rollers so that they form a cylindrical shape which can then be welded along one side. Smaller plates are rolled in-house, whilst the thicker plates have to be sent out.

There are also strict guidelines for welders to follow which are detailed in the weld procedures, which specify the type of welding rod to use and how many runs to perform. If too thick a run is put in then the heat necessary to perform the weld can alter the properties of the metal on the edge of the join and make it susceptible to failure. Other weld defects, caused by damp welding rods, insufficient cleaning between weld runs, inadequate purging and so on, may also occur. All welding rods must be kept constantly at 40°C to prevent them from becoming damp. Some are also baked for a number of hours before use at a much higher temperature. All welding rods booked out of the stores during the day must be booked back in at the end of each day if they are not used, and these are subject to the procedure 'storage and control of welding consumables'. All instructions are passed to the welders from fabricators who are, in turn, monitored by lead hands. The lead hands are also fabricators and although they hold a degree of responsibility for timekeeping, materials handling and safety, they have no authority – ultimate responsibility is held by the technical director.

Once assemblies or vessels are welded together, and after they have been inspected, then they are fitted to the skid by the fabricators and the whole package is put together. Finally it is packed and prepared for dispatch according to the procedure 'preparation for dispatch'.

Although procedures are laid out for almost every activity which the company undertakes, these are rarely followed to the letter. Problems arise during quality audits when employees are asked to describe their activities in detail, and these are checked against the written procedure. In theory someone should always notify the quality manager of any discrepancies before an audit. The problem is worsened when the discrepancy is not caused by the job holder but by somebody else who has an input to the procedure. In this case the job holder sometimes attempts to cover for the person causing the discrepancy, feeling that to explain the situation properly would be tale-telling. In this way non-conforming practices remain hidden.

The idea that blame will be attributed to the person not conforming with the system is also the cause of many welding defects going unreported by the inspector. Instead they are put right quietly without notification to any higher authorities. In this way improvements in these systems are not made, as difficulties never come to light. There is some justification for this attitude, however. If a fault is made, for example in welding, then that fault could be an error on the part of the welder, or of the welding equipment, of the lighting in that part of the workshop, or of the general atmospheric conditions there. It may even be that the welder who has made most mistakes has simply performed most of the welds. However, when I sat in on a non-conformity meeting during my fieldwork, it was solely the welder who was attributed the blame without any attempt to investigate the cause.

THE QUALITY SYSTEM

In 1989 Logos obtained a BS5750 quality assurance certificate. Since then the system has been revised and refined. Originally the BS5750 was sought as a method of increasing sales and gaining a better reputation for quality amongst customers. Further it is usual for companies with BS5750 rating to seek orders with similarly rated companies. Thus obtaining the BS5750 was probably necessary in order for the company to remain in business, owing to the high-quality nature of Logos's products.

The sophistication and precision of Logos's products has increased enormously over the last ten years. Quality assurance early in the company's history was almost exclusively done by visual inspection. However, with increasing sophistication has come tighter inspection standards, and now almost all aspects of a job have to be carried out in accordance with prescribed operating and inspection. These are not simply control but also assurance procedures, containing the percentages and methods of inspection required but also detailing aspects such as welding practices. As the company's products began to increase in precision, and therefore required further inspection, much of it was carried out externally. Eventually, however, an employee was fully trained in inspection methods, and with the exception of radiography (an X-ray of the weld identifies any internal faults), he is able to fulfil most inspection requirements.

Quality assurance on the shopfloor is carried out according to strict procedures. The stores books out materials to the fabricators only when the certification for that material has been thoroughly checked by the certification clerk and the material has been established as conforming to the purchase specifications. However, there are sometimes problems here as goods inwards inspection is the jurisdiction of the notoriously understaffed stores. Goods are not checked immediately on arrival, therefore faulty goods cannot always be returned. The stores supervisor always signs for items as prior to inspection. On one occasion a large quantity of plate ordered from British Steel was kept in the stores for some weeks before it was released for use. Only then was it found to be totally different quality steel to its description on the certification. Fortunately, British Steel were prepared to take the material back and replace it. However, there were residual fears that had the material come from a smaller company it could have taken an expensive court case to force the replacement of the material.

Once the material is booked out onto the shopfloor it becomes the responsibility of the fabricators and welders to ensure that its treatment is as specified in the quality plans. This includes adhering to the correct weld procedures. After each operation (fabrication or welding) has been carried out a coloured sticker is placed on the item. This signals that the item is ready to be inspected. A sample of items is inspected by outside inspectors from the British Standards Institution and from Lloyd's Register in order to maintain insurance on the completed products.

I observed an interesting attitude to quality at Logos when, one afternoon, some results from the radiography lab arrived at the inspector's office. As the operatives realised that the results had arrived they stopped work and gathered around the inspector's office. The inspector analysed all the plates in turn, putting the few that showed faults to one side. The operatives started to ask 'Who's made the cock-ups, then?' The atmosphere was quite excitable. Finally, the offending welder was identified and was sent off to repair the job to the sound of light-hearted jeers from his colleagues. This and other similar incidents indicated that a culture of *competition for quality* had somehow evolved on the shopfloor. It was not clear whether or not this culture had been deliberately orchestrated.

Lack of supervisory control was viewed positively by operatives: one young man told me how much he enjoyed working nights on a job that was in danger of being late. His satisfaction arose from the fact that although a specified amount of work was laid down there were no senior staff to supervise. There are two aspects which relate directly to the lack of supervision at Logos which are worthy of discussion here. These are the implications for inspection and the consequences concerning materials handling. Firstly, however, it should be made clear why there is no supervision. Bob Pike, the technical director, had been with the parent company for a number of years. When Logos was set up he was brought in as the third partner because he knew the company and had the necessary technical expertise. At this point Logos was fairly small and thus had no real need for a separate shopfloor supervisor. As the company has grown, however, Bob has found it impossible to relinquish control of the shopfloor and refuses to bring in supervision, feeling that an hourly walk around the shop is sufficient:

I don't believe in this 'I'll find out by your weekly or monthly reports'. I don't believe in that, I want to know what the problem is as it's happening or before it happens, not bloody after. I believe very much in hands-on management. Well basically that's my 'old woman' role, you know, that's the open office progress chase role. But that's either a quality or a failing I've got, I'm not saying that someone else would do it that way. I just have to try and be aware of everything that's going on. I always like to say 'Yes, I know' when somebody tells me [something].

The advantage of this set-up is that shopfloor operatives appreciate the autonomy given them in their work, and respect Bob's technical expertise. However, there are disadvantages too. A lead hand explained:

I mean there's nobody . . . apart from Bob Pike, who has his hourly wander round the shop. I mean in between him coming in and out you get a group of them who stand together who can stand there all day and just look busy when Bob appears. I don't know what spurs it on but all of a sudden they'll have a spate of doing nothing.

Further, because there is an unofficial supervision requirement, the inspector takes on a partial role as supervisor. This leads to a situation when quality control and scheduling are in opposition, i.e. there is a requirement to 'get it right' versus a wish to process the job quickly. The problem at Logos is that although there is no official supervisor, part of the responsibility falls at the feet of the inspector. Thus Trevor performs two opposing roles, and therefore holds some responsibility for each. Inevitably there will sometimes be pressure on him to compromise inspection for the sake of speed:

Inspection here is partly supervisional as well as inspection in a lot of cases because there's no shopfloor management . . . you tend to get responsible for production as well as inspection and quality which is wrong in a way, because before you know where you are you're looking at the pressures of time, which you shouldn't do with inspection. . . . You should be saying 'Well, I'm sorry I can't help you, it's wrong, I shouldn't let that go, it doesn't make any difference about time'. If you've run out of time or whatever, it's up to somebody to override that at the end of the day if they want to, but to me to reject and say it cannot go out. That's what you should be doing, but in a way you get so involved with production that you tend to be a bit, 'Oh, I'd better get this on the wagon to send to such a place', and you know, you're involved in production side of the general running of the place as well.

The second problem is that of materials handling. Because both carbon steels and stainless steels are used at Logos there have to be strict codes on their handling to prevent contamination. Contamination arises when carbon and stainless steels come into contact with each other. Carbon molecules infiltrate the stainless steel and thus cause rust and areas of weakness. There are regular 'lectures' to the shopfloor workers on the importance of keeping these steels separate, and the shopfloor itself is split into two halves for work on each kind of steel. However, although the lectures seem to have the required effect for a while, sooner or later the operatives become complacent. The only semi-formal supervisiors are the three lead hands, who are more experienced and can deal with technical enquiries from inexperienced operatives. One lead hand complained that he held responsibility without authority:

> One bad area we've got is contamination of stainless steel with carbon steel. The big thing is that they walk across stainless sheets, which you're not supposed to do because the carbon dust off grinding picks up on your shoes and leaves it on the plate, and if the plate's left for a couple of months, all of a sudden you've got rusty footprints all across the plate. What a lead hand hasn't got is the authority, if you like, to reprimand somebody. A lead hand isn't a foreman. I can't say 'Get on with what you're doing' sort of thing or do this or do that. I can ask them nicely but I haven't got the authority to make somebody do that.

Mike outlined other materials-handling problems:

> There are lots of things like that, like one of the classics is that . . . you've seen these people putting this acid cleaner on, that is a never-ending saga, it's been going on now for four years. The correct way to use that system is, they're supposed to have a special applicator, it's like a stirrup pump which pressurises a container, then you spray on the acid in a fine mist, and that's the way you apply the product. Now we bought an applicator, and because the operators, instead of when they finish with them washing them out and getting rid of all the traces of acid, they leave the acid in, it rots the machine, it rots the seals at the ends, they can't pressurise it. They come in three weeks later, say 'This has only lasted three weeks – it's useless', and then they revert to applying acid to the vessels with a mop, an ordinary floor mop! That then does not give an even layer of acid, so you've got some areas where you've got thick layers and some areas where the mop doesn't reach, and . . . when you wash it off you've got all these streaks on it. And that's been going on for four years.

He went on to criticise the technical director, to whom he has mentioned this problem several times. He described a further event symptomatic of inadequate direction from shopfloor management:

> I walked out there the other day and they had glass cylinders on a bench at eye height, pressure testing them with eight-bar, which is 150psi. No eye protection to any personnel in the shop; if one of those had shattered they could have blinded somebody. They weren't aware of the danger or anything.

The rest of the company is also governed by the BS5750 quality assurance system. For example, the procedure for purchasing ensures that items are only bought from approved vendors and that orders are expedited in a controlled fashion. Other procedures ensure the smooth and swift passage of documentation through the established system.

INVENTORY CONTROL

The inventory control system at Logos is based loosely around a just-in-time (JIT) system. Once an order is finalised the drawings are completed by the design office. Items are subsequently ordered from the drawings. A complete product may take several months to complete, in which case items which are needed for initial production and those with the longest lead times are ordered first. Subsequent expensive items are ordered after stage payments from customers have been made. Before the designs have been completely finalised the drawings are referred to as 'provisional'. When the items required have a very long lead time they are sometimes ordered from provisional drawings. Examples of such items are flanges which have to be specially machined for each job to exact specifications. Each of the flanges costs around £600. The problem is that as the drawings are only provisional they are sometimes changed, resulting in the obsolescence of the ordered flanges. Often, since items are specially machined, they are of no use to other jobs, thus thousands of pounds' worth of stock lies idle: the whole top floor in the stores is given over to redundant stock.

The actual layout of the stores also seems inefficient. The room has one large entrance at the front of the building and consists mainly of large shelving racks which bow under the weight of metal components. The top shelves are quite high and can be reached only by ladder. However, extremely heavy items are still placed on the higher shelves. Furthermore, very large items cannot be placed in the stores as the entrance is too small and storage space is inadequate. At the beginning of a job when many items are arriving, these have to be stored in the only available space – the main workshop – where they risk contamination.

Another problem is that of welding consumables. The appropriate welding consumables, such as rods, are not marked on the drawings even though the process of working out these requirements is a simple one. Thus, there is no formal requisition for such items. Instead, they are controlled by the stores supervisor who must maintain certain stock levels. The problem is that if the levels he maintains are too high he is reprimanded by the technical director. If, however, the levels are too low then all of the rods can be used in a day if the welders switch to a certain kind of steel. This issue is even more complex as some welding rods must be baked for twenty-four hours before use. Thus if rods have to be ordered, usually on a two-day lead time, and then baked, there is a three-day delay before they can be used. All consumables are ordered by the stores supervisor. Visual systems (how many are left in the box) are used for small nuts, bolts and rivets. Larger boltage is ordered according to the drawings.

On the whole the stores is understaffed, with only one person performing all duties. He finds that he needs to come to work early and leave late in order to cope with his usual workload. He has asked for help but as yet this has not materialised. The buyer has overseeing responsibilities for the stores but he is still learning to cope with his own job and is not motivated to get involved with the stores, so he has little involvement. There is an annual stocktake which necessitates the stores supervisor working Sundays. However, the planning engineer has a tendency to remove spare stocked items unrecorded, which soon renders the stock list obsolete.

Work in progress consists of part-finished pipework or other components which will become part of a final package. They are usually stored on wooden pallets or fixed onto the framework on the shopfloor. The control of this simply involves ensuring that all cast numbers are correct so that these items will fit into their appropriate slot on the package, and making sure that all materials-handling considerations are borne in mind.

EQUIPMENT/TECHNOLOGY

The level of technology at Logos is very high. Although their products are simply constructed by welding together various pieces of metal, the kinds of metals used are very highly developed. For example, Duplex steel takes a certain amount of skill to weld. Further, the welding technology is sophisticated and the company is prepared to take a gamble when investing in new capital equipment if future gain is likely:

There's an ongoing programme at the moment on that welding lathe outside, to try and get more and more towards automatic welding, you know. We've spent forty thousand quid on that this year and we've not seen any results from it yet. But the light is at the end of the tunnel now, we are starting to get the results we want. So yeah, we are continuing to try and improve our production process.

(Bob)

The company is obviously in favour of investment in new equipment. However, there were complaints on the shopfloor about grinding weld preparations involving, for example, grinding a 45° angle onto the edge of a pipe or plate. Often this had to be done manually, creating a lot of unpleasant dust. Bob's view on this subject is as follows:

I've been looking at a machine that will do some weld preps but it doesn't fit the bill. That's one side of the coin; the other side of the coin is that our lads have got such an easy life, they've been mollycoddled so much and they work in such a nice factory they don't want to do unpleasant jobs. And whereas in other companies grinding is considered a day-to-day job, because it's one of the less desirable jobs . . . and of course if you can make it better and easier you want to do that. I've been looking at a machine which costs £18,000, £20,000, but it's too limited. It would only do probably 40 percent of the weld preps we have to do, so it just doesn't justify it.

It is almost exclusively Bob's responsibility to find new equipment for the shopfloor. He does this mainly by searching through trade magazines, although he feels he cannot do this during work hours as it would be seen as leisure not work by employees. However, his attitude to computers is odd given his engineering background. When asked about computerised scheduling he explained to me that he needs experience to do his job, not some 'fancy computer'. He is, however, strongly in favour of computerisation in the offices.

Computers are used in design calculations and production of drawings. All the accounts are computerised, and PCs in the main office run word-processing, CAD and database programs. Further, standard formats have been developed for paperwork such as quality procedures, quotations and other forms, as well as programs for tracking paperwork as it passes through the factory. The quotations are put together impressively with large, clear typefaces, and CAD drawings and calculations read into the text. The employee who has responsibility for putting the quotes together has his own PC and laser printer at home, purchased for him by the company. There has been investigation into the possibility of computerising the stores, but it is felt that the memory needed to store all the required details would make the cost of such a system prohibitive.

There is also a fairly high degree of technology in use during inspection. The inspection equipment includes alcrometers (for measuring the thickness of paint) and a helium sniffer for leak-testing of vessels. The alcrometer is an important piece of testing equipment, because if too much paint is applied in a certain area and it thus fails to dry, then as the next layer is applied solvents from the first layer are still evaporating, and thus causing the top layers to 'pickle'. If too little paint is applied then twenty years in the North Sea may wear down the paint sufficiently to cause corrosion.

Although Logos is a relatively small company it does undertake development work. For example, at the present time one employee is researching a quick-release mechanism for the top of a pressure vessel. The engineer responsible for this design work was a young man from Hong Kong, and during my interview with him some interesting things came to light. I asked him to talk about the differences between working in Hong Kong and England:

> I think that in Western companies, the people, they tend to work independently. For example, if your boss gives you a job you have to solve it independently or solve it yourself, it is hard for you to ask anybody for help, for some reason. But in Hong Kong they try to solve the problem in a group rather than just one person.

I feel that as Logos is the only company where Eric has worked in Britain then this comment is perhaps more relevant to small firms than British firms. I thought about the people he could go to at Logos if he had a problem. There was no one else in his area of design. However, Logos have at least partly solved this problem by sponsoring Eric to do a part-time PhD at a nearby university. Many aspects of his job and his PhD overlap. Furthermore, if Logos were to go to the university directly and ask for information they would have to pay a fairly substantial fee. By sponsoring Eric they have access to all this information in exchange for his PhD registration fees. This was a very good way of overcoming the problem of technological isolation which many small companies experience.

RECRUITING AND TRAINING

Recruiting at Logos tends to become more informal as the status of the position decreases. However, even for positions further up the hierarchy, recruiting does not adhere to any formal procedure. At one time during my fieldwork the technical director was trying to take on a new fitter. Bob sat at his desk and asked if anyone knew a fitter who was looking for work. The buyer, Vic, said that he did, so Bob asked him whether he thought he was any good. Vic replied that he thought he was very conscientious, so Bob asked where he lived. Vic told him that his friend lived locally so Bob asked Vic for the man's phone number. The second incident was when I suggested incorporating a formal recruiting procedure into the BS5750 system. The idea was rejected as being 'the right thing to do but impossible to carry out'. Furthermore, several members of the company were related to each other in some way which suggests a practice of recruiting informally. John, a labourer, explained how he came to be working in the factory:

> Originally I'm from Liverpool, but I came to live down here cos me girlfriend is from [the local town]. Her mum is Christine who works in accounts. I've got a little boy and she's due to have another baby anytime now, so I stayed down here, decided to try and get a bit of work down here. I've been here ever since. Basically I just came to do that bit of landscaping the garden, cos I used to be a landscape gardener.

Informal recruiting is seen as a good thing almost universally. In this way it is felt that company members would not put their reputations at stake by recommending someone who would not be entirely conscientious. Furthermore, the new recruit will feel gratitude to the person who recommended them and thus work harder in order for that person to feel assured that they have done the right thing.

Even if jobs are advertised in the press the actual interview and appointment procedure is a little amateurish. I asked Vic about the recruitment procedure for taking on a new stores supervisor, as this had happened within the last six months:

> When the stores supervisor was recruited I was asked to interview the stores supervisor, he couldn't make it here until about quarter to five in the evening and when the guy turned up I went to show him round and tell him what the job was, and he said 'I've done all this' and I said 'Well okay, fine, we'll just go back in the boardroom and have a bit of a chat and try and get to know each other' and as he walked out he said 'See you on Monday', and I said 'Sorry?' He said 'Well, I start on Monday'. I said 'You start?' He said 'Yeah, I got a letter this morning from the directors saying that they'd already employed me'. Now I'm supposed to be his boss. It's a good job that there wasn't a total clash of personalities because it could have been devastating for the stores if there had.

In a similar vein to many aspects of work life at Logos, a pretence was made to involve staff members in the recruitment of their colleagues and subordinates. However, the real choice was made by the directors who failed to even inform Vic that his new colleague had been taken on. This procedure is becoming less adequate as the company grows as it is only people in a certain area who understand the particular skills which are required. Further, the people responsible for hiring sometimes have little or no understanding of what the job actually entails, thus people who perform well in interview situations but are perhaps not the best suited candidates for the job are taken on.

A rather lengthy anecdote from Mike is worth recalling here because it tells the whole story of how and why a new employee was recruited, and also indicates some of the consequences of this:

> What annoyed me when Dean left was their attitude that 'We can get another buyer tomorrow, they're two a penny'. You can get in a buyer who can get you pickled eggs and sweets, but you can't get buyers that are technically aware. He was totally ignored you see, especially by Ian Glover, because he always thinks it's a personal attack on him [to leave], but you're going to a better job. Instead of saying to Dean Murray 'Yes, we'll give you a company car' it cost them over four years . . . even if they'd given him £5,000 worth of benefits they would have saved Bill Morris's salary, and a lot more, basically two-and-a-half people do what Dean does. And the chaos that occurred . . . I mean the buying is not as efficient as it used to be. . . . Now I'm not saying that is Vic's fault, he's not a buyer, he was never a buyer. . . . But Jim Grosvenor decided they could cope with that and now it's an embarrassment to them and I always, if I've got the opportunity, remind them of it.

A further aspect of the inadequacy of recruiting at Logos is their attitude towards taking on women. Women are not considered at all for technical positions. This is of course illegal, but is seen as justified by the company's directors. James Grosvenor had no qualms about explaining this policy to me:

> In specialist engineering . . . there's no substitute for being . . . I don't know what it is . . . it's just the way we're made chemically, whatever it is . . . but we see it every time we come across it. . . . You're not going to like this . . . but the simple strength of a beam or the strength of materials is something that . . . the way materials operate, the way engines work, the way engineering comes together as a product . . . it's a masculine thing. It's just one of those things, it's not feminine . . . it's

chunky, it's dirty, it's greasy . . . you very rarely come across women engineers. If you ask Bob he'll say he's never met a good woman engineer. There is always a difference in concept and view that you know, the hairy-arsed engineers . . . I mean you don't get women being scrap merchants' sons who end up as engineers, do you? . . . So, well we haven't really looked at that and I must admit I suppose that we would be guilty of discrimination in that we would tend to disregard a woman applicant for an engineering position.

Women employees are also well aware of this attitude. I asked Judy, the document control manager, about her hopes for promotion:

I don't believe I'd be allowed to move to a more senior position within this company because I don't think women are particularly viewed as worth employing in engineering. That is the opinion of our technical director. That's one of the things that I feel strongly about.

Furthermore, the inequality does not simply stop here. Judy is paid £4,000 per annum less than her male counterparts. When I asked the finance director about this point he replied that she was paid top rate for a 'girl in [this city]'. Judy was in fact paid the same salary as the company's secretary. It is possible that in smaller companies where very few managers exist on the same hierarchical level, women may be compared in terms of status with other women rather than other managers. Judy is viewed as a highly valuable employee and as such is paid a 'high wage' . . . for a woman.

Training at Logos is basically split into two categories, shopfloor and staff training. Shopfloor employees are trained by their peers but also by the local branch of what was the Engineering Industry Training Board. This organisation monitors apprentices through their college and on-the-job training. It also makes sure that new apprentices carry out new operations in order to constantly improve their skills. Apprentices keep a logbook of all the tasks they have carried out. On the whole the standard of shopfloor training is regarded as good, if a little frightening at first:

It's very good, if you get with a good bloke who's willing to tell you what he's learnt, then it's okay, but there's nobody on here who if you say 'Can you help me do this?' they'll say 'Oh, it's dead easy, you ought to be able to do that'. They don't do that, they actually show you how to do it.

However, training in the offices is not as rigorous. Whilst visiting the company I was lucky enough to observe the introduction of a new estimator.

There is a BS5750 procedure for the induction training of new employees. None of the actions detailed in this procedure were carried out to train the estimator. On his first day he simply sat at a desk reading Logos's quality manual. On the second day he began putting together a full quotation. The first quotations he did were small ones, and the idea was that he would work up to the larger ones. However, the other estimator was working very hard in order to keep up with his own job and was given no extra time to train his new colleague. Frank, the new estimator, had previously performed a similar function but, coming from a larger company, had narrower experience involving more standardised components than those used at Logos. Thus he required at least some retraining to do his new job. Frank had also been unemployed for some months and was terrified of losing his new job. At the same time he was worried about disturbing John, the company's existing estimator, as he was kept extremely busy.

Another account of initial training, by Vic, was also fairly disparaging:

I had a three-hour turnover when I came here, that was all I had. It wasn't even induction training . . . I wasn't shown the system or anything, I was expected to know it. I mean they knew full well from my background that I was not an engineering buyer. I don't think anybody else realised, because the minute you walk in [it's] 'Oh, we've got a problem with this job and can you ring these people?', and you haven't got a clue where to start. So I came in on the Monday morning and sat at a desk with things in the tray which weren't finished that I knew nothing about but was expected to know about. Dean had invented the purchasing system. I knew purchasing systems but I'd never used one like he'd done. They wouldn't let me change the system. I got the old 'That system works'. I would've changed a lot of things. I would've changed the purchasing role for a kick-off.

Even though Vic was told not to change any aspects of his job when he was first recruited, many jobs within the company have been personally built up by the individuals who first took them over. The way that jobs have evolved is that employees take on a task until they can do it well, and then they take on something else to fill the time. People take on jobs until they can no longer cope with any more work – in other words filling their personal capacity. However, this means that some employees perform many more functions than others, according to their ability, and this does cause some friction. It also makes comparison of jobs at similar levels in terms of status and value very difficult.

On-going training appeared to be slightly better. A file of various relevant training courses was kept in the personnel records along with the training record of each individual employee. Money had also recently been made available to improve the training of existing employees. This action is primarily to satisfy Section 4 of BS5750 on training.

Finally, one aspect which struck me as odd during my fieldwork period was a statement by one of the directors about a young project engineer, Ian: 'I mean technically he's a little weak but he's under Bob, and Bob will be bringing him on as someone who he can delegate overall responsibilities to'. Ian has already completed eight years of training from apprentice to project engineer. He was taken off the shopfloor and brought into the office as a project engineer. What is strange about this is that Ian is young and has few formal qualifications. He is also extremely traditional in his attitude. In my opinion there are other project engineers, more capable both intellectually and socially, who would make better managers. I feel that the reason that Ian has been chosen is that he resembles the present engineering director in background and has adopted many of his attitudes. What is surprising is that the other directors do not consider that a perfect clone of Bob would not perhaps be the best choice for his successor, even though they recognise some of the problems which Bob's character already creates, such as inability to delegate.

But on closer inspection there may be reasons for this as Jim Grosvenor felt that, 'the trouble with graduates is that you give them a couple of years and the money which they can get elsewhere is totally out of proportion to what we can give them'. There is also an awareness that training employees where the end result is a recognisable qualification may make their skills transferable. There is thus a reluctance to train certain employees, or to provide training for particular functions, in case these employees then take their skills elsewhere.

CULTURE AND CONTROL

To examine the issue of control it is certainly necessary to look at the evolution of relationships within the company. One respondent gave me a particularly dramatic account of this:

> When it was the eight of us, there was the three directors and five young lads. I'm the last of them, I'm the sole survivor of the original five, and we were all young, all about the same age, and we were all trainees but we all, if you like, had abilities to learn, and we were all self-taught, nobody here gave us any training. But we all had that same attitude, and every one of us got on, and if they weren't any good they didn't survive, but out of it all came a strong team.

He went on to explain how the directors had done well to gather an unqualified but capable and fairly cheap team around them. However, because of the high turnover of new members, the team remained discrete without the integration of other recruits:

You see . . . when we were a young team and we were sort of poor . . . we were always promised jam tomorrow . . . I'll give you a story. I was earning about £8,000 a year and a local company phoned me and said 'Do you want a job? We'll give you £14,000 a year', and I accepted and everything. I accepted just before Christmas. I . . . said 'Look, Jim, I've been approached by another company, they've offered me a job and they've offered me this much money'. And he fell through the floor, and went on a massive exercise of trying to persuade me to stay, and they succeeded, he made a play to my sentiments . . . you know, we had a Christmas night out and I was surrounded by them all, all night trying to get me drunk and make me feel guilty leaving them in the lurch and one of the things was that me and Dean Murray, the other buyer, we were like brothers, and there was myself, Dean Murray and Jim Grosvenor who were all together and talking about our ambitions, and Jim was saying 'Who knows, if we're successful you'll become successful, you'll have directorships and shares' and all this, you see. . . . I mean the ironic thing was that we knew that Logos was going to be successful because we were committed to it. We knew that we had it in our destiny to be able to make Logos successful, but you see what's happened is . . . we've become very disgruntled because . . . what happened was a gap grew, we were still going along this trench at the bottom and slowly Jim Grosvenor and that were climbing up out of the trench and walking on the top. And the following year Dean went in to see them and he asked 'When are we going to see the fruition of these promises?' and they just said 'Well, we feel that we're giving you the right rate for the job, it's what everyone else gets in the area', so they basically admitted, then, that they were never going to give us anything. . . . When Dean Murray left I almost went with him because it was like losing my right arm. You see what they were afraid of was giving in to Dean over that would mean that it would have a knock-on effect, I'd have to have it, you see they missed a crucial step in the company's development . . . as they grew out of the trench and left us walking along the bottom, what they should have done was split half the people walking along the bottom and said 'Right, you come up here to this level and become senior managers'. They still have the majority on the bottom, they should have created a third tier, instead they just had a bottom tier and a top tier with huge columns in between, well that's unstable . . . twelve months ago the situation was worse than it is now because what's happened is they've climbed back down a bit. They've had to come back down a bit because we were treated like . . . bottom of the trench and we just stuck there and said 'Well, okay, if that's how you're treating us' . . . and we just passed everything up, and they said 'Hang on, what's going on here'. So they've changed tactics actually. They're not as open as they used to be, we used to know what every penny was spent on, but now everything's hidden away, there's lots of things we don't know . . . well no, we know everything that goes on, because there's somebody in this company who knows everything and it's passed on from one to the other, we know things . . . turn the tape off!

Logos has thus gone from a tightly-knit team which needed very little direction to the point where employees were so disgruntled that they required almost constant supervision, until a compromise had been forced. Promises were made in the early years which have never been honoured, and this has caused some employees to leave. Emotional bribery is used as a form of control, and guilt is used to persuade employees not to leave. Employees have developed their own informal 'resistance' in the form of strategies for dealing with iniquities. Further, they have built their own channels for the dissemination of the information which they require.

Another aspect of Mike's account is his discomfort with the growth of the company. The analogies he uses to describe the company in its early stages are very positive and there was apparently a very close working relationship between him and his colleagues at this point. He obviously views newcomers in a negative light. This is very interesting as there is evidence to suggest that he and other long-serving colleagues are blocking newcomers from joining the 'core group'. Conversations with staff were peppered with familial analogies, including accounts from those who feel part of that family and those who do not. For example, Alan said:

There's been quite a few that have come and gone. Well you've got the likes of . . . well the old campaigners like Judy and Stan and Mike, Mike Jones, and they've got their own . . . well they're like a little family unit aren't they? All the other latecomers are . . . well it's difficult to get in you know. . . . It's difficult to get under the skin.

One final point which I feel is of particular interest in Mike's account is his assertion that the company would grow because he could make it grow. Perhaps this is another reason for his staying with the company. From the organisation studies literature it would seem that few employees actually feel that what they do has much impact on the company for which they work.

It would be wrong to suggest in any way that all employees are dissatisfied, however. Many of the shopfloor operatives expressed great pleasure at working for Logos. One of the fitters said: 'With a small company everybody knows each other, it's like tightly knit, isn't it? That's why we don't need foremen on our backs – because everybody can trust each other to do the work'. And this is a recurrent theme on the shopfloor, that satisfaction is gained through autonomy. Indeed there would probably be great difficulty in introducing a supervisor as any kind of higher authority would almost certainly be resented.

Andy's statement about trust is also part of a wider theme. It seems to link into the 'culture of quality' discussed earlier. Many shopfloor employees expressed pride at being involved in the construction of elaborate products. This was enhanced by scores of photographs of completed products along with a selection of their creators, which line the walls of the offices and shopfloor, and there are certainly management practices which encourage this kind of feeling:

> We have do's like the Christmas dance and that, and a disco, once a year, plus Jim Grosvenor took us up [a local leisure centre] on the jet skis and all that, and got a bus for us straight after work and bought the drinks. I mean you don't get that with a big company, do you? So they look after us. Plus we've got all the perks – we've got a pension going for us and we're in BUPA.

Finally, when asked to list the major events in the company's history, almost all employees cited moving to larger premises and achieving the BS5750. It seemed unusual to achieve such unity of opinion even in such a small company, and therefore I would conclude that not only is the BS5750 important externally to customers of Logos, but it is also at least partly a determinant of the company's culture.

Of course, this is but one aspect of culture and in order to examine its relation to control in more detail it is necessary to link some of the preceding data to wider issues. It is my feeling that the leadership of the company is based around patriarchal and paternal management styles. The paternalism is obvious in the ideas of benevolence which underpin events such as the jet-skiing and the Christmas party. However, this has been taken further in the form of the company's purchase of a caravan in North Wales which employees can book free of charge. Finally, a quote from James Grosvenor summarises this attitude:

I would like my employees to enjoy working here, I want them to feel that it's a better place to work than anywhere else. Happy, healthy little employees, with smiles on their faces . . . I think a trade union is a sign of bad management. We've never had unions, and nor has my father ever had unions even when he employed three or four hundred people. I think one man who came along and tried to start a union was fired because of that, because really they just create animosity. If anyone has problems they can talk to me, Bob or Ian.

Again the company's attitude to trade unions reflects an autocratic patriarchal style. Another example, already referred to, is the practice of pretending to involve employees in the decision-making process and then ignoring their input.

As far as the employees are concerned this attitude is resented to a much higher degree by those working in the offices than those on the shopfloor, and this is probably because they have less autonomy. This is highlighted by Bob's assertion that he likes to find out what is happening before it has actually happened. This implies that he is constantly asking his employees for information rather than waiting for it to be given. Furthermore, the tight control in the offices is exaggerated by its lack on the shopfloor. Thus there is in evidence a certain amount of conflict between shopfloor and office personnel. A description of the office atmosphere is given by John:

I don't like the working atmosphere in the office, everybody's quiet and very . . . intimidated. I mean I love a good laugh, but I've got to the point now where I just don't put my head up, I just get on with it . . . and I just don't think there's any need for it, you can do just as good a job – probably a better job – if your morale's a little bit higher and you're allowed to use your imagination. Okay, if you're busy then you just get stuck in, but there are odd times when you just want to come in and talk about the boxing on Saturday night. But Bob Pike is looking over your shoulder to see if . . . and everybody seems to be the same. They just keep their heads down and don't say anything, there's no banter. . . . It's certainly not a very nice atmosphere.

This is further compounded by the fact that this kind of discipline certainly applies more to newer employees than to established ones and also more to women than to men. For example, some of the men who have been with the company for a long time are allowed to talk for over twenty minutes about their social lives or their children and so on, yet if the same conversation is held by the secretaries then they would be told off within minutes for 'gossiping'.

Logos is generally a more unpleasant place for women to work than for men. The walls are adorned with very explicit calendars of naked women. Of course, there are women in the company who do not find this offensive, but there are also those who do. One young woman told me that she once stuck a 'Confidential' sticker over part of a calendar. When the calendar's owner saw this he became very angry and shouted at her for defacing his personal property. Furthermore, sexual harassment is fairly common and 'being cheeky' back is not tolerated. A woman who used this strategy was labelled 'cocky' by the men.

STRATEGIC OPERATIONS

The firm is controlled by three directors who have split the functional areas between them. James Grosvenor manages finance and training, and holds overall responsibility for the BS5750. Ian Glover manages sales and estimating, and Bob Pike fulfils the roles of production manager and supervisor, and is responsible for all things technical. The two other managers, both under James Grosvenor, are Judy, the document control manager and Mike, the quality manager. All other employees who perform an administrative role are given the title 'Senior' before their job title, although these are by no means equivalent in terms of status or pay.

There is a fair amount of tension between the directors. Sometimes this is referred to by other employees in terms of class differences. James and Ian are both upper-middle class whilst Bob would almost certainly not identify as such. Bob explained to me how the friction has become managed:

> [Director's meetings are held] when we feel we can talk to one another instead of . . . (laughs). It depends whatever mood one or three of us are in and whether we're hating one another or loving one another, or whether we want to talk, or we don't want to talk. . . . Well, we're all human beings, you have to sort of find when your body rhythms are all in a positive direction rather than a negative direction, because if they're in a negative direction we just end up falling out and you get nowhere . . . at one time we used to have regular meetings, and if you were all in the wrong mood . . . we were ready to close the company down. . . . So now we're a bit more mature and a bit more water's gone under the bridge and we sort of ride it now. We're totally different characters, totally different characters. Some people say that's the reason we've been successful, it might also be the reason that we haven't been as successful as we could, who knows?

Communication within the company is variable. On the whole it is felt in the offices that those on the shopfloor are better informed. Mike talked about how the growth of the company has adversely affected communication in the office:

> Now as the company's grown and as this office has grown, I mean it was, when there was eight of us in that office four or five years ago, every person in that office knew what everyone else was doing, what they were working on; there was a lot of interface and discussion. Now what's happened with the expansion of that office is that there's, if you like, mini-departments starting to appear, and within the departments people are doing functions, so they are liaising with their supervisor but that's not getting back to another department. There are at times breakdowns in that awareness thing.

This shows how informal communication systems may have been adequate when the company was in its infancy but that a need is now emerging for something more formalised. Of course the production meetings are a vehicle to formalise some of these aspects, but as they are held rarely and are not particularly valued by management then at present they remain rather ineffectual. Eric also talked about communication:

> Actually this company, the communications are really complicated. There is a grouping problem. I think that problem will exist in every company or organisation, it depends on the bosses' attitude and how they control it, if it is not serious it is alright, I think it is controlled well here, but the problem is because it's a small company there is no formal communication root, so every time you approach a person you have to know that person first and how to talk to them, otherwise you will not get a result.

The benefits of informal communication systems are all linked with the benefits of being small. However, Eric does acknowledge some of the difficulties associated with informal communication and it is possible that the problems will come to outweigh the benefits if the company grows much more. I feel that his reference to a 'grouping problem' refers to the shopfloor/office and core/peripheral employee split. It was not obvious that the directors did anything to control these problems.

SUMMARY

The layout of the factory is much improved since the company moved to larger premises. The new premises have been purchased with the foresight of possible expansion in the future. However, a singlehanded attempt to organise the positioning of equipment on the shopfloor without consulting employees has led to inefficiencies in the welding process.

Scheduling is sometimes very haphazard and even a simple method such as using working hours to calculate capacity is not always considered. The deficiency in this area often leads to conflict between staff members. Further, overtime is usual, with shopfloor operatives working on both Saturdays and Sundays and occasionally through the night. The production process is governed to a certain extent by the BS5750 quality system. However, its official procedures are frequently bypassed as they are considered too long-winded or obstructive. Another problem with the BS5750 is that it is based around existing work practices without a thorough assessment of these beforehand. Thus, it not only reinforces bad habits but also prevents these habits from being changed. This compounds processual inertia (the reluctance to update and improve existing processes).

The quality system, although fairly well developed, is also occasionally evaded. However, the introduction of the BS5750, along with the autonomy attributed to shopfloor operatives, has created a strong 'quality culture'. This appears not only to give operatives a strong sense of pride in their work but also sets up competition between them to avoid making mistakes. Problems with quality assurance arise from the dual role of the inspector through his involvement with supervision, and the possibility that he will thus ignore errors to save time; and also from the lack of attention to materials handling.

The space allocated to the storage of materials is too small as are the human resources. The ordering of items from provisional drawings leads to the accumulation of expensive and unusable stock. Goods-inward inspection is poor and there is the potential for a disaster at this point. Finally, as welding consumables are not ordered from drawings, unnecessarily large stocks have to be kept, but even these will not prevent a stock-out under some circumstances.

The level of technology at Logos is fairly high. There is a good programme of ongoing investment in technology and capital equipment. The company even organises special projects to investigate the potential expansion of technology within the company. However, technology is avoided as a management tool, especially in the area of production; here computerised ordering, stock control and scheduling could bring benefits.

Shopfloor training is fairly comprehensive and is overseen by an external organisation. However, the training of office personnel, especially induction training, is weak and has been given a low priority. There is hope of improvement in the future as the company is beginning to recognise this deficiency and take steps towards its improvement.

The management style is patriarchal and paternalistic. This works particularly to the disadvantage of women and newer company members, and causes an unhappy and constrained working culture for some members of the office staff. However, many shopfloor operatives and longer-serving members of the company pointed out the benefits of working for the company and the good atmosphere.

Strategic issues are controlled by three directors through a fairly even split of duties. As time has passed they have learned to deal more effectively with any conflict which arises between them. The communication system which has worked in the past is becoming inadequate. Investment in capital equipment will probably ensure the further capability of the company to pursue its present policy of improving quality and diversification.

5 FranTech Ltd – soldering on!

INTRODUCTION

FranTech was founded in Raj's (the present owner-manager) garage in 1970. It manufactures electronic and electrical equipment predominantly for a few large customers. The company continued to operate from Raj's home for about eight years, after which it moved into a small rented warehouse-type workshop. In 1983 the company moved to its present location. From 1978 to 1989 Raj had a partner, but he left FranTech over a row, so the business is now a limited company with 90 percent of the shares owned by Raj and 10 percent by his wife. Raj started the business because others whom he viewed as less competent than himself were getting better jobs. This gave him the confidence to run a small business. The company has since grown through a series of large orders from abroad and has subsequently obtained a BS5750 Part I certificate and two Smart Awards for innovation. It has strong contacts with both engineering and management departments at various local universities, and indeed there are academics on the company's board.

FranTech now employs about fifteen full-time employees, two out-workers and various other temporary staff. Last year the company employed about thirty employees, but this fluctuation in company size is not unusual and is primarily caused by the more unstable sub-contract side of the business.

LAYOUT

The factory is a small two-storey unit on a 1950s industrial estate. The layout is shown in Figure 5.1. The main entrance leads onto a small corridor which runs into the rather dilapidated main office. This office is occupied by the owner-manager Raj, Joy, the receptionist-cum-secretary-cum-administrator-cum-accounts-clerk-cum-storekeeper, and Harry, the purchasing manager. Various awards, certificates and pictures of Raj meeting assorted dignitaries cover the wall. A smaller rear office contains various filing cabinets in which old invoices and other paperwork is kept. This is also home to 'Ability', the production schedule system.

Beyond this the ambience improves somewhat. A cramped stores (cramped because it has been moved from a more congenial site which is now sub-let to another small company manufacturing and repairing tachographs) overlooks the shopfloor where rows of benches are situated.

Two staircases lead up to the 'development area'. Prior to refurbishment it was possible to see the sky in a number of places through a yellow corrugated plastic roof. This has now been camouflaged with a bright white suspended ceiling. In the corner of the development area is a smallish box built out of two false walls incorporating windows and a door. This is the boardroom. Finally, above the area let to the tachograph company, there is a huge area which contains old boxes and crates (I was told some are filled with Raj's daughter's old clothes and the remaining house contents of a friend of Raj's whose business went bust and took his home with it).

SCHEDULING

New jobs are entered onto the computer. The printout from this shows the job number and description, and the departments through which the job is expected to travel – these include purchasing, kitting, production and test. An expected and actual processing date is displayed for each department. In this way jobs can be tracked around the factory and targets are set so that jobs can be diagnosed as falling behind schedule early on in the system.

This printout is then updated by Raj, who fills in target dates for each stage according to his own experience of the time taken for such jobs. He also decides which jobs to start immediately and which to put off until later. This is where one of the first problems with scheduling begins. Jobs which are held back are not marked and as a result are frequently forgotten. This should not happen in theory as the job will be entered on the schedule as being located in the office. Thus, by looking at the location of new jobs and comparing them with the delivery date it should be possible to see easily when jobs must be initiated in order to complete on time. However, no system exists to check this, and occasionally the first time these jobs are remembered is when the customer phones to check on progress, or when an audit is carried out.

Further updates during the week are noted on the printout with locations being changed and jobs being written on or crossed off the schedule as

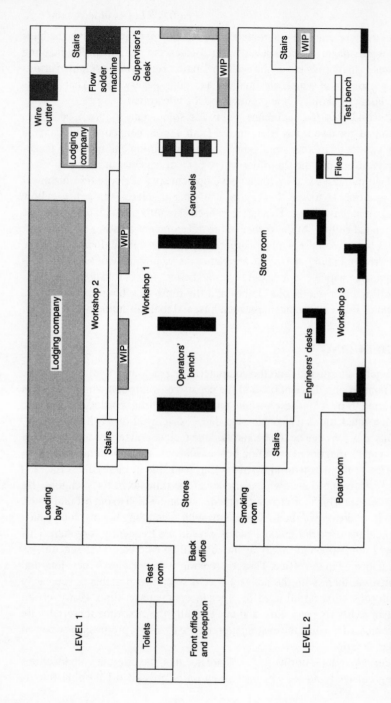

Figure 5.1 Layout of FranTech Ltd

required. At the beginning of each week this production schedule is updated on computer, noting all the jobs which have moved from one department to another, cancelling jobs which have been dispatched, entering new jobs and marking on new URGENT stamps. This is carried out (in theory) by the project nominees or section leaders. However, it is frequently overlooked, so the schedule bears only nominal resemblance to the actual position of jobs.

On an audit of the production schedule – examining each job to discover its actual location – I found that about half of the jobs were in the wrong place. Audits are carried out infrequently and haphazardly. One problem here is that when Raj carries out such an audit he insists on 'bollocking' people when the relevant item is not in its rightful place. An audit is thus very stressful and employees prepare themselves for confrontation.

Another problem with the scheduling system is the setting of priorities, as these appear to be constantly changing:

> In the past, I've scheduled everything out and everything is ticking along smoothly, and he [Raj] might go out with one of his friends who is a customer, and he'll ask me to do their job early, and change everything round just as a favour.

(Jill)

But these kinds of problems are not simply caused by Raj, they are also caused by the very nature of the business environment and small firm–large firm power relationships. For example, at one point during my fieldwork I attended a scheduling meeting. Halfway through, the telephone rang. It was a large sub-contractor wanting their order brought forward. It was the day before the Easter holiday. There was no way around the problem, as Raj realised that if he turned them down they would probably take their business elsewhere. So the employees were asked to come in over the holiday even though most of them had made their own plans. But they seemed neither surprised nor very concerned and some told me that they had been expecting it anyway: this was not an unusual occurrence. In fact, enough of the employees cancelled their holidays for the job to leave the factory before the new delivery deadline.

PROCESS

Upon the receipt of an enquiry the job must first be costed. This is based on a bill of materials. The bill is put together for standard products using existing parts lists but uses the design drawings of new products. All components are then priced according to the latest catalogues. However, other parts, such as casings or panels, are priced according to the previous year's invoices which are filed for one year only. Labour cost for standard jobs is calculated using a set charge of £12 per hour for operatives. This price is neither current nor fixed. For example, the charge may be lowered to compete against a competitor's bid. Max, the trainee supervisor, has recently completed a project for a college training course which he undertakes on day release. As part of this project he asked all the operatives to fill out time sheets during assembly. This represents the first attempt to systematically record a time for each job. Raj has yet to be persuaded to use the system.

Labour for development jobs is very difficult to calculate as design is very rarely completed on time. Raj attributes this to the optimism of the design engineers in estimating design time, but from Mark's account below it is obviously a very difficult process:

> If you get the time wrong you've got the cost wrong, so a lot of thought goes in at the start with how long something's going to take, so you can easily overrun your budget, particularly where software's involved. . . . If you take this job at the moment . . . the manual on it's that thick. Maybe if we'd have got the manual first we'd've realised that it wasn't as simple as we think. So, that part of it's probably taken ten times as long as what we thought. So we've changed the target now from aiming to make a profit on the job to breaking even. So we're probably effectively losing something like £10,000 profit.

Orders are received either verbally or in the form of a fax or some other kind of written request. When an order arrives at the factory it is noted in a job book and a job file is initiated. No action should be taken on a verbal order until this has been confirmed in writing by the customer. There are basically three kinds of job: the first requires a design input (these are passed to a nominated designer); the second are straightforward manufacturing jobs which are orders for an item from the company's standard product range (passed to the production manager); the third are processed only through sales. This involves buying in some item which is then sold without further processing. These are passed to the purchasing manager.

Once the job file has been raised, a job nominee appointed and the relevant paperwork signed, it is entered into the computer. When a new job has been initiated it begins life in the purchasing department. This department is made up solely of Harry, a retired manager from a large retail organisation. For simple build jobs, usually for a sub-contractor, and sometimes for development jobs, the information arrives in the form of drawings. These drawings arrive in varying states of orderliness. Mark remembered one of his first tasks upon arriving at the company:

One of the major things I started off here was what was known as the India job, a thirteen-off of a particular pair of items, and it became my project to get rid of it because it had been going a few years when I arrived. There was stuff everywhere associated with this job and it became very obvious that the problem with it was the documentation we had – all the wiring diagrams we had were wrong. So I spent a lot of time getting it right and making sure that the next one we made was built to those drawings. It was only really when we got rid of the last one that we got them completely right because everybody who made one found something else wrong. So what we'd done was we'd got a job from [sub-contractor A] that was a straight build job to their design and it turned into a nightmare because their drawings were all wrong. We eventually made the decision that we wouldn't work to their drawings again, we would put them on our CAD system so we could alter them at will, because trying to get [sub-contractor A] to alter their drawings was impossible.

Unfortunately, jobs often arrive as straightforward assembly jobs. Everything is assembled according to the drawings and sometimes it is not until the job goes to test that faults are discovered. The faults are then traced back to the customer drawings, and the drawings then have to be altered. This of course involves some development work, but FranTech is not usually paid for this. Furthermore, it is extremely difficult to get customers to modify their drawings. Thus, the next time the same job is received the same problems may be encountered, as Gayle, a shopfloor assembler, said:

> If we came across a problem and it was our own problem on our own boards, then we put an engineering note in for a change, for the parts list to be changed next time, the layout to be changed next time or whatever, but because it's somebody else's we can't make the changes, we have to phone up and they'll say 'Yes, you can do this' or 'You can do that', but it doesn't make them go back and change their original paperwork. So when you do the job next time, unless somebody's got previous job knowledge of it, we run into the same problems again.

In theory each job is scrutinised and the long lead-time items ordered. The shorter lead-time items are put on one side and ordered later to keep stock to a minimum. In practice the whole purchasing procedure is governed by the amount of money owed to the various suppliers. An invoice will not usually be settled until a new order is required from that supplier. This precarious juggling act is a necessity forced onto the company by a lack of equity to fund working capital. It is not uncommon for the bailiffs to arrive at the factory.

Because of the nature of the industry, and being a small company within that industry, an enormous amount of job knowledge is required. Harry discusses some of the complications:

> There are a number of constraints really, it's not always buying the cheapest. Although in my function, uppermost in my mind is cash, both cashflow and also what we pay for an item, but it doesn't always follow that if you buy the cheapest it's always the cheapest in the long run, because you've got to take into account procurement charges, postage and packing. Some companies deliver free, which would have an influence on the actual price of the goods, and also length of delivery. Very often we're working on a pretty tight schedule, so delivery is of the essence. . . . I've got a broad picture really of every job that's going through, and therefore I would know what jobs are urgent, what jobs are not quite so urgent, what we can get away with. Well, perhaps it's not right to say that but . . . you get a feel from a certain customer what his requirements are as opposed to somebody else, and you're flexible enough to say 'Well, perhaps that one can wait until next week but this one is urgent' and things like that.

One potential problem here is that Harry is already over the age of retirement and carries all this information in his head. Thus, when he leaves the company finding a replacement for him will be very difficult.

A further complication of the purchasing process arises from the financial predicament. If there is a lack of funds in a particular month and a required item is expensive then purchase will have to be delayed until the following month. By the time the following month arrives the item must be purchased urgently, incurring a penalty payment and thus pushing up the cost of the job enormously.

The production process consists primarily of soldering components onto a board which is carried out either manually or with the aid of a flow-solder machine. Some items cannot be flow-soldered as they are unable to withstand either the heat of the solder or the after-solder wash. All this information should be marked on the paperwork which travels with the job, but this information is frequently missing or filled in incorrectly. Thus, it is the operatives who flag up discrepancies or make decisions to go against the paperwork if they feel it is necessary.

Shopfloor work is carried out by two women assemblers and two male supervisors. The company recently experienced a serious decline in orders and laid off ten people from its thirty-five members. Major redundancies appear to be cyclical. It is nearly always shopfloor staff who are made redundant. Such redundancies are caused by the company's partial reliance on sub-contract work. This kind of business is very precarious as under recession conditions sub-contractors are likely to retain work in-house in order to keep their own operatives in work. For example, just before Christmas one year the company was undertaking sub-contract work for sub-contractor D, organised in terms of a monthly order which had continued throughout the previous year. One afternoon, sub-contractor D phoned the company and told them without warning that there would be no more orders, that they were to stop what they were doing immediately and send the part-finished work back to be completed in-house. In spite of incidents like this, FranTech plans to expand its sub-contract work in the future:

> The attraction of [sub-contracting] is that there's no risk, all you're doing is employing some more labour. So long as you've got the space and you've got the equipment, so long as it doesn't cost you anything then it's no risk because you take the labour on and then you dispose of it like we did before Christmas. But you've got to harden your heart to getting rid of people. . . . It certainly looked bad before Christmas because it looked as if it wasn't going to stop there. We virtually got back to the core people and if it had gone on any longer we'd have had to get rid of some core people.
>
> (Mark)

As redundancy pay cannot be found for the engineers who have been with the company longer, they are not really susceptible to such fluctuations in firm size. Further, as long as it can be funded, development work continues in the hope that a saleable product will eventually be produced. Most of the development centres around the S400 series, a control board insert for a standard PC which enables the control of information fed into it from an outstation (for example, one of these measures faulty cans in a bean canning factory). The remainder of the development work centres around meter test equipment. The design work usually involves obtaining a data sheet from a competitor and attempting to produce the same equipment at lower cost. The company also has a maintenance contract with sub-contractor A, one of its largest customers, for the care and repair of equipment supplied to them. The contract, which takes up about a quarter of one engineer's time, is longstanding and renewed annually. Apart from building PCBs the company also does sub-contract work in the form of constructing wiring looms.

Once individual items have been assembled, they are passed to inspection. If the item represents a completed product it is then tested. However, the company also produces large units of equipment of which the assembled items may only be a small component. If this is the case then these items travel to another workshop where they are tested by the mechanical assembly engineer, who also fits together all large items of equipment and tests them as a complete unit. Finally, completed items are packed by the shopfloor supervisor for dispatch. Packaging is recycled from incoming parts. Delivery to the customer can be by the company's own transport, through carrier, or by customer collection.

QUALITY

The quality system is nominally based on the BS5750. It is structured around inspection at intermediate stages of production and electronic testing of the final product. The first quality issue concerns the incoming documentation sent by the customer with orders. Because of the two different types of work undertaken by the company there are different considerations for each. The first kind of documentation that will be considered is for development work. This documentation is generated internally by the company's engineers. Recently a conscious effort has been made to control this kind of documentation, and as such it has changed from 'a pile of sketches' to being entered and properly updated on the CAD system. Thus, many of the problems, for example design and drawing faults, have been eliminated.

The other problem, however, is customers' paperwork:

> Very often we work to poor documentation and it's difficult to force a customer to give you good documentation because the reason he's giving you the job is that it's a messy job and he doesn't want to do it himself. So he's deliberately giving it to you because it's got poor documentation.

This amounts to an inadequate specification from the customer which makes it impossible to match quality to customer needs. It is easy to see why these problems occur for externally initiated products, but why do the same things happen with internal jobs? There appears to be an anti-paperwork (and in this respect anti-quality) culture. The problems caused by this are real enough. As Nicky explained, most of her time is spent:

> Probably chasing round other people when they haven't done something right. They'll put . . . instead of putting an ECN [engineering change note] in saying that something's wrong, they won't tell you exactly what's wrong or how to put it right, so you've got to go and find out how to put it right yourself [she explained that all the engineers are bad at

paperwork]. It's because Raj keeps saying 'Don't bother with that now, do it later when you've got more time', so it gets forgotten.

So the anti-paperwork culture is at least partly created and reinforced by the owner of the company and pushed downwards. This is reinforced by reactions to BS5750. When news of a forthcoming BS inspection is received there is a 'clean-up' operation where the gaps in ongoing and completed paperwork are hurriedly filled in by any available personnel. Thus, employees collude with Raj to present an 'image of efficiency'. Once the inspectors have left, practices return to normal.

The next failure of the quality system occurs in the stores. The system of vendor rating, after the monitoring of delivery which is controlled in the office, originates here. Joy told me about the system which used to be in place (there was no evidence that this system was still in operation):

> I used to do vendor appraisal when I was in stores. At the end of each month I used to check how many items we'd received from companies, check how many items we'd actually sent back due to their error or due to our error. . . . Things that are incorrectly supplied and that's their fault then they'll be warned about it. . . . That will also reduce the vendor ratings because you can't rely on the customer to send the correct items, you've got to check every item.

When components arrive at the company they are inspected by the store-keeper for both appropriateness and damage. Frequently, if a component has been damaged in transit it will be sent back. However, sometimes this process involves a compromise whereby the delivery lead-time of an item is taken into account. For example, one morning while I was working in the stores, a quantity of engraved front panels arrived. These panels were black and the surface had been etched away to reveal the required digits in white. Not only were the digits imprecise, but several of the panels were marked with white scratches where they had been poorly packaged. I brought this to the attention of the storekeeper who agreed that some of the panels were rejects. I filled in a goods returned note accordingly and passed the items back to the office. Several minutes later they were returned to me and I was told to book them in as usual. I informed the storekeeper, who took the panels to the mechanical assembly engineer. This engineer confirmed the panels' inadequate quality, especially in view of the fact that these were for a defence project where the quality required is higher than usual. An argument followed, with the engineer refusing to use the faulty items and Raj refusing to send them back. Eventually it emerged that there was a penalty clause on the finished product and replacement parts would not

arrive before the delivery due date. Thus there was no alternative but to use the sub-standard panels.

Another aspect of the inadequacy of the stores function is the control of the components. Firstly, many of the components used by the company are static sensitive, which means that certain precautions must be taken. Initially, the items must be kept in anti-static boxes and handled by people wearing protective clothing who are wired to an anti-static bench. The problem with this is that the stores area has recently been moved to allow space in the factory to be sub-let to another company:

> We have to be quite strict on static. All the benches have got curly bands and the anti-static straps, we all wear anti-static coats when we're working with them. The only place where it could tend to go wrong is in stores because stores is such a funny shape. When it was over there it was in a square box so no matter where you were in the square box you were actually tied to something. This desk isn't anti-static and that was one of the big kick-ups I had when we moved the stores over here, it just wasn't anti-static. I had row after row with Raj, but he's the boss.
>
> (Joy)

Another problem is the control of personnel entering the stores. To begin with, many people enter the stores area without the protection of anti-static clothing. But of even deeper concern is what they do when they get there. I have already explained that all components are purchased for a specific job and that they are consequently placed in the appropriate kit. The problem starts when one of the engineers from the development area requires a component:

> He [Raj] also allows people to go in the stores who shouldn't really be in there. If they want a component and they realise that there's another job being built with that component on they will take it. They don't mark down what they're taking, so everything gets confused. So with some jobs you're thinking 'I've got that', and so you don't worry about it until you actually come to fit it and it's not there. Other jobs, it says something's not there and it is there because it's just been dropped in. So you can be sitting waiting for something and it's actually gone into stock.
>
> (Joy)

So, once again, the paperwork is ignored. If the engineers marked down what they had taken then at least it would be possible to reorder the missing component, and if the parts lists were properly updated then there would be no time wasted or confusion at the production stage. The inadequacy of paperwork could be overlooked if it presented no further problems, but actually it represents a good deal of wasted time for the drawing office supervisor, the shopfloor operatives, the office administrator, the storekeeper and the buyer.

The straightforward aspect of building a job appears to fit within a culture of quality. Most of the operatives appear to recognise the importance of quality. One told me:

> In inspection, afterwards you look for the same things, the same faults that you look for when you're building, so hopefully it gets checked twice. The person that's doing it should hopefully build it correctly and take some pride in what they're doing and hopefully you've got somebody who knows what they're looking for when they inspect it.

She continued by describing some of the constraints on the quality of inspection:

> For the shopfloor [the goals are] to get the work out on schedule and to the best quality that we can manage. Unfortunately because of the way things go, you don't get the time to spend on the job. You don't sit down and do the job from start to finish and then go on to something else, you get halfway through and then you're stopped and you go onto another job, and then it's suddenly 'Everybody leave whatever job they're on and rush to get it out' so things, instead of being plodded through, are rushed through.

However, in the long run inspection should be overridden by the test procedure. This is the next stage in quality checking and involves electrical testing using meters and oscilloscopes to check that the correct voltages and signal are in the right places at the right time. Here again, however, problems were found. This account from Mark shows how some faulty items slipped through the test procedures and it ends with one of the most amazing accounts of the kinds of things which may go wrong at a small factory:

> The first thing I found when these things [were returned by the customer] was that the test procedure was inadequate, so I thought I'll do one and I'll write a new test procedure – so when I started to test [the returned items] I noticed that they went backwards, what other people had obviously done was just swapped the wires over. What I did was worked my way back saying 'I know the wires are right' – so I went back to the electricity meter and they were wrong there. So I got [the electricity board] to come in and they didn't believe me to start with, well they came up with this fanciful tale that all [this city] was like that – I

said 'pull the other one'. Anyway, I think in the end I believe that all [this city] *is* like that. . . . What I found amazing was that this place has been going, what, fifteen years, and they make electricity test equipment, and for fifteen years they've had the things going backwards. They've known that you have to swap the wires round, but the next person who comes along makes exactly the same mistake. And the same thing was happening with drawings and things, it was all in people's heads.

So, in a company which manufactures electrical and electronic equipment, the input to the factory had been reverse polarity for fifteen years! With respect to quality, poor-quality items were being dispatched to customers because the test procedures designed to find out if the products were working correctly were inadequate. What is more, even though all the engineers were aware of this, nothing was done to improve the system until a new member decided to tackle the issue. Furthermore, it appears that this behaviour is inadvertently endorsed by the owner-manager.

INVENTORY CONTROL

The system devised to control the storage and traceability of bought-in items is very thorough. Ordered items are documented on a purchase order card filed in the office in date sequence. When the goods are received in the stores they are unpacked and inspected. The inspection process takes two forms: the goods are inspected for damage and they are also checked against the vendor's delivery note and then in turn checked against the purchase order. In this way the quality, quantity and accuracy of the order are inspected. As each item is inspected it is ticked off against the order and delivery note and a GRN (goods received note) is filled in. The GRN details the item, the item's order number and the job number for which the item is required. This information is all taken from the purchase order. When the GRN is complete, one copy is filed in the stores and another copy is attached to the delivery note for filing with the invoice in the office. If at this point faulty goods are discovered then this information is noted on the GRN and a goods returned advice note is completed and sent back to the vendor with the faulty items.

Once this has been completed then a ticket bearing the GRN number is attached to all goods. This ensures full traceability of all goods kitted or put into stock. Once this process is complete the items must then be placed. Items for stock are put into their appropriate boxes on the shelves and booked in on a ticket in each bin, showing the quantity of items, the date they were booked in, and the name of the vendor. The remaining items are then kitted.

In another area of the stores are large bins. Each of these is labelled with a job number and a production traveller giving the details of the job, and a parts list. As the components are placed into the bins they are ticked-off on the parts list so that any component shortages are immediately visible. If more than the required number of items for a particular job are received then only the required number are placed in the kit. The remaining items should always be placed in stock.

However, although the system should ensure full traceability and complete control of all components this does not happen in practice. Firstly, goods are sometimes removed from their packaging and left loose in their bins. This removes the GRN number from the goods rendering it impossible to locate either the date when the items were bought or the vendor of the items. Secondly, items are not always detailed on the parts lists. This is because the engineers who make up the lists sometimes assume that the purchasing manager will know what other items are required. This is usually true but if he is rushed or concentrating on other things then this is overlooked and essential items are not ordered. There are also other reasons why the parts list may not be complete:

We've had an instance since you've been here where a printer had stopped halfway through a parts list, so a page was missing. It wasn't obvious at all that it was missing, so it was kitted and they came to build it and a quarter of the parts were missing, and one of the parts was on something like thirteen weeks' lead time. Can you believe, for instance, that even on jobs that we've been making for years that the bare board can be missing off the parts list? It's not a disaster so long as you've got some in the cupboard, but the job goes on the shopfloor, no bare board, none in the cupboard, haven't ordered them, so you pay through the nose to get boards in a week when if you'd known before you wouldn't have to have paid three times the cost, you could have got them in twenty-one days' delivery at no extra cost.

Thirdly, because there is no full-time storekeeper and people are frequently moved about, items become forgotten, lost or not properly booked in. An example of this was when I was working in the stores and a shipment of switches arrived. I was booking the items in when I was transferred immediately to another area. When the next person went into the stores he picked up the switches, saw they had been booked in and placed them on the shelves. When I returned I saw the items on the shelves and assumed they had been crossed off the parts list. A week later the engineering manager arrived to enquire about the switches which had not arrived. The job was late and only held up by these items. I embarrassedly pointed them out on the shelves and was gently reprimanded for not crossing them off the list. However, this kind of incident reflects a much more general trend which is that as a result of people being moved before the completion of a particular task, jobs are not completed properly and the system falls down.

A final aspect of kitting is that for defence work the customers' own parts lists must be used. These customers use their own parts numbers and descriptions. They may supply some components but the majority are bought by FranTech. Unfortunately, component numbers from other suppliers bear little resemblance to their descriptions on the customers' parts lists. Thus, for someone with little job knowledge it is virtually impossible to match incoming goods with the parts lists. If the order code from the company supplying the parts was added to the parts list when components are being ordered then it would be a simple process to check them off. As it is it takes many hours and some expertise to match them all up, even for some of the more experienced staff.

Work in progress should be controlled through the scheduling system. This should detail the position of every job travelling through the factory. However, as I have already explained, it is rare to find all of the items in their correct positions. In fact it is not uncommon during an audit to find many missing items jumbled together, without their labels or documentation, in a heap on an engineer's desk. This makes it virtually impossible to trace each item without the help of the engineer concerned.

Finished goods stock is kept to a minimum. It is usual for most items to be shipped immediately upon completion. However, some stocks of smaller, less valuable goods are kept.

EQUIPMENT/TECHNOLOGY

The level of technology within FranTech is quite high. There are computer terminals in the office and in the development department. These PCs support wordprocessing, desktop publishing, CAD and other development software as well as accounting/administration and scheduling programs. All development drawings are recorded and updated on the computer and all invoices, delivery notes and shipping tickets are printed automatically. Assorted other control software is used in the production of the S400 control boards, and the company's software design is quite sophisticated.

The company also owns some production technology. This includes a wire cutter, purchased at a massively discounted price from a bankrupt company. It has quickened the process of wire cutting by a considerable amount. Further, there is the flow solder machine, which passes PCBs over a bath of solder securing many components at one time rather than having to hand-solder each component.

Equipment has also been purchased specifically to increase the speed of the production of batches of PCBs, in the form of carousels. All the components which must be fitted onto a board are pre-formed to the shape of the holes into which they are placed and put into bins on a circular wheel. There may be up to five of these wheels on one carousel. A computer is then programmed with the layout of the components of the board. The operator then simply picks out a component from the relevant bin (the machine will buzz if she puts her hand in the wrong bin) and places it on the board where a light spot indicates the correct position. Here again the machine buzzes if she puts the component in the wrong place. This greatly increased the assembly speed, especially in conjunction with the flow solder machine.

This system should greatly increase not only speed but also the accuracy of the position of components:

> It's more effective on a large batch, once you've taken out the programming time. If it's only for a small batch it probably isn't really worth doing, but it can cut the assembly times by a third, and it also improves the quality because it's very difficult for the operator to put the wrong component in the wrong place. . . . So, theoretically, it's impossible to do it wrong.

> (Max)

However, the technology is not viewed universally in this way. For example, an operative's account of the same equipment was as follows:

> It's good in a way, but it can lead to mistakes in another way because you could go onto the machine and the machine tells them where they should put the components. They don't always check the resistors that they're putting in, so there's more mistakes that way. You get, 'This is a bit boring: press the pedal, take a component, put it where the dot is', and it can lead to boredom because there isn't a lot of thought in it, because they're already pre-formed so you just take them out of the bin and put them in a hole on the board, like Raj says a monkey could do it, just stuff the boards.

So obviously the technology is not infallible in every instance. It also does not cope with components being placed on the board the wrong way round for example, which for some items means that they have completely different electrical properties.

Although the company owns quite a lot of equipment, considering its size, it also has access to other sources of technology:

We've got close tie-ups with [sub-contractor A]. Take a storage oscillo-scope where it actually remembers the picture – we borrowed one off [sub-contractor A] and we have got access to equipment that we haven't actually got ourselves.

(Mark)

This is a good example of the positive advantages to small firms of links with large companies.

There also appear to be disadvantages to the technology level. For example, the carousels, purchased for sub-contract work, are practically useless for small batches. When the sub-contract work came to an end the company was left with very expensive pieces of redundant equipment for which it is still paying. Joy also spoke of Raj's technological commitment sometimes having negative consequences:

The stores was going to be computerised, in fact we had it all on the computer two or three times and then he [Raj] goes to someone else and sees a better system and he likes that one so we have to change every-thing again. And the last time it was on it just got completely wiped off, with no hard copies or anything so that was it, *the end*.

RECRUITING AND TRAINING

The first aspect which needs to be examined when looking at recruiting is the requirement of the employer. Raj explained to me the qualities he considered important for potential employees: 'It's mainly the motivation, the appearance, the discipline, manners, that sort of thing, you know, the sense of humour.' Skill or ability are not at the top of the list. The emphasis for a new employee, then, is 'fitting in' rather than being competent. For example, Raj gives an account of someone who didn't fit in:

There was a guy, he was a first-class worker, he was made redundant because he was a troublemaker. But nobody could do as good work as he could. But he didn't have a sense of humour or he was not motivated or whatever, he was a bloody good worker.

Raj also has contradictory ideas about what characteristics are required from a manager: 'I expect him not to come to me with problems, but to come to me if there is a problem. I expect him to come up with solutions, and if there is help needed I want him to offer that. It is essential to come to me for help in time'.

Part of this represents Raj's inability to delegate, which will be dis-cussed in more detail later, but it also shows the absence of a clear idea of what is required in the recruitment of managers. This is perhaps borne out in the way employees are recruited into the company. I found little evidence that any formal recruiting methods are used. For example, one new employee taken on while I was at the company was usually referred to as 'the plumber's son'. This is because a plumber who did some work at the company remarked that his son, who lived locally, was unemployed. Raj then phoned up the son and asked him if he wanted a job. Other accounts bear out the informal recruiting policy:

> I didn't apply here, I bumped into Raj one day. I knew Raj because he'd been trying to get work off our factory and about a year before I finished there he'd actually managed to get some work – he said how was I getting on, and I said 'Fine apart from the fact they've fired me'. He said, 'Well, I'm looking for somebody – do you want a job?', so I ended up here.
>
> (Mark)

> Well, it was just that I worked for [sub-contractor D] and I left to have my baby and I was at home and Raj came and asked me if I wanted to do it. He knew a next-door neighbour, he'd worked with Raj, and Raj had asked him if he knew of anyone that could assemble boards, so that was it. I've been here ever since.
>
> (Marion)

Training, on the other hand, has been more formal. Some use has been made of educational establishments. Assistance with the cost of training is also sought from government grants and schemes. Raj outlined some of the more recent training which had been undertaken by employees:

> Take Max, he's going to a day release; Mark, we've sent him to do the courses on the new European laws and things like that. I mean obviously, as it is he's very well qualified. I got some help [to pay for training] from the TEC. We've sent her [Nicky] to do her Higher National Diploma. Brian used to go to night school; we sent him on courses. But a lot of other people have done training and then left us.

So, the fear of creating transferable skills is also a constraint imposed by Raj on the training choices for employees. This is emphasised by Joy:

> You know that I do the payroll and everything. There's a lot involved in payroll, you've got to know the law as well as wages and pay. I wouldn't expect to go on an expensive course or anything. I think that Raj feels women are far less a secure investment than men are. I don't know why, because I'm comfortable here and until I'm made to feel uncomfortable

and physically made to leave, I shan't be interested in going. I mean at the age of thirty-eight I'm not going to start wandering around looking for another job.

So, Joy obviously feels that she has not had sufficient training and would like to go on other courses. Raj has arranged for specialists to come to the factory and train Joy in-house but will not allow her to attend a course, probably through the fear of her obtaining a recognised qualification which would be of interest to other employers. However, this does not seem to be considered in relation to the engineers in the factory, as many of them have obtained HNC or other qualifications during their employment.

Another aspect of training is the programmes for shopfloor workers. Gayle told me about the training which used to be offered and compared it to the current training methods:

> When I first arrived, Jill put us on small jobs – wipers – it's a very small board and I did one and she checked it, and if you had a problem she'd go over that problem with you. We were shown everything and checked that we could do it before we were allowed to go on. Now they give them the job, wait for them to finish and then say, 'This is wrong, and that's wrong', whereas when I did mine you were watched, not constantly, but you were checked regularly. So faults were put right soon and not waited till you were finished, so you weren't so demoralised when you got to the end of the job.

However, when Jill left the system left with her and thus the training programme is now less thorough. Although there is a document outlining the general aims of training, no training procedures were written down. Furthermore, time constraints prevent employees from doing work which does not appear to contribute directly to the firm's productivity, so efforts are directed towards urgent work:

> Well the normal procedure is, if we were recruiting we would request that the operators be fully experienced so that cuts out the training, which if you're recruiting people you need them to start work now, you need to get them onto the seats now and producing. If you've got to start training people in this sort of business, if they didn't know anything at all about the job and they're straight in off the street it could take, I believe, six weeks to fully train somebody. I do the training, as well as everything else . . . and in the situation we're in it isn't very easy to do it because output is the king and you've got to try and push them on farther and quicker than you would probably like to, so the training doesn't always either get finished properly or even get started properly,

because they get dragged away to do other things. If they make a mess of it they get moaned at. It isn't their fault because they weren't shown how to do it in the first place. I would love to sit down and do them a full training course, right through the whole lot of it, but it's very rare. We rely on large companies to train them for us.

(Max)

Max's reference to large companies training FranTech's workforce is an allusion to the company's tendency to employ redundant employees from larger organisations. This improves in times of high unemployment, when FranTech can pick and choose those with the greatest experience. Although this is no guarantee that new employees can perform effectively in smaller companies where work is more varied, it does go some way towards relieving the costs of training. However, the concept of large firms training FranTech's employees does not end here, as Mark explains:

What Raj tends to do there is to send you down to [sub-contractor A]. I mean when I came I went down there to find out what it was all about. So it's using the customers to do a bit of training, because it's in their interests as well that we learn about that, and that's free.

So sub-contractor A put Mark on their own employees' training course. In this way the costs of training for FranTech are reduced by using their customers' facilities. Obviously having well-trained staff in a sub-contract firm is valuable to the sub-contractor, and thus they are willing to foot the training bill. Finally, Max gave me an account of his training in the stores. He was expected to take it over from the storekeeper who was made redundant:

I think I was given two hours of explaining how to go on. In all my experience in the industry I've never had to work in stores before, so I was totally green to it, I didn't know how the system works. So I got the manual thrust at me and told to read that, and then just get on with it.

Max's takeover of the stores was further complicated by the fact that the previous storekeeper refused to show him how her job had operated. This was not a personal dispute with Max, but rather because she felt she had been made redundant unfairly. She felt that the reason she was laid off instead of Max, the trainee supervisor, was a matter of sex discrimination. Raj explained that the reason for the redundancy was that Max had PCB skills while Anne did not. However, Max had only been with the company for two weeks at this point and it must be said that the stores are now in almost total chaos. There is also scepticism amongst the workforce about what exactly Max's PCB skills are, and that it was felt Max could be trained to manage the stores but Anne could not have been trained to perform a trainee supervisor's job.

A final point which should be mentioned here concerns the continual fluctuation in the company's size. For production workers it was universally acknowledged that when the company is small then the work which they carry out is more varied and may include not only assembly, but also inspection, kitting, pre-forming, loading the carousels or even working in another section altogether. On the whole employees preferred to stick to their own jobs, and thus less tension is created in this area when the company size is larger.

CULTURE AND CONTROL

The owner-manager, Raj, is ultimately responsible for all aspects of the running of the company. This causes some problems. One of Raj's special talents is selling – he has an unusual rapport with customers which does not involve being polite and friendly to customers. Instead these relationships are conducted with very little conciliatory behaviour on Raj's part and it is not unusual to hear him swearing animatedly at a customer on the phone. However, the customers with whom he deals obviously appreciate that this is Raj's natural behaviour and so do not take offence. Rather, it reinforces their notion that they are dealing with a straightforward and honest person. However, although selling is one of Raj's strengths, it represents only a small part of his overall duties. The problem arises when the company grows in size. When this occurs, Raj, because he finds delegation difficult, transfers his attentions from selling to the internal company operations. Thus, employees become frustrated with his interference, while selling is neglected.

> I think also because he's built the company up from something very small – I don't want to use the word interferes – but he can't let somebody get on with it. Even though he knows they're quite capable, he wants to be involved in everything all the time. Whereas he could leave you in charge he tends to be checking up every five minutes. I think that's because he's built it up from something very small, but as it's grown he's kept in the middle, in the heart of it.

Because selling becomes secondary at times, orders become fewer and the company contracts, laying off employees. In this way a cycle is created whereby the company's growth is never maintained.

Another aspect of the company structure is that there are concentrations of management staff in certain places. As Gayle says:

There's too many chiefs and not enough indians. There's too many people organising and not enough people doing. We have Raj, and then Mark who's in charge of test, and Doug who's our supervisor, and Max, who is trainee supervisor. That's four people, there is only three women on the shopfloor and two trainees. I'll be leaving in three weeks, so there'll be two full-time and two trainees with four people over them. Somehow the mathematics of that don't work out.

And yet there are no full-time sales staff. Another interesting characteristic of the company is its collection of people who appear to simply drift in and out undertaking small sales and other tasks. While I was with the company there was one man who was undertaking some selling as a favour to Raj. His business had gone bankrupt and he was 'keeping his hand in' doing work for Raj. Another man in a similar position was being paid on commission for such work. Yet another whose business had gone bankrupt had teamed up with Raj in order to grow a new business within Raj's factory. There were also two students and myself working in the company during my visit, all conducting relatively complex projects for Raj. One of these students was brought in to take over the graphics work, while Nicky, who is usually responsible for this, was displaced onto the shopfloor.

Moving people around is one of Raj's preferred interventions and this causes some tension within the company. It must be said here, though, that it is almost without exception the women who are moved whereas the men are usually allowed to stay with their own jobs. Of course all employees' jobs are varied, but women may be moved to the office, the stores or the workshop, whereas the men will usually be left in their own departments. The problem is that the women's versatility does not lead to increased status. For example, Mark says of Nicky:

> I think Nicky is extremely versatile. I mean she does testing, which is unusual for a woman, you don't get many. She's the only woman that I've bumped into that's actually got a technical qualification, so I think she's done very well for herself. As regards her versatility here she does everything – CAD, she can test things, she can assemble, she can do the accounts, she's probably the most versatile person here. I would say as regards sex discrimination there is none, Raj will have you doing anything you can do.

However, the fact is that Nicky is paid less than the lowest-paid man (apart from the two YTS trainees). Furthermore, Gayle feels that the atmosphere at work is:

> Them and us, upstairs and downstairs really. The workshop is lowlier,

we are the scum-of-the-earth kind of thing, not as important. Out of the whole factory there's about four or five people who have to clock in and they're all shopfloor. They're all basically women as well. As far as the us and them, you know the technicians and whatever and the shopfloor, there's men and women and men will always get further. The men are paid more. Not for what they know, just because they're men . . . I just think everybody should be treated equal and not like us and them. Management should realise that women are as capable as men and treat us the same. If that was dealt with then a load of other problems would go as well. A woman can tell Raj something and he'll query it; if a man tells him something he'll think about it and put it into practice, whereas if a woman says it he'll say 'Why?' So unfortunately if it's mentioned by a man there's more chance of him doing something about it.

Furthermore, there is an almost total split between the descriptions of the company culture between men and women, where men describe the culture positively and women negatively.

Terrible – the way you're talked to and the way you're treated. Generally you're talked to as though you're a piece of dirt, and he [Raj] will just totally ignore you if you ask him something, or if you're talking to somebody he'll say 'Why are you all standing around here talking?' and he doesn't know what you're talking about, whereas men can get away with anything basically.

(Nicky)

Joy equates the atmosphere of the factory directly with Raj's mood: 'If he's in a good mood everything goes along swimmingly, if he's got one on him everybody sort of retreats back into their shell and they don't want anything to do with anybody'. While Max made a similar link, his overall assessment of the atmosphere is more positive:

Things are said in the heat of the moment sometimes which . . . err . . . perhaps if he'd given it a bit of thought he wouldn't actually say it. But I think people accept that and that's the way he is and he never alters; you either like him or you don't, you take him or you leave him. He's not a bad man, he's a good person.

Other men in the company were even more positive about the workplace culture, while still seeing Raj's role as central in setting the tone:

I suppose it's like a lot of small companies, it has more of a parochial sort of touch to it. It's not terribly formal. Hopefully people are reasonably friendly to one another and I don't sense very much backbiting or some of the rather nasty things that come into certain businesses. . . . Raj is the sort of father figure in many ways, he means well, but sometimes of course he can be quite irritating to people (laughs).

(Harry)

I'd describe the culture as being a family business. Most of the people have been here a long time. I mean Brian, Peter, Nicky, Marion, they've all been here ten years plus probably. So obviously they must be happy or they wouldn't be here, would they? I think basically it is an easy company to enter, they're basically a friendly lot. I think it's a very open place, I think that's the way to describe it. Certainly Raj is very forthcoming (laughs), he isn't the sort of person that would say nothing and fire you after three months without having sworn at you fifty times in between – you'd get the idea things weren't going well.

(Mark)

So there are basically four themes which have emerged from the accounts. Firstly, there is the issue of sex discrimination. Of course this is not unusual in any small firm and this fits with the family analogies and Raj as father, using a paternalistic form of control. However, what is unusual is the degree to which this is recognised and resented amongst the company's female employees and this has an evident effect on the company's culture. Second is the theme of constant interference by Raj. This too is resented enormously as it leads to employees feeling that they are not trusted to carry out their work effectively. It is recognised, though, that this is inevitable up to a point when the owner of a company also manages it. The third aspect is the movement around the company of certain employees. This, too, is resented as people are quite protective about their own jobs and do not like to be moved to another or to have someone else doing their job. Finally, I wonder if the overwhelming theme for me has been emphasised enough by my respondents. I was very surprised at the level of emotion within the company. Virtually no attempt was made by employees to manage their feelings and thus there was at times an almost electric and highly volatile atmosphere. All of the respondents talking about the atmosphere referred to this, but a particular case occurred while I was in the factory: I witnessed a woman shout at Raj who had blamed her for something she was obviously not responsible for, and practically throw some papers at him. After this she slammed the door and marched back to her desk. Raj sneaked out of the room, taking me with him, and told me: 'I think I'll give her a bit of time to cool off'. No further action was taken over the incident. I feel that this represented a certain freedom of expression which I have not encountered in workplaces before.

STRATEGIC OPERATIONS

> We started off doing odds and ends for little companies . . . who didn't
> really need the quality, and slowly we had to work towards the quality
> and get BS so that we could take on better stuff. Which we do now. . . .
> We use better components and better materials than we ever have done
> before. If you're working with good stuff then you're happy about it.

(Marion)

As Marion explains above, the company has had a policy of moving
towards the higher quality end of electronics manufacture. This has been
part of a conscious plan to increase profitability and to obtain sub-contract
work from, for example, defence industry firms. To prove this strategy the
company obtained the BS5750 about five years ago. This has been the key
to orders from some of their now major customers.

One of Raj's plans for the future is to widen the company's customer
base. Presently three customers account for about 65 percent of all orders.
The company is also rather heavily in debt primarily due to some development work which was undertaken for another company, who then took the
design and promptly declared itself bankrupt. A legal battle followed which
took up even more resources and won only a tiny amount of compensation.
The money which Raj owes was lent to him to cover this period by a
personal friend.

The most frequently mentioned strategy at FranTech is survival.
Although the company has now been in business for many years the size
fluctuations are a constant reminder that things could and do go wrong.
Over and above this the goal appears to be increased batch sizes and
standardisation although this too presents some problems:

> Standardisation is very very important . . . so that we can keep the cost
> down, but the difficulty is that, because of the business we are in, and
> because we are so small, it is such that if we've got to compete with the
> big boys we can't because it's not a mass production. So the only way
> we're going to survive is by making specials, you know niche markets
> . . . but as far as possible we will have a hardware module and a software
> module so that we can pick up modules and produce a flexible kit to suit
> the customer's requirement.

So the aim appears to be to standardise as far as possible whilst retaining
enough flexibility not to have to turn away any large orders.

There are three kinds of product which need consideration in any grand
plan for the company's future. These are the S400 control equipment, the
meter test, and the sub-contract side. The plan is to grow the sub-contracting

in order to cover the development costs of the other two product lines. This seems rather odd considering their disastrous prior experience of sub-contracting. However, as I mentioned earlier, there may be the possibility of an extended agreement for such work in the future which would help to stabilise output.

There are also plans to move into a new product area. Fred, the man I mentioned earlier whose business has recently gone bust, had £20 million worth of orders when the bank foreclosed for the sake of £200,000. Thus, a partnership between Fred and Raj may not be as risky as it may seem. There may, however, be some dangers associated with this decision. At this point no one in the factory knew of Fred and Raj's plan for Fred to gradually buy Raj out as his side of the business expands:

> The risk there is that it could rapidly outgrow us; I mean he had 150 people before, you couldn't get 150 people to fit in here, so he might rapidly outgrow us and move out. It's a very big break to actually move into bigger premises and there's a lot of money involved.

I feel that perhaps with the help of Fred the business can be built up. In many ways Fred is also a charismatic leader like Raj, and this may smooth the transition to Raj's retirement. However, this could easily create hostility as the plan is very secret and there are several others who probably see themselves as a candidate for next managing director.

SUMMARY

On the whole the layout of the factory is fairly logical although the general ambience could be improved, the only drawback being the location of the engineering and test departments upstairs. The size and shape of the stores and its potential to cause static problems is also a difficulty.

Scheduling is very haphazard. The Ability program only works in so far as it allows checks on the position of items and work in progress; it does not create any proactive action. The printout is not regularly updated or taken particularly seriously. Interference in the scheduling process from Raj interrupts workflow and so causes resentment from many staff members. A situation where almost all jobs are urgent is common, which really makes a mockery of the scheduling system.

The processes employed by the company fall into two categories, design and assembly work. The assembly work is predominantly the placing and soldering of components onto PCBs but also includes wiring and mechanical assembly. The development side of the business employs qualified engineers to develop new products for FranTech and to modify or design particular items for customers. The administration system which facilitates these processes is not seen as necessary by many employees or by the owner. Thus paperwork is almost always incomplete and there are major hold-ups while missing information is traced. Further, very little work is actually organised by the supervisors. Instead, organisation of shopfloor work is undertaken predominantly by assembly staff.

The quality system in the company is governed in theory by the BS5750, although parts of this have completely broken down. Quality checking takes the form of visual inspection and electronic test. However, inspectors are sometimes not qualified or experienced enough to perform such a task and test procedures are inadequate. Thus, faulty items are sometimes dispatched from the factory. Again many of the faults in the quality system originate from inadequate paperwork, for example poor or inaccurate customer specification. Finally, there is a trade-off between quality and time which leads to faulty goods being knowingly dispatched in order to achieve the required delivery date.

Inventory control is one of the company's biggest problems. The stores is chaotically run and this appears to be due to the absence of a full-time storekeeper. Furthermore, the lack of discipline in the stores leads to engineers 'pinching' components from kits without leaving any record that they have done so. Having a variety of people working in the stores means that kitting operations are repeated or missed out and that assembly workers' time is wasted in compensating for this lack of organisation. Finally, the short lead times for the assembly of products combined with the necessary reduction of stock means that items are continually awaiting shortages of components and can thus not be built as quickly as they might be.

The level of sophistication of equipment and technology is very high for a small firm. The company has a computer network system and advanced manufacturing technology such as the carousels and flow solder machine. However, better use of existing technology could be made by, for example, computerisation of the stores.

Human resources management tends to be rather informal. Recruiting requirements tend to be centred around personal qualities and 'fitting in' rather than skill and ability. Furthermore, recruiting is most often by word of mouth rather than formal advertising. Training is variable. Engineers tend to be trained conventionally, through college courses on day release, whereas production and office staff are trained in-house. Training for shopfloor personnel used to be better organised under the previous supervisor. However, when she left the training programme was not recorded and so it was not continued. Further, time constraints impose limits on the amount of 'non-productive time' which new employees can spend on training. Finally, as the company expands or contracts so the nature of the work performed by shopfloor personnel changes, becoming increasingly fragmented with decreasing size.

Control in the company is not achieved by means of a standard management hierarchy or authority structure. Very vocal disagreements frequently break out but these are tolerated and seen as normal. There are concentrations of management personnel in particular sections which do not appear to derive from any particular rationale. Moreover, some of these managers are viewed as incompetent and superfluous by workers.

The culture of the company appears to depend on the mood of the owner-manager to a large extent. Most of the women who work at the factory perceive a clear split between the favourable treatment of men over the unfavourable treatment of women, and thus see opportunities blocked in terms of promotion and training. However, on the whole Raj is seen as a likeable and affectionate character, and employees see their own growth very much through the development of the firm.

The strategic aims of the company are to begin to sell a product which they have developed themselves over a number of years and to try to recoup some of the finance directed into this venture. Further, the company hopes to develop a standard product line whilst remaining flexible enough to service their large customers.

6 Small firms and production management

INTRODUCTION

As was stressed earlier in this book, there are certain tensions between what has thus far been written about the role and form of production in the small business sector and the practicalities of the way in which small firms actually function. In part this stems from the scientific tradition still at the heart of much production research, which inevitably influences the methodologies chosen and therefore the research outcomes and prescriptions. There is now widespread agreement that the problems of small firms production are more attitudinal and cultural than technical in nature, an observation which should have an impact on the kinds of studies conducted. Amongst the key effects of these problems are:

> Companies have a policy of taking all work that is offered with little attention to whether the system can cope with it. The outcome is a compromised production system.
> Failure to do any corporate planning beyond budgets. This results in panics, purges, wasted energy and information overload.
> Reliance on financial information for control purposes and an absence of operational shopfloor measurements. In these circumstances firms have no information on how well or badly they are using their resources or whether they are satisfying their markets.
> Failure to make the full use of people through creating a climate where they own problems. This inhibits the most powerful resource in any business – people – and often creates negative situations. . . .
>
> (Lawlor 1988: 21)

As a final point I would like to include an extract here from a study by Watkins which has great affinity with my own work, and, I feel, 'sets the scene' for the discussion which follows:

The crises experienced by the sample firms would fill several books of case studies. They included fraud, flood and fire – declining total markets, the unexpected loss of a major customer, the emergence of an aggressive competitor – exporting disasters and the removal of tariffs; chronic shortage of capital, sudden dramatic cost increases and unpredicted cashflow crises – the failure of new technologies; strikes, unionisation disputes and legal actions for unfair dismissal, the defection or sudden death of a partner, key manager or skilled worker, personality conflicts and unwelcome takeover bids.

(Watkins 1983: 41)

Testimonies such as these point to the irrationality or at least 'bounded rationality' of small firm owner-managers. They also give an indication of the intensely complex nature of small firms management and the importance of context in examining and understanding the management *process*. As Ram (1992: 24) argues: 'Management activity may not be "rational", but that does not necessarily mean that it is not comprehensible within a certain context'. Thus, in the case studies it is shown that 'rationalities' or ways of looking at things have developed and become accepted. There are conventional wisdoms which have evolved and become 'firm-specific rationalities'. This is explored in more detail in Chapter 9.

By using ethnographic techniques I have obtained a broad picture of the ways in which production is managed in small companies, and how this may often be in direct contradiction to the suggestions made from within the operations management canon. To reinforce this I shall be rehearsing some of the findings from my three case study firms, and discussing these alongside the existing literature.

LAYOUT

Hill (1987) has classified types of layout. Process layout refers to the bringing together of similar process capabilities, that is items of equipment which perform the same function. Product layout, on the other hand, implies placing equipment in a sequence which reflects the order of the processes to be performed on the product. Hill relates these to the size or stage of growth of the small company, acknowledging that small firms are likely to use product layout when small, but that a switch to process layout is preferable with increasing firm size. Finally, a return to product layout is required with a move to high-volume production which comes with further growth. This approach implies that the concept of small-firm growth is largely unproblematic. As most small companies do not grow, and only a tiny minority ever reach the point of large batch or mass production, it is difficult to imagine which recommendations should apply. Further, in my case studies, other factors, such as the possible contamination of components and the physical size and shape of the factory, constrained the layout. Further, the relative status of different functions and personal relationships between people also impacted on such decisions.

The most common constraint on the factory layouts was lack of space. This was of course very variable. Whereas, for example, Logos's only problem area was their stores facility, Wellmaid suffered cramped conditions in almost every area of business. The owners of two of the three companies had no office space for themselves. This may seem relatively unimportant but had some surprising consequences. For example, at Wellmaid, the manager's desk and phone was separated from the main workroom only by a row of filing cabinets. The problem for the directors was that they had nowhere to discuss sensitive or private matters. Thus, they would huddle together discussing things at normal volume until they reached a particularly sensitive piece of information, when their voices would drop to a whisper. Employees at the company found this aura of secrecy and conspiracy disconcerting, even though the discussions were almost certainly around finance or other managerial worries (Holliday 1992a).

At FranTech, Raj had been forced to relinquish his office space in order to accommodate another company which had taken up lodgings in the factory. The consequences of this may have been that the company seemed unprofessional, especially since Raj being based in the reception area tempted him to answer the phone directly. This automatically betrayed the size of the company to potential customers.

In contrast, Logos portrayed a very professional image as each owner-manager had their own office, except Bob who preferred to be 'in the middle of things'. Furthermore, the offices were decorated and pleasant and the factory space purpose-built. Photographs of Logos's products adorned the walls, all designed to inspire customer confidence.

In all three companies storage space was limited and badly designed. At Wellmaid, the cardboard templates used in pattern cutting covered every available inch of wall space. Because of this, patterns which shared a particular template had to share this piece. Thus, it was only key individuals who knew where to retrieve certain parts of the templates, and even when these individuals were present templates would take time to locate. There was also insufficient space to store off-cut material or end of rolls. Thus, particular rolls of fabric were difficult to identify and off-cut fabric was folded in a box, leaving creases which rendered it useless. At Logos, certain larger materials such as steel girders and plates had to be left outside where they could be damaged by rain or passing traffic. Further, the layout of the stores was impractical in that large heavy items were stored on high shelves only accessible by ladder.

This, and the wooden stairs connecting the production and test areas at FranTech, were not only inconvenient and dangerous but probably in contravention of health and safety laws. Finally, at FranTech the stores was extremely cramped, and since it too had been relocated to facilitate the tenant company, was not properly designed in order to prevent static contamination of components. All these problems were really due to the lack of funds of small companies and thus their limited available space and limited time for solving such problems.

At Logos employees had not been properly consulted in the planning of layouts. The shopfloor layout and the fixed extraction ducting at its perimeter meant that heavy part-finished goods had to be moved around the shopfloor. The lack of a solid partition between work areas for stainless and carbon steels also showed a lack of layout planning, all of which could have been avoided. However, it would now be too costly to rectify them. Similarly at FranTech, having the production and test areas on two different floors necessitates the carrying of part-finished items up and down stairs.

Finally, although Logos probably had a good opportunity to plan the layout of their new factory, this is not really so for the other companies. Part of the problem of layout in these firms, along with cramped space, is the way that the layouts have developed over time. Instead of the implementation of layout plans there has been a gradual evolution of the shopfloors. The consequences of this may be seen clearly at Wellmaid where a new machinist must find a sewing machine somewhere amongst the existing vacant machines. As these machinists are likely to be recruited by friends or family members then the most obvious place for them is next to their recruiter. Thus, instead of workstations being laid out in terms of their sequence in the production system, they are *ad hoc* and placed in terms of their social preference. This finding clearly supports Ram (1992: 120), who depicted two different layout diagrams of the machinists in his study. These drawings clearly contrasted the 'rational' layout and workflow with the actual, clearly irrational, one (see Figure 6.1).

SCHEDULING

Lockyer (1983) states that scheduling is the key to efficiency in production. Scheduling involves loading tasks to parts of the process and organising the start and finish times of jobs to meet the delivery requirements of the customer

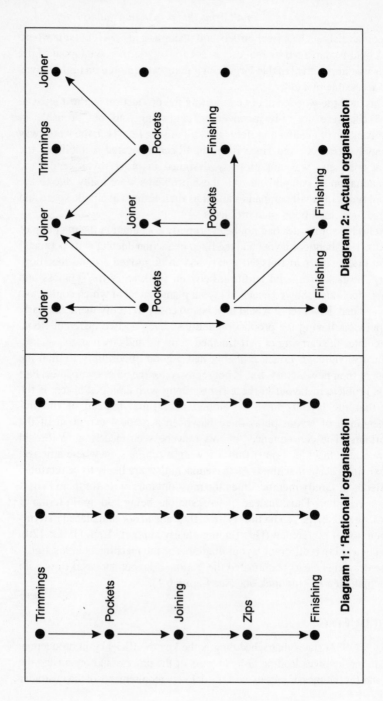

Figure 6.1 Rational versus irrational organisation of workflow (after Ram 1992)

or demand forecast. Failure to schedule effectively results in customer dissatisfaction and subsequently lost orders, and is thus a key dimension in the success or failure of small firms. Inadequate scheduling in the case study firms is also shown to impinge directly and heavily on other aspects of production such as purchasing, quality and even employee morale.

Scheduling in all three case study firms was very problematic. At Wellmaid there was the URGENT/CURRENT file, at FranTech the URGENT stamped job list printout and at Logos no written statement of intent at all. In all three cases the job details, including how long the product was likely to take to manufacture, were kept in the owner-manager's or line managers' heads and calculated using past experience. Thus, if at any point these people are absent the whole production schedule was unworkable.

This is perhaps most surprising at Logos where some of their other systems were rather sophisticated. However, it is also most worrying at Logos as they employed by far the most complex production system, especially since it was project-style manufacture. Bob at Logos did explain that he occasionally used a bar graph to calculate 'man-hours' needed for a job. At Wellmaid the same kind of system was probably sufficient for their needs. However, at FranTech it was shown that their production schedule did not operate in any proactive sense, and instead only enabled a check on progress. Furthermore, the FranTech study showed that due to short production lead-times and constant switching of priorities every job became urgent, and therefore the schedule was based around the most vociferous customers rather than any internal plan.

For all of the companies, much of the scheduling was considered 'automatic' and therefore unproblematic. Thus, as jobs were initiated, their total completion time would be 'intuitively known' by the relevant manager, but other details were not considered necessary as each function would trigger the next into action as the part-finished product moved onto the next stage. This worked well providing there were no hold-ups. When a hold-up occurred it would be up to the owner-manager to resolve. Thus, the actual scheduling systems were all reactive and not proactive. The person responsible for scheduling thus became a problem-solver rather than a planner. The idea that scheduling is on the whole straightforward, and that more sophisticated control techniques are unnecessary, supports Hankinson (1989), particularly as some of my respondents appeared to boast about the fact that scheduling was kept in their heads and that they had no need for mathematical or other methods.

The implications of the poor quality of scheduling were evident at all three companies. Firstly, at Logos, the owners built in a kind of 'safety time'. Thus, shopfloor workers were given times in which to complete production which they saw as unreasonable. The operatives rushed to complete the job and then at the last minute they were given one or two extra weeks to complete. This practice was disliked by operatives who complained that they were initially given unrealistic targets. This made them rush their work, not allowing them time to ensure its quality. The extra time found at the end of the job was thus infuriating. This had led to a situation where production deadlines were not always taken seriously and also promoted an atmosphere of stress or panic in which the operatives worked.

At Wellmaid the inability to schedule effectively meant that jackets had to be cut as one-offs instead of as part of a large order. Cutting out one jacket is less efficient as it takes the same time to cut sixty jackets. Finally, at FranTech poor scheduling not only led to a situation in which every job became urgent but also led to jobs becoming 'lost' within the system. This usually happened as a job moved from one department to another, as each department leader was responsible for updating the schedule for jobs passing through his or her own department. Consequently jobs which were not seen initially as urgent were put on one side and forgotten until the cutomer phoned to progress the order, at which point panic action was called for.

A final point which I will address in this section is the impact which the *dis*organisation of production actually had on shopfloor workers. Ram (1992: 113) commented in his study that 'there seemed to be an expectation that [operatives] should also remedy problems in production that stemmed from a lack of managerial competence'. This can be shown most clearly at FranTech, although elements of this problem were also in evidence at the other two companies. At FranTech purchasing was scheduled according to the delivery dates and incoming components were put into kits. When enough components had arrived to enable an operative to begin work the job would be assigned. However, as there were other constraints on purchasing, it was rare that all the components needed to build a product would arrive together. Thus, the operative would have to complete what she could with the available components and then switch to another job. Further, if components arrived in large batches, which they frequently did, the operative would then be transferred to assist with kitting. This was because of the lack of personnel assigned to this function. The operative would also have to continually monitor the incoming components in order to see if a vital part for her current job had arrived. Thus, operatives spent more time organising their production than building products, despite the existence of two supervisors. Similarly, at Wellmaid machinists would have to organise their work in terms of chasing missing garment pieces from the bundles of work which they were given, or compensating for poor cutting by machining thicker or thinner seams in order to hide this in the finished product.

PROCESSES AND SYSTEMS

It is probably necessary at this point to re-state that Wellmaid, the clothing company, manufactures in small batches while Logos is ostensibly a project-based company. FranTech, the electronics firm, uses large batch, small batch and jobbing-style production, a strategy not recommended by Scherer and McDonald (1988), who suggest that an attempt to serve both custom and standard markets results in extremely unstable businesses. Hill (1987: 22) explains the importance of matching production processes to the product and this is certainly supported by my findings:

> In practice, good operations managers tend intuitively to appreciate what their plant can (and cannot) do profitably and competitively. This intuitive understanding generally develops through experience – usually costly experience! They take on a job which they feel they can do, but then realise that it is somewhat different to most of the orders previously taken on – they find that it takes up more resources than expected, that there are unforeseen technical difficulties, and that it has priorities through the whole production process affecting other products/services. The result: a failure to meet the profit margin on that job, additional inefficiencies elsewhere and an undue allocation of management time and effort throughout.

Both FranTech and Logos have BS5750 quality procedures in place, although their systems are by no means comparable in terms of sophistication. However, when either company receives an order, in theory it should wait for written confirmation before production is commenced. In practice, however, whether or not written confirmation is requested depends on the size of the job. Small jobs in both companies will often be conducted 'outside of the system'.

The companies also vary in the level of bureaucracy employed. At Wellmaid the only internal paperwork comprises small slips of paper with the cutting schedule marked on them. At FranTech, paperwork travels with the job throughout production, and a certificate of conformance is required for incoming material. At Logos an enormous amount of paperwork is required, including material specifications, design drawings, production drawings and specification books. Procedures are documented for every task and no part of production can be changed without written consent from the customer. Quality plans and weld procedures are required for every job and welders must be qualified for each different kind of weld undertaken. This is kept in hand by the document control manager. However, at FranTech no one has this responsibility, and thus the paperwork used is chaotic: production travellers which should be kept with the job are not; design faults are not updated and thus the same mistakes are made again and again; employees dependent on efficient paperwork waste many hours cross-checking information. Thus, companies cope with the degree of sophistication of production with varying competencies.

Hankinson (1987) described small firms' pricing as a 'neglected art'. He found that the firms in his study did not prioritise pricing. They wanted a 'fair and reasonable return' for their products which led them not to adjust prices in line with inflation and to maintain prices at a lower than market level. He also discovered that firms did not know what their production costs were, and did not attempt to monitor them. He concluded that the firms could have charged a much higher price for their products especially as they operated under a Z-shaped demand curve which allowed some variation in prices without a variation in demand. This is borne out in my case studies. For example, while I was working at Wellmaid, the company finally conceded to increasing its prices by 12.5 percent without any outcry from customers.

Pricing is contingent on many factors. All of the companies have a standard cost for labour and overheads, although these are not really kept up-to-date, nor are they thoroughly calculated. For example, a standard rate of £12 per hour to cover labour and overheads is used at FranTech. This has remained the same for at least the last three years. Furthermore, the price given is dependent on the amount of work already being undertaken by the company. Thus, a higher price is given when the company is busy and vice versa. None of the companies appear to be able to produce an accurate breakdown of individual product cost. Furthermore, both FranTech and Wellmaid are very wary about increasing their prices and aware that they probably underprice their products. Thus, the emphasis is on keeping costs down rather than increasing product prices. Logos, on the other hand, does not charge a minimum price for its products, rather it uses its quotation as both an indicator of costs and as a sales device, by concentrating on giving it a very professional image.

The companies vary enormously in the degree of development and design work which they undertake. At Wellmaid, another company's product would be copied in a different fabric or with some other slight variation in design, usually requested by the customer. This work would be completed by one of the owners who would unpick a garment brought to the factory by a customer, make a pattern from this and then make any modifications required by the customer. The modified garment would then be cut out and sewn up by another of the owners to iron out any design problems, such as modifying the pattern to make the sewing easier. Once the design is completed the first few garments are sewn by one of the owners to set the piece-rate.

At Logos there were no standard products and thus each new order required a considerable design input. FranTech really fell between these two. At one end of the scale it would make copies of more expensive equipment by obtaining design drawings from other companies or dismantling a rival product in order to produce layout drawings. At the other end of the scale the company has developed a series of control boards through its own design engineering base. In fact, one engineer who had been with the company for about fifteen years had spent five years almost exclusively on the design of these boards.

Logos undertook some other design work which went beyond that required for straightforward production. This work was undertaken by a young engineer. His difficulty was in technological isolation, not being able to work in a team on a particular design. However, this was solved by his enrolment for a PhD, through which he was able to source the technical expertise of his university department. Finally, it should be said that his design duties were not looked upon favourably by other employees of the company. He was frequently criticised for 'doing nothing', 'being under no pressure' or 'having his nose in a book'. The culture of the company preferred employees to be 'involved', which meant actually being seen to perform a physical activity. This culture was confirmed by the technical director who explained that he would not search for new equipment in trade magazines during office hours as this was seen as reading for pleasure rather than working. Thus, the firms in my study tended to copy other companies' products rather than develop new ones, as Edwards (1983) also found. Where innovation did exist, as at Logos, this activity was not viewed favourably by its employees, thus the process was inevitably discouraged.

In all of the companies there was no thorough costing of development activities. Development costs were not seen as worth calculating, firstly as they were largely labour costs which tend to be downplayed anyway, and secondly because such costs were not seen as recoverable. The first issue is interesting. In the companies there was a strong emphasis on controlling material costs. Fabric was rarely thrown away at Wellmaid, and at FranTech the blowing of a component worth about £5 was seen as a major crisis. However, the cost of time was not viewed in the same light. For example, in one company an employee was summoned to a meeting ten miles away in order to deliver the owner's diary to him. The information required could easily have been given out over the phone. Thus, the costs of time and materials were not viewed equivalently. Secondly, the costs of development were so high in relation to the product costs of low-volume output that they were not seen as reasonable. Thus, quotations or even invoices to customers would drastically underplay development costs. One owner told me that if he tried to charge the real costs the customer would laugh at him.

All this appears to militate against the possibility of new product development in small firms, and yet small companies have a reputation for innovation on account of their entrepreneurial culture (Cannon 1989). This is a myth which has been exploded by many writers. For example, Rothwell (1989) found that the concentration of small firms on innovation varies considerably between sectors of industry. In particular, where capital and/ or R&D requirements and entry costs are high, small firms have played a smaller part.

PURCHASING AND INVENTORY

[M]anaging inventory consists of two major elements that are closely related. One is getting the various items into the factory or store at the time they will be needed. This activity involves knowing what and how much to order, when to order, and what price to pay. The other element is making sure that the items are used to produce a profit.

(Mulvihill 1969: 3)

Other studies looking at inventory control have been of the 'action research' variety, sending experts and academics to attempt the implementation of particular systems in small firms. For example, Ashcroft (1989) conducted a study of the implementation of optimised production technology (OPT) in one 'relatively' small manufacturing company. Rhodes (1979) continued in this vein by examining the use of 'economic order quantity' in small-batch manufacturers. He showed that such a method produced a required order size of between one-quarter and one-tenth of the batch sizes acceptable to suppliers. Thus, some conventional operational research methods used in large organisations are fundamentally inappropriate to smaller firms. Consequently it is also important to look at the special conditions of small firms in order to examine why such measures are not taken spontaneously. The attitudes of owner-managers thus begin to appear. Hankinson (1989: 40), investigating output determination by small firms, explained that:

Efficient operation of any system also requires a minimum level of work in progress to ensure that when a particular resource finishes a task, another is waiting to start. All this was accepted by the . . . firms, but what was much less well appreciated was that overfilling the system was potentially just as damaging as underfilling it.

This is supported by the FranTech case study where not only was there a huge amount of WIP but, through its disorganisation, much of it had become top priority, thus making a nonsense of the scheduling and inventory control systems. Further research linking owner attitudes and inventory control asserts that some managers realise the importance of inventory control but lack the knowledge of how to handle it with their limited resources, and that some are unaware of the existence of inventory problems. Indeed, many small business firms do not keep any records at all (Saladin and Hoy 1983).

Thus, this kind of research begins to show some of the reasons for the inadequacy of small firm inventory control. This is more closely related to this study which shows the actual nature of inventory control and purchasing in three small companies.

All of the companies in the study were aware of the need to keep stock to a minimum. This was not through any aspirations for a JIT inventory system, but rather through the necessity of having adequate cashflow, and thereby not tying up capital in excessive stocks. Thus, minimal stock is viewed as constraining rather than, as Mulvihill (1969) suggests, a conscious strategy for cost control. For example, none of the firms intentionally kept finished goods stock, although Wellmaid hoped to keep stocks in the future of complicated or small items in order to buffer them against seasonal variations in demand. This aside, all the companies were dependent on timely and efficient purchasing to ensure that the right materials were available at the right time, and not before. FranTech and Logos also made use of stage payments in order to fund the acquisition of parts for products with a long production lead time. Thus, purchasing became inextricably linked to inventory control. Chase (1981) identified practically no research on purchasing in his review of research on small firm production.

Logos was the only firm to have a full-time buyer, although he had no technical expertise, and therefore purchasing became a kind of team effort between him and the project managers. Furthermore, he had little purchasing experiences and tended to buy from a vendor without comparing the prices with other vendors of the same product. Finally, there was little or no communication between the buyer and the estimators, thus items were sourced from different vendors to those contacted for the budget. This contradicts work by Gupta (1988), who celebrates the benefits of small firms' communications, stating that the inventory control system becomes meaningful when accurate schedules are available and when assessments of production rates are realistic. While the business is small, he argues, personal interaction between managers may be sufficient to accomplish these tasks.

Both FranTech and Wellmaid relied on directors or managers to perform the buying function alongside their other duties. For Wellmaid, this was a relatively simple task, as their main component, wax cloth, was purchased from only one supplier at a time. Furthermore, only three suppliers for this grade of material exist in Britain, so vendor selection was rudimentary. At Logos and FranTech, however, vendor selection was much more complicated. Both companies had dozens of suppliers, and both operated a BS5750 approved vendor system. This involved monitoring suppliers on price, delivery and quality, although as explained in the case studies neither of these companies carried out this process very effectively. In fact, the system itself is rather clumsy for use by those companies with many suppliers. Furthermore, both companies worked outside the system when they felt this was necessary, thus unapproved vendors were approached in times of need.

All the companies in the studies were working to tight deadlines since, firstly, their customers tended to be large, and as they too were aware of the necessity of keeping small stocks the delivery lead-times imposed were short and not really open to negotiation. Secondly, because cashflow in these companies was limited, purchases were made as near to the sale date of the product, allowing the companies to recover their costs as quickly as possible. The companies have managed to counter this to a certain extent by encouraging their customers to make stage payments; however, this is not always possible. The consequences of this for Logos and FranTech were that the paperwork which they were working to was not usually thoroughly checked before purchasing commenced. At FranTech in particular, customers' paperwork was frequently sub-standard. Thus, the wrong components would be ordered from faulty documentation. Further, long lead-time items at both FranTech and Logos had to be ordered from provisional paperwork in order to receive the items on time and meet the required delivery date. Later the paperwork would be updated and some components changed. Thus, wrong components would be ordered from provisional or incomplete paperwork. In either of these cases the companies were left holding obsolete stock, sometimes worth thousands of pounds.

A third problem associated in particular with FranTech was that because of low quality of the company's own paperwork, important items would be missing from the parts lists. In one instance this led to a hold-up in production when components had been ordered, but not the PCBs on which to mount them. This had been due to the printer printing the parts list running out of paper halfway through and thus not printing out the vital components. Furthermore, due to cashflow limitations, it was sometimes impossible to source expensive items in a given month. The consequences of this and the previous problem were that items then had to be procured quickly, incurring penalty payments from suppliers.

The fourth problem is poor quality items. If an item is ordered and arrives at the appropriate time but the quality is poor, then there is often no time to reorder a replacement. Thus, faulty items are used in production. This can have two consequences. At Wellmaid, for example, faulty cloth meant that garments had to be cut around the faults, thus leaving a large amount of scrap. At Logos and FranTech this could mean obtaining a concession from the customer which might lower the price, or even that the product was rejected. As shown in Figure 6.2, this becomes a vicious circle where limited cashflow imposes low stocks which leaves the companies open to inappropriate or poor quality purchases. This in turn decreases revenue and so perpetuates the cashflow problem.

Another potential problem at Wellmaid and FranTech is the extent to which all the buying information is kept in the heads of those responsible for purchasing. In both companies there is little or no documented information concerning vendors. The buyer intuitively knows which vendor will be able to deliver quickly or cheaply. At FranTech the buyer, Harry, is the only employee able to adequately interpret some of the customer parts lists. The potential inconvenience of this is shown in the Logos case study when the new buyer had great difficulty taking on the job. Disruptions are thus caused by a reliance on the person rather than the function. An employee leaving a key position can have disastrous implications when the functions of the task are not documented.

Lin (1980) appears to show a greater understanding of small firm operations than most, through an assertion that inventory control systems for small businesses must be inexpensive, comprehensible, easy to use and not too time-consuming. However, most of the inventory and control systems discussed in books and journals deal with complex mathematical models beyond the grasp of small business owners. Instead, Lin recommends a two-bin system that can be easily and cheaply implemented.

At Wellmaid the system of stock control is entirely visual. This applies to raw materials, work in progress and finished goods stock. Work in progress is clearly labelled and thus easily traced, as is finished goods stock, except that this is constrained by lack of space so that jackets are bunched tightly together. This system generally works well, except for some minor exceptions. Firstly, if incoming fabric is not checked for quality and one or more rolls are faulty, then although it appears that a certain number of rolls are in stock some may be unusable. Secondly, rolls which are part-used should be clearly labelled so that they can be easily

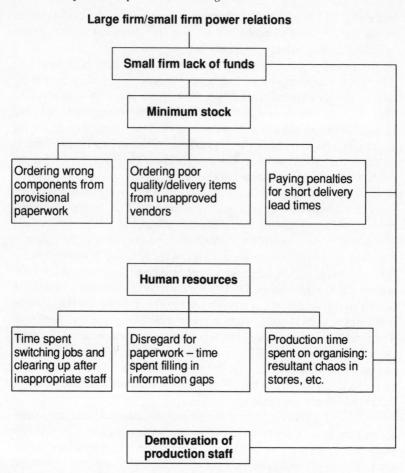

Large firm/small firm power relations

Small firm lack of funds

Minimum stock

| Ordering wrong components from provisional paperwork | Ordering poor quality/delivery items from unapproved vendors | Paying penalties for short delivery lead times |

Human resources

| Time spent switching jobs and clearing up after inappropriate staff | Disregard for paperwork – time spent filling in information gaps | Production time spent on organising: resultant chaos in stores, etc. |

Demotivation of production staff

Figure 6.2 Small firms' funding: the vicious circle

identified for re-cuts. At present much time is wasted trying to match shades of cloth from about thirty rolls. Finally, off-cuts should be stored somewhere more visible. At the moment they are placed in a box so that only the top layers are visible. However, solving this may be impossible due to lack of space. On the whole, however, a simple visual stock control system, combined with an annual stocktake, appears to be adequate and appropriate.

At Logos an annual stocktake also contributes to the inventory control system. However, though a complete list of all items in stores is made, when items are subsequently removed they are not crossed off. Thus, the list is quickly outdated. Logos and FranTech both have very thorough systems for the full traceability of items held in the stores. Both companies use a system of numbering all parts along with keeping documentation which ensures that information such as full part description, date of purchase and vendor is kept for each number. However, both systems fall down, at Logos when parts are not attributed a number, and at FranTech when small items are removed from their packaging. This appears to be caused in both companies by the relatively low status attributed to the stores function. At FranTech there is no full-time storekeeper and at Logos only one storekeeper is employed where 'one-and-a-half' or two people would be more appropriate. Perhaps this is because the stores is not seen as contributing directly to production, and thus new employees are taken on to build products rather than to control their inputs.

A huge majority of the inventory kept by Logos was work in progress, as its products were so large and took so long to build. Thus, new pieces which were built were then affixed to the frame of the unit where they stayed until the project was completed. Similarly at FranTech many jobs of varying sizes were at various stages in the production process. Where these jobs rested tended to depend not on machine availability, but rather on the number of components required for completion as well as operator availability. The problems associated with control were similar in some ways at both FranTech and Logos. At Logos the issue was of controlling contamination of stainless steels, where as at FranTech it was of controlling static. Finally, at FranTech, the chaotic scheduling system led to many items of work in progress becoming lost either physically, or in terms of not being included in the schedule. This would only be discovered when a customer phoned to progress an order or the item was stumbled upon.

For consumable items, such as studs, nuts and bolts and so on, all companies used a simple visual system and this appeared to work well. There was a problem at Logos with welding consumables, which could be easily determined from manufacturing drawings. Thus, many of the problems tend not to be caused through system design but rather through a non-adherence to the system in place. There appears to be no call for more sophisticated techniques such as materials requirement planning (MRP) or other operational research methods. The origin of the non-conformance with inventory control systems seems to stem from an anti-bureaucratic culture, which is perpetuated by management. Thus, paperwork systems are seen as irrelevant by those with responsibility for them. The consequences of this directly impinge on production through shopfloor workers having to check paperwork and the components with which they work before they commence assembly.

Finally, Gregory *et al.* (1983: 476), in their study of batch production decisions, add to the list of contingencies which influence inventory control in small firms. Although the study was carried out to find general solutions for use in the improvement of small firms operations, their research forced them to acknowledge some of the idiosyncrasies which render such tools somewhat less than universal:

> There was a batch size governed by the size of a trolley which would pass between the banks of machinery; the delay by a day or two of acceptance of deliveries at the end of the month in order to extend by a month the discount deadline; the need to ensure that, when coloured yarn was used in a production batch, it came from the same dye batch: a batch size in a sequential production process which dwindled owing to reject materials and pilfering; the stage at which sub-assemblies were made being governed by their immunity to shelf damage. The influence of tax relief on stockholdings [and the] . . . power of the large firm as both creditor and debtor can also have serious implications on the stocking policy.

These aspects arose in the study of just twelve manufacturing companies. Thus, the relevance of universal production systems is highly questionable.

EQUIPMENT AND TECHNOLOGY

There has been much research into small firms' use of new technology, and many attempts to link its adoption to small firm growth or success (Dodgson 1984/5). Many studies have found that larger companies (not surprisingly) attempt the implementation of new technology rather than smaller ones (Libertore *et al.* 1990). This might appear to be common sense when the financial conditions of small companies and the costs of new technology and its implementation are borne in mind. Further studies have looked at the kinds of technologies introduced and concluded that smaller companies tend to purchase secondhand equipment from their larger counterparts, which they may then rebuild or modify (Oi 1983). This is supported by this research when, for example, one business owner purchased a loom which weaved wiring harnesses for aeroplanes. He then converted it from a unidimensional mechanical machine by breaking the mechanism and incorporating a computer numerical control (CNC) unit, allowing programming for different wiring operations.

Other studies have attempted to link the introduction of new technology to small-firm success. For example, Steiner and Solem (1988) suggest that successful companies tend to change their production technology and product-mix more frequently in response to industry advances and changing customer needs. However, we must be wary of claims which link technology and success, as other factors may be involved. For example, why did the companies choose to implement it in the first place? Is this indicative of a more enlightened approach by their owners? How far is technology the sole variable governing success, and how far is it a symptom rather than a cause of success?

Technology is also prescribed as a panacea to promote company growth. Meyer and Roberts (1988) see the creation of an internal 'critical mass' of engineering talent as central to the building of a distinctive 'core technology' which in turn forms the foundation for effective product development. This, they argue, represents the best opportunity for rapid growth of a young firm.

Finally, perhaps the most useful studies have linked new technology and owner attitudes. For example, Garsombke and Garsombke (1989: 44) found that firms which did not adopt new technology saw few barriers to its introduction, but that those which did saw many problems (including time, money, knowledge and staff constraints):

> Firms [which had implemented new technology], however, experienced many indicators of successful performance: increases in output, improvement in material flow, lowered inventory safety stocks, and increases in sales and profitability. It would seem that entrepreneurs who adapt to new technologies are realistic about problems that their small firms need to overcome, but that such realism does not inhibit them from making changes in automation, computerization and robotization.

It appears that the technology employed by the companies has more to do with industry sector rather than firm size. For example, although Wellmaid and FranTech employed the same number of workers, the level of technology was far higher in the electronics company than at the clothing company, as indeed one might expect. Wellmaid employed virtually no technology other than sewing machines, scissors, (manual) studding machines and an electric cutter. Other than this they had a computer for dealing with financial items such as invoices and statements. In fact they had not even heard of many kinds of technology such as CAD/CAM.

Both Logos and FranTech employed a high degree of technology, which included the use of computers for wordprocessing, CAD and accounting and financial control packages. However, the level of technology employed by the companies does not necessarily impact on the sophistication of production organisation. This supports Gupta (1988: 17) who explains that:

While investments in significantly better production machinery may be made, the further investment in control systems – which save money rather than make it – will often not be made.

At Logos, the products manufactured were very hi-tech for the mechanical engineering industry and the levels of skill and job knowledge required for both production and inspection were significant. At FranTech the technology level of the products was defined as being reliable, using tried and tested components, but not at the cutting edge of development.

Both FranTech and Logos have invested fairly heavily in capital equipment for improving production. Wellmaid has implemented the more cautious approach of leasing most of its equipment. At Logos the payback has taken longer than expected but on the whole the investment will be proved worthwhile over the next few years. FranTech has been less cautious. The equipment in which it has invested, and for which it is still paying, was for the improvement in batch production methods used in sub-contracting work. However, since their major sub-contractor terminated its contract with the company these items of equipment have been severely under-utilised. This is consistent with Hankinson's (1989: 41) point from his study:

> Excess capacity was widespread. . . . If outputs had been raised to the full capacity level then the majority of the firms would have suffered no financial hardship. . . . Yet there was little evidence that subsidiary production was specifically employed for the reduction of excess capacity.

In addition, Anoochehri (1988) suggests that increased planning horizons could be achieved, since communication and the sharing of information between manufacturers and their customers could result in smoother demand: if manufacturers are informed of the production plans of their customers, they can meet their needs more effectively. However, this does not acknowledge the kinds of power relationships between small and large companies. Unless the larger sub-contractors have a vested interest in helping out their small suppliers such communication would not be likely. Large firms do not inform small suppliers of their plans because there is no economic rationality for doing so.

Thus, it is unlikely that FranTech's investment will pay back in the near future. FranTech does, however, borrow equipment from its customers free of charge. By forging good links with customers this kind of practice has become possible, providing it is in the interests of large customers and is a very efficient solution to the problem of technological investment.

Although FranTech introduced production technology to reduce the possibility of human error, this has not necessarily been achieved. One shopfloor worker complained that the work had become so boring that it was performed absent-mindedly and thus became open to more human error than when she performed the work manually. This was in direct contradiction to the feelings of her line manager who felt that the introduction of CAM would improve quality. Perhaps there should have been more consultation before such equipment was introduced.

Finally, the two more technologically sophisticated companies had attempted or were attempting to computerise inventory control. It is difficult to say whether this would be of benefit to either company as the systems already in place are not used properly. A computerised system could suffer the same degree of misuse. At FranTech the inventory was, at one time, computerised. However, through carelessness the whole system was erased and the company has never bothered to reinstate it. It can thus be assumed that its advantages were outweighed by the time-costs of reinstating it.

STRATEGIC OPERATIONS

In the area of strategic operations the literature is dominated by planning. This involves studies of the extent, sophistication and time horizons of small business planning, or linking planning to effectiveness, success or stage of growth. For example, Bernolak (1981) recommends that small firms can often enhance their performance by improving their planning and forecasting variables such as sales, inventories, direct and indirect labour requirements, utilisation of plant, equipment and tools, utilisation of energy, water and consumable materials. Marucheck and Peterson (1988) recommend microcomputer software for use in the areas of business planning, production planning, master production schedules, capacity management and MRP. They claim this is suitable for small businesses in view of their having better lines of communication, a flexible workforce with broader job responsibilities, and a leaner management structure which is close to daily operations.

Firms employing forecasting and aggregate planning techniques financially out-perform those firms that who do not employ these techniques, according to Riggs and Bracker (1986). Orpen (1985) related planning to performance and found that the extent of long-range planning was unrelated to company performance, but that high-performing firms appeared to use a more formal planning process and a longer time horizon than less successful firms.

Almost in contradiction with this is Robinson's (1979: 19) assertion that 'simplicity, not sophistication is critical. Rather than specialised forecasting techniques, a simple and rational planning process appears more likely to aid and be adopted by the small business'. He goes on to give us greater insight into the actual planning systems employed by small firms:

> When decision-making in the small business environment is considered . . . it is likely to be characterised by intuitive 'seat-of-the-pants' speculation based on the owner's experience and dealing with present, operational issues. The owner/operator has minimal time, resources and skills to engage in sophisticated forecasting. Furthermore, the owner has moulded his (or her) [*sic*] decision-making activity through repeated crisis management, focusing on day-to-day decisions with relatively short time spans.
>
> (Robinson 1979: 20)

Elsewhere, Robinson and his colleagues related the type of planning to stage of growth:

> At Stage One, SP [strategic planning] is principally directed at enabling the firm to improve its ability to gain a foothold in the marketplace (sales growth). Thus, as the results suggest, there appears to be a trade off between sales growth and profitability in Stage One. At Stage Two, SP concentrates on the firm's growth (sales and organizational size) as it seeks to become an established, viable competitor. After growth is achieved, SP in Stage Three firms emphasizes growth stabilization and profit improvement to insure the firm's long-term viability in its products and markets.
>
> (Robinson *et al.* 1984: 52)

Finally, Lawlor (1988) found that strategies in his study firms were frequently confused with budgets and sales targets. Again, however, such models assume growth in defined stages which are largely treated unproblematically.

All of the companies in the study stated that growth was one of their aims. However, the questions when? how much? and by what strategies? could not be answered. There was much reference to the recession and the fact that things might get better once this was over. It was felt that the end of the recession may trigger an increase in orders which would lead to growth, but none of the companies attempted to employ aggressive strategies to seek new markets. Thus, growth was something which happened to a company, not something which a firm actively pursued. All of the companies had strategic aims to increase the number of customers with whom they traded, although this was difficult for Logos as only a few very large customers exist for their products. FranTech aimed to expand its sub-contract work in order to fund its own development projects. However, the main concern of all of the companies, especially FranTech and Wellmaid, was for survival.

The instability of such firms is illustrated in the FranTech case study, where the company nearly ceased trading over one bad debt. Both the other companies agreed that one large bad debt could put them out of business. All of the companies traded in fairly turbulent and highly competitive markets, and this could to some degree explain their short planning horizons. This characteristic makes a nonsense of the claim that small firms could easily implement JIT systems (Ettkin *et al.* 1990). As Anoochehri (1988: 26) explains:

> To fully adopt JIT, a manufacturer needs, (1) a relatively stable demand, (2) the ability to produce in small lots just in time to meet the demand of the next work station or customers, and (3) the ability to receive raw materials at the right time and in the right quantity.

Despite this, he goes on to recommend JIT systems for small companies. Small firms are in fact unlikely to be able to secure JIT agreements with large suppliers as their purchasing power is too small to be in the interests of the larger company. The alternative then is to source from a small supplier, thus guaranteeing some bargaining power (Anoochehri 1988).

However, it is the very instability of small companies which leads them to choose larger companies as suppliers. As one bad debt could wipe out a small firm then other small firms are not necessarily trusted suppliers, as they could cease trading before vital components are dispatched. Furthermore, delivery promises from small suppliers were often broken in the study firms. It is my experience that small firms will frequently promise delivery dates that they cannot possibly meet. Worries about not obtaining replacement orders are a long way behind immediate survival. It is possible, however, that this is more to do with the present economic climate than the nature of small firms.

Logos differed slightly in this respect from the other two companies who really only planned for six months in advance. For example, Logos did look at payback periods for expensive items of capital equipment and had begun negotiating a licence agreement with a U.S. company.

Another aspect which all the firms had in common was their desire for standardisation. Each company had hopes to create product lines which they could make from standard components, without a design input. At FranTech this took the form of opting for sub-contract work in large batches for which they could use their specialised equipment. Logos hoped to provide a line of products for which they could provide spare parts.

Wellmaid, too, hoped to eventually increase their batch sizes. However, each company had to ensure that they retained the necessary degree of flexibility which would prevent them having to turn down large orders. Thus, rather than aiming for flexibility, which is frequently extolled as one of the virtues of small firms, the companies aimed for standardisation and dedicated equipment. This was moderated by a desire to never have to turn down a large order. Thus, flexibility, rather than a competitive strategy, was forced upon the firms through necessity. This rather militates against the flexible firm and flexible specialisation debates (addressed later). The results of this kind of policy were noted by Lawlor (1988: 20):

> Over the many years since [the study firms] began, a complex mix of orders had been accepted which the manufacturing system found increasingly difficult to satisfy . . . the result is a do-it-all plant which satisfies no strategy, no market and no task.

A further characteristic which all the firms shared was poor communications. Communication channels were unusual as the functional departments were not like those found in management textbooks. For example, at Wellmaid, these were cutting, sewing and paperwork. It is thus imperative that information from the director responsible for paperwork is passed on to the other two. Poor communication systems were manifest in several different ways. Firstly, where a company had more than one director, there was conflict between them. The firm with only one owner (FranTech) had started with two partners but relations between them had become so strained that one had left. This conflict appeared to be due to several reasons but one which was frequently put forward was lack of communication. This took the form of one owner accusing another of secrecy or withholding information. In fact, in two firms relations were so strained that the directors were unable to discuss issues as and when they came up, but rather had to wait until they were 'all in a good mood'.

Secondly, directors were perhaps overly secretive in passing on information to employees. For example, at Wellmaid, employees were not informed about the imminent opening of a factory shop. Furthermore, it was not unusual at FranTech for Raj to cancel or hold back jobs without telling anyone else what he was doing. Employees or line managers were not informed of different production priorities, neither were they party to adjusting these priorities. At Logos even identifying job progress was very difficult for employees who were not directly involved in production of a specific job, and thus there was a strong desire to build up some more formal communication channels. The latter example perhaps shows the way in which increasing formalisation of communication channels is required with increasing firm size.

Finally, communication of employees' grievances to employers was shown in all companies to be extremely difficult. Some issues were discussed but others were not. Furthermore, employers' rejections of unions ensured that even when an individual was informally nominated to communicate such issues to management, they felt unable to tackle some aspects for fear of personal retributions. Thus, communications in all of the companies has been shown to be poor, and evidence from the only company which had achieved substantial growth showed that communications had actually worsened rather than improved with time. The informal channels which had been sufficient when all personnel shared the same office and sat near to each other were now fundamentally inadequate, yet no plan of action to overcome this problem was in evidence.

Strategic decision-making tended to be a rather informal, *ad hoc* process in all of the companies. Furthermore, such decisions were really taken using limited information, as information is expensive and time-consuming to collect. Thus, decisions tended to be made on a trial-and-error basis. A company would try a particular course of action for a limited period and then change to something else if it did not work. How quickly the change was made depends on how disastrous the consequences of the action were. For example, FranTech decided to build up its sub-contracting activities until the sub-contractor withdrew its orders. The new strategic objective was quickly modified to place emphasis on the company's own product range. When it became obvious that the income from these products was not sufficient, sub-contract work was sought once again.

All three companies had either chosen or worked towards a particular market niche. Wellmaid deliberately pitched their jackets at a niche just below the high-quality end of the market. Their aim was to create jackets using high-quality fabric, but to make the jackets less intricate and therefore cheaper. By doing this they felt they could compete effectively without becoming one of the sweatshop-style enterprises at the lower end of the market. Perhaps the most successful use of the 'go up-market' strategy has been by Logos. When the company started it was a 'backstreet fabrication shop'. After securing the BS5750 the company deliberately became more specialised and in doing so finely developed the skills of its workforce. The outcome of this is that the company now only performs precision metalwork jobs and has design and skill specialisms in this area. This has enabled the company to move to the most profitable end of the mechanical engineering industry and this is reflected in its growth.

Obtaining the BS5750 was part of a grander plan for FranTech and since they obtained the certificate they have moved into the manufacture of higher quality products. Ostensibly this means a move from small customers to large customers. This enables the company to simplify production, since it entails a switch in orders from small to large batches. In many ways this policy has paid off except that just before Christmas 1992 one of these large customers pulled out, precipitating the redundancy of thirteen FranTech employees.

At Logos, as there are three directors, most decisions tend to be made by consensus. As two of them are fairly like-minded, the third is often over-ruled. This has caused considerable tension over the years which is not lost on their employees. One employee referred to this tension as 'the class thing'. This was because employees perceived the engineering director as working class and the other directors as upper class. The strategy used at Wellmaid was that one partner passed on little information to the other two and consequently tended to make most decisions herself. This also created tension between the partners. Major decisions however, were consensual although as only one partner had access to most information she could be selective in what she passed on to the others. Finally, at FranTech senior managers were consulted about major decisions, but their advice was frequently rejected. Furthermore, the outcome of decisions was often not communicated to managers who would become informed through customers or suppliers or other external parties. Tension arising from decision-making was therefore also evident at FranTech.

It was very rare for employees in any of the companies to be involved in decision-making. Decisions were made on the basis of intuition. When I asked Raj how he went about pricing, for example, he pointed to his stomach implying a 'gut feeling'. No employees in any of the companies were consulted in the making of pricing decisions. Much of this behaviour appeared to stem from a distrust of any other person with the company's welfare. This also led to owners' assertions that they would never step back and hand over the running of the company to a manager. This was characterised by Rita who said, 'If we can't do it how can anyone else?' Only one owner had directly delegated some of his responsibilities so that he could spend more time on leisure activities. This was seen, not only by the other directors, but also by employees, as him not taking his job seriously enough.

By examining some of the small firms operations management literature a reader could be forgiven for thinking that production in small firms is simply operations management writ small. I have challenged this by pointing out some of the contradictions inherent within the literature and by comparing this with my own findings. The next three chapters deal with some other issues raised in the case studies in more detail.

7 Recruiting, training and flexibility

In this chapter I bring together three key themes which emerged from my reading of the small firms literature and through my empirical research in Wellmaid, Logos and FranTech. The first two, recruiting and training, are closely related to the third, flexibility. A considerable debate around the issue of flexibility – something some writers see as both synonymous with the small business sector and as its most positive asset, but which others see as either myth or as wolf in sheep's clothing – has considered, among other things, the recruiting (and dismissing) patterns of small firms (numerical flexibility) and levels of skill and training (flexible specialisation). In order to get beyond the hype of the flexibility debate, this chapter foregrounds its discussion in a consideration of the recruitment and training procedures described by other small firms researchers, and those disclosed in my three study firms. This analysis leads into an overview of the flexibility debate informed by these findings.

Recruiting at the three companies in this study was conducted overwhelmingly by word of mouth. This included both shopfloor workers and managers. If it was heard on the grapevine that someone had been made redundant from a competitor it was not unusual for them to be contacted and offered a job. This practice can be partially explained at Wellmaid by the company's extreme difficulty in recruiting trained workers, attributed to the fact that many sewing jobs were available in the area. However, as Steiner and Solem (1988: 55) found:

It is also interesting to note that although all of the companies in the[ir] sample compete in the same labor market, successful companies stated that adequate labor was available at competitive wage levels, while less successful firms stated that this was not the case. Where direct comparisons could be made within comparable industry classifications, no actual differences were found between wage rates in successful and less successful enterprises.

However, it has been argued that sewing is no longer seen as an attractive occupation, particularly amongst younger women (Ram 1992), owing to long hours and low pay. Phizacklea (1990: 24) explains that women sewing machinists are some of the lowest-paid manufacturing workers since:

> First, they enter the labour market labelled as inferior bearers of labour because they occupy a subordinate position in social relations prior to their entry into the labour market. Second, it is argued that they can be paid less than men because they are partially dependent upon [men's wages] . . . for the costs of their daily and long term reproduction [a position which trade unions have done nothing to challenge in their fight for a 'family wage']. Third, it is within this context that men excluded women from the skilled craft guilds, so women were denied access to socially recognised skills. Fourth, while the Factory Acts passed in 1834 were seen to provide protection for women . . . the acts defined women as minors and also provided a legal underpinning to the notion that a woman's rightful place was in the home caring for her husband and children.

The implications of this are summarised by Elson and Pearson (1981), who suggest that women do not do 'unskilled jobs' because they are the bearers of inferior labour. Instead, the jobs that they do are deemed 'unskilled' because women enter them *already* determined as inferior bearers of labour.

This point is perhaps most aptly illustrated by my positioning, during the fieldwork, within Wellmaid. Traditionally, the job of pattern cutter within the clothing industry is a skilled job, done by a male worker. But within half an hour of starting my participant observation in the company this was the job which I undertook. I was, however, never allowed to use a sewing machine. Thus, a so-called skilled job was given to a complete novice with no experience. As Wellmaid is an all-woman company, they had a female pattern cutter. She was not paid any more than the machinists in the company, and therefore her job was obviously not seen as more skilled. Finally, it should be said that the wages at Logos for welding were four times those at Wellmaid for machining, yet as an outsider I would say they required similar degrees of skill. Thus, the shortage of labour described at Wellmaid is not a labour shortage *per se* but rather a shortage of cheap, flexible and female labour, a point also discussed by Ram (1992).

Workers in the companies were frequently given jobs by virtue of their 'family' status. This process is inextricably linked with the most important quality which an individual can bring to the job, which is to be able to 'fit in' with the existing workforce and company culture (Ram and Holliday 1993). Almost all employees were interviewed only by the firms' owners and not by their immediate superiors or co-workers, meaning that new employees' skills were not properly investigated. At Logos, for example, interviews were dominated by the owners 'selling' the company to the interviewee and not vice versa. JobCentre and newspaper advertisements were rarely used. This supports the idea that small-firm recruitment is based more on the personal judgement of the owner-manager and less on tangible skills or qualifications (Cowling *et al.* 1988).

A factor which must be influential in the inadequacy of recruiting is the limited skills of the entrepreneurs. Watkins (1983) asserts that none of the factors in the prior experiences of the owner-managers in his study (such as education, professional studies or work experience) had been an appropriate or adequate preparation for the task of actually owning and running their own businesses. None of the business owners in my research were well versed in management education. Only one had attended a formal course.

Discussing the problems of entrepreneurship education in general, Curran (1988: 31) has noted that its need may be uneven:

> Production [education] usually requires less attention because owner-managers, whatever their other business skills, often know quite a lot about the goods or services their business is based upon either from previous work experience or the knowledge required is relatively limited.

However, it could be argued that an owner-manager can have a great deal of product knowledge without knowing how to organise its production. Even modest production levels require a knowledge of or ability to develop quite complex systems for scheduling, inventory control, quality control and so on.

One overriding factor which the case study firms perceived as an important consideration in recruiting was the price of labour – low labour costs were always attractive, hence the excitement caused by nearby redundancies. Rainnie (1989) suggests that small firms in the traditional manufacturing sector deliberately recruit disadvantaged work groups from 'loose' labour markets in order to minimise wages and the threat of industrial action. This is reinforced by Oi (1983: 148):

> The composition of employment systematically varies with size. An increase in firm size is accompanied by a rise in educational attainment,

a higher fraction of employees in salaried supervisory positions, and relatively few part-time workers. . . . Wage rates (average hourly earnings) climb with firm size . . . the hourly wages in the largest firms [studied] were 49.6 percent above wages in the smallest firms. When the effects of worker characteristics (sex, race, education, job tenure etc.) were included in the wage equation, the adjusted difference fell to 24.7 percent.

Thus, smaller companies tend to recruit from disadvantaged labour groups. What this implied for the companies in my research was a trade-off between the level of skill possessed by an employee and their cost. Thus, people with few formal qualifications and limited experience were recruited to fairly demanding positions. Promoting employees already working in the companies was also a favoured strategy for economy, and for two further reasons. Firstly, job descriptions in the companies tended to be vague and eclectic. This appears to be due to the variety of tasks which people in the firms were required to perform. There were more jobs than employees, and thus the tasks were shared between workers even if the portfolio of tasks given to each employee was unrelated. Also, in the companies which had grown, employees tended to have created their own jobs. Therefore, although they had been recruited to perform a particular function, the necessity may have arisen for that person to take on more jobs, or to change jobs altogether. Thus, as employees became competent at performing their tasks, and thus had more free time, they took on other tasks to ensure that they were kept occupied. It was therefore doubtful that an 'outsider' would comprehend the complex of activities that any one employee would undertake.

The second reason for promoting internally was that the person would probably already be enculturated into the organisation, and thereby understand the requirements of the owners. Thus, employees were recruited according to their degree of alignment with the goals and attitudes of their employers. The problems associated with this include the fact that new ways of doing things never get introduced. I have called this processual inertia: doing things this way because they have always been done this way. However, this characteristic has also been identified by other writers:

[S]enior managers are often not brought in from outside . . . but are promoted up through the company. Often promotion is dependent both on the efficient execution of a particular line management function over a number of years and, more ominously, on an acceptable 'conformity' of behaviour and acceptance of traditional organizational structures. As a result, new senior managers tend not to question or challenge the managerial system or company attitudes and this does nothing to encourage either organizational change or new product development. This promotional 'conservatism' is particularly observable in tightly-controlled family businesses, in which the owners' paramount concern in bringing new members to the boardroom table is that their own position and attitudes are not challenged. The new manager, ideally, is required to be *plus royaliste que le roi.*

(Mason 1973: 31)

Also, people with skills complementary to those of the owners are not recruited or promoted as their talents are not recognisable to the existing bosses (Lowden 1988). This is in direct contradiction with the more romantic small firm proponents, such as Anoochehri (1988), who suggests that smaller manufacturers have greater flexibility and a more entrepreneurial culture, as is discussed in greater detail below.

A further important selection criterion is that the potential employee is already trained. At any of the case study firms, the collapse of a local company in the same industry is viewed with relish. This leaves a pool of redundant, trained people willing to work for low wages. A very small minority of employees were ever offered training by the companies. Employees who were trained tended to be YTS recruits or 'apprentices'. In this way their training was at least partially funded by the state. None of the companies felt able to afford training for other new employees. Thus, the more responsible the position, the less likely it was that the new recruit would be given training. This was also a contributory factor to the companies' reluctance to employ graduates, who were considered too expensive for their initial ability, while developing them for the future was not seen as worthwhile either, since it was assumed that they would find better jobs elsewhere once their training was complete.

Closely related to this is the fact that the owners of these companies all showed a reluctance to train existing employees using external courses. As Adams and Walbank (1983) found, the emphasis in small firms tends to be on skills acquired by experience rather than formal education or training. In my study firms, this was on the whole apparently due to the fear that funding people to obtain recognised qualifications would encourage them to seek more lucrative employment elsewhere. Thus, external training was only given to those employees who had been with the company for a long period and who had therefore proved their loyalty. This was not automatic even if the need to develop a particular skill was evident, as shown in the Wellmaid case study where the pattern cutter was held back from learning to use the electric cutter.

Thus, that training which was given tended to be internal and inadequate.

At Wellmaid this involved a new machinist watching another for two hours. At FranTech the employee would immediately begin production under partial supervision, and at Logos a new office worker would read the quality manual and then begin his or her job. Training for the use of new technology was usually carried out by its supplier. A further problem associated with this was that existing employees, although they were allocated to train new ones, were rarely given time off to spend with new recruits. Thus, they were expected to train another person while maintaining their productivity. Being a new employee in any of the case study companies is a very stressful experience. The exceptions to this are apprentices at Logos, whose training is controlled by an external training association and is very thorough.

Of course, the reason for the paucity of training is lack of time and money. Adams and Walbank (1983) found that owner-managers are generally reluctant to spend much time on or to invest in formal education or training. Further, Griffith and Dorsman (1987) found a disparity between the intentions of firms concerning training and actual practice – many managers in their survey recognised the importance of training, yet very little was actually spent on it.

The perceived expense of training is both in terms of non-productive wages and in terms of materials which may be wasted. One way of diminishing these costs is through the use of government schemes, such as YTS or ET, although such schemes were not so much viewed as apprenticeships as cheap labour for unskilled tasks. However, the companies must still fund another employee to carry out the training. FranTech has managed to overcome some of these difficulties, for a minority of employees, through making use of the in-house training programmes provided by its customers. In this case a large customer is willing to fund one extra person on its training scheme as this ensures an employee at the small supplier with the relevant expertise. This training has been accessed through the development of close links between a large customer and its small supplier.

The tight time budgets of small businesses not only restrict training opportunities because labour (and labour-time) is a scarce resource. Limited time also affects the choice of training programme by inhibiting the collection of information on which to base any decision. Thus, the owner-manager is likely to choose the first satisfactory solution to the immediate problem, without looking for an optimal solution and so preventing further problems from developing. This process is termed 'satisficing' (Tait 1990). A further aspect of this is that the owner-manager's knowledge of education and training is likely to fall far short of perfection, owing to the probability that he or she has limited direct experience of these facilities.

Comparisons of the level of training in small and large firms show that the initial fixed investments in recruiting and training employees are likely to be greater in large firms, for two reasons:

> First, smaller firms with shorter, uncertain lives have less opportunity to capture the returns. Second, training yields higher returns when workers must be taught to conform with prescribed production methods. Large firms are thus provided with more incentives to design pay and personnel policies which can reduce labor turnover, thereby increasing the returns to firm-specific human capital . . . job tenure (years of service with the current employer) is positively related to firm size.
>
> (Oi 1983: 150)

Griffith and Dorsman (1987) found that small firms have very different training needs to larger firms, but that nevertheless the need is great. The pace of change of new technology has led Holland (1984) to estimate that between half and three-quarters of the industrial and commercial workforce may need some retraining. However, he notes that two-thirds of firms in the UK spend less than 0.5 percent of annual turnover on training, and it can be presumed that small firms are some of the worst offenders. Training is often seen by entrepreneurs as a luxury and this is reflected in the way that technology users in small firms are taught. As the case studies show, most small-firm training is done on the job, and the smaller the firm the more likely the training is to occur purely on-site.

A study by Watkins (1983) indicated another problem in the attitudes of owner-managers. Employees of small firms are some of the most likely groups of people to become entrepreneurs, especially in industries which require low initial capital investment, and in companies which experience regular crises (Cooper 1986). Many people join smaller companies simply to determine a market for a similar product or to develop the wide-based skills necessary in the initial stages of business start-up. Hence it is understandable that owner-managers are reluctant to develop the skills of those people who are most likely to become their competitors. Watkins (1983) found that one-fifth of all owner-managers in his survey had a fear of developing their managers for this reason. These fears are apparently not unfounded: one engineer at FranTech told me that his only motivation for joining the company was to learn how to run a small business.

A final observation on recruiting and training which emerged from my fieldwork is the notion of core and transient workers. At each company there were a number of people who had been with the firm for many years, in some cases since its inception. These people were happy with the working methods employed by the companies as well as with the social situation. There were other employees, however, who arrived and left within months.

The best illustration of this comes from Wellmaid, where the employees fell roughly into two categories – fairly satisfied and very dissatisfied. The satisfied employees had all been with the company for a number of years whereas the dissatisfied ones had generally been with the company for only a short while. The main reason given by them for their discontent was money, but some also mentioned that the work was difficult. The satisfied employees all said that they enjoyed the work as it was set up in the factory. The system used was make-through (the whole garment is made up by one machinist). The satisfied machinists thought this was common practice, whereas the dissatisfied ones thought that it was not. Finally, the training methods used for newly recruited machinists involved the machining manager completing one or two garments in front of the trainee before sending her to do the same. The trainee is subsequently allowed to ask questions for a few weeks before she goes onto piece rate. New employees who have only worked making up small pieces of a garment in previous jobs are totally out of their depth trying to make-through a whole garment. They thus become demotivated and demoralised and, as they go onto piece rate, underpaid. Inevitably this situation can only be endured for so long, and so they tend to leave within a few months. On the other hand, the fully trained machinists who have come from other factories on a make-through system find the task of making the whole garment infinitely more pleasurable than simply putting together small pieces. In fact some of the women had left other factories when the firms tried to fragment the tasks.

This outcome can also be witnessed in the other companies where inadequately trained workers are thrown straight into an unstructured work routine. Some appear to thrive on this chaos, whilst others sink. The swimmers become the core members of the companies whilst the sinkers leave quickly, thus becoming transient workers.

It should be mentioned that this view in part contradicts the argument put forward by Curran and Stanworth (1979), who explain that older workers in small firms are likely to seek employment in larger companies in order to combat the inherent insecurity of the small firm. This counters my findings in that a number of older core workers had been with their companies for many years and expressed no desire to leave. Rather it was the younger, transient workers who expressed their ambitions in terms of a career in another organisation. This core/transient split might best be approached through a critical reading of prevailing ideas of the flexibility of the small business sector.

The flexibility debate has become one of the dominant theoretical perspectives on small firms, although it consists of a plurality of conflicting definitions and models, notably those popularised by Atkinson (1984) and Piore and Sabel (1984), and critiqued by Pollert (1988).

During my research I certainly found no evidence of Piore and Sabel's (1984) 'democratically regulated enterprise culture'. The idea of small firms co-operating to manage competition would be alien to my respondents. Instead, particularly in the case of the smaller companies (FranTech and Wellmaid), they existed in a cut-throat, dog-eat-dog world where they battled to secure orders, labour and survival. The feeling of insecurity in these two companies was evident in the panic-stricken atmosphere of daily working life. Conversely, the large customers had almost complete price control over their purchases, being fully aware of the needs of their small suppliers and the lengths to which they would go to secure an order. In addition, the notion of flexible specialisation rests upon the creation of a new 'artisan' worker through the adoption of programmable technology (Bagguley 1990). However, the few examples of such technology in use in the study firms (most notably at FranTech) were responsible for deskilling rather than enhancing the 'craft' content of work. Thus, far from fitting the 'libertarian' flexible specialisation ideal of Piore and Sabel, these companies were much more in line with Atkinson's (1984) conception of numerical and wage flexibility in the 'flexible firm'.

None of the companies in this study sold exclusively to end-users. A large proportion of all their production was for sub-contractors. Thus, they made up the flexible labour force advocated by the 'flexible firm' model. The consequences of this were, firstly, that full-time workers were taken on and laid-off according to the state of the order book. Secondly, the smallest companies used a good deal of part-time, shift- or home-workers in response to changing demand. Shift work was used when there was no time to recruit extra labour and there was strong pressure to comply with new rotas through implicit threats to job security and so on. Thirdly, there was a further core–periphery split within the companies themselves. Periphery workers were employed on part-time or temporary contracts which left them with few benefits or legal protection. All of the companies were anti-trade union. Taken together, these indicators are not intended to point out the exploitative practices of the *petite bourgeoisie*, but rather that such practices are imposed on small firm owners by the price controls inflicted by their larger, more powerful customers. Thus, if the order book was empty or the profit margin cut then so too were the owner's earnings.

Thus, in the era of equal opportunities, moves towards the ideal of the flexible firm can be seen to inhibit progression towards equality. The middle-class, well-educated manager in the large corporation may well benefit from its equal opportunities programme. Meanwhile millions of small firm workers in secondary labour markets will see a decline in their standards of pay and conditions. Part-time rates of pay are invariably lower than their full-time equivalent and rights such as sickness, holiday and maternity pay are not usually available to part-timers. Thus, the flexible firm is likely to uphold or increase inequalities due to racism, sexism and classism (Pollert 1988). These themes will be returned to later, in a discussion of the function of 'familial ideology' within small companies.

A further important strand of the flexibility thesis is that firms have moved away from the price-based competition symptomatic of the mass production and markets of the Fordist era towards competition based upon quality. However, numerical flexibility militates against the sustained achievement of quality. This is for one very simple reason: achieving quality on sub-contracted work involves job knowledge both in problems and interpretations of paperwork and in recognising potential weaknesses in the product. Through the deployment of temporary labour for individual projects there is no opportunity for such job knowledge to accrue. Thus, each time a new order for the same product is placed the same problems are encountered and resolved from scratch. There is no learning curve whereby quality can be improved via quicker and more effective problem-solving techniques. This has certainly been recognised by one of the sub-contractors to FranTech, and thus the wisdom of such flexibility is being called into question.

For Atkinson core workers were specialists or multi-skilled, and periphery workers were semi- or unskilled operatives. However, I prefer to use the terms core and transient for the following reasons. The term core worker is intended by Atkinson to reflect a highly skilled specialist employee who becomes core through the indispensability of her or his skill. Periphery workers are unskilled or semi-skilled labour. Thus, the core/periphery split is based on economic factors such as profit maximisation. Bearing in mind that my study unearthed few 'highly trained specialists' the same parameters cannot apply. Rather, the core/transient distinction focuses on whether or not employees 'fit in', either socially or with the existing idiosyncratic working methods employed by the small companies. Thus, 'core' is not a parameter of skill but rather of social acceptability or social location within the context of a familial culture. In the following chapter, the importance of the family, both in terms of actual blood-ties and affinal relationships and as a prevailing cultural metaphor deployed by small firm owners and workers, is assessed in more detail.

8 Management control and family culture

In this chapter I turn attention to the ways in which employee relations are managed in small companies. From the case studies it should be clear that small firms both exist in and create a complex and continually renegotiated social landscape which impacts directly onto management control systems. In particular, I explore the deployment of familial ideology as a technology of industrial relations (which are themselves constituted to a great extent by social relations in the workplace), considering the mechanism of 'negotiated paternalism' (Ram 1992) as a way of taking account of the complex web of obligations and freedoms bestowed on both employers and employees.

Initial studies of industrial relations in small companies tended to follow Schumacher's (1974) 'small is beautiful' philosophy. Many writers put forward the idea that small companies somehow overcome the antagonisms between management and workers which exist in large organisations (e.g. Bannock 1981). This was endorsed by the Bolton Committee's dismissal of small firms industrial relations in just four pages of their 400-page document. Although this utopian view was embraced to a varying degree by politicians, academics and the small business community, it has also been heavily criticised (Curran and Stanworth 1981), and the industrial harmony view is no longer predominant, at least within academic circles. Conversely, there has been a tremendous growth in the opposing view, that small firms are the sites of some of the greatest industrial injustices towards employees.

Mason (1973) has described the small manufacturing firm as a centralised productive unit in which power is concentrated at the top. Further, many researchers have emphasised the autocratic and patriarchal nature of small firms management. For example, Scase and Goffee (1982) assert that there is no place in the small firm for senior staff who do not agree with the owner, whilst Rainnie's (1985) work on small firms industrial relations described tight supervision, scarce unionisation and authoritarian management control – in his view, 'small *isn't* beautiful'.

WE ARE FAMILY

More recently the notion of a familial culture has been used to examine small firm social relations (Holliday and Letherby 1993; Ram and Holliday 1993). There have been a range of studies that have deployed metaphors and labels with familial connections to work relations (e.g. Dick and Morgan 1987; Rainnie 1989; Scase and Goffee 1982). However, such studies are rather similarly polarised in their views of the 'family firm'. As with the industrial relations theorising, at one extreme lies the 'small is beautiful' school, which would suggest that small firms are just like *happy* families; at the other end of the spectrum is the analysis which states that small firms are not happy places – in fact they are run by tyrannical autocratic managers – and are thus not like families at all. That such a polarisation exists is not surprising given that the popular image of 'the family' is at odds with the sociological realities of family life.

My research adds to this by providing a much more detailed insight into the operation of 'family' ideologies within small firms. 'Family' members as I see them in this context may be blood or affinal relatives or those enculturated into the family ideology, that is the employees who gain 'core' status through their social relations with small firm owners. Thus, small firm workers may not be related to other workers in, or owners of, the family firm but may nevertheless identify as 'one of the family'. So, while there was evidence of substantial family involvement in the case study firms, the 'family culture' pervaded the whole company, not just the blood or affinal relationships present. Thus, 'core' workers can be thought of as 'family' members.

Dick and Morgan (1987) have highlighted the importance of the family as a recruitment channel. They found that family networks ensured a supply of 'reliable' workers and acted as a continuing mechanism of control over workers. Moreover, the family offered an important element of flexibility to a management operating in a competitive environment. While workers from the chosen families benefited in that they had privileged access to jobs in an extremely harsh economic climate, the relevance and rationality of the family to management was clear. Extensive familial involvement is depicted as a boon to management, primarily because it is cheap and supervision is made easier (Ward 1987). Viewed in this way, the rationality of the use of family labour seems beyond question. However, the use of the 'family' in key positions can, in important respects, serve to constrain management.

As is the case in most small companies, the grapevine was still the most effective system of recruitment for my study firms. Generally, the process involved the owners asking their workers to encourage friends and relatives to come to work for them. The whole process was very informal. These particular channels of recruitment made it more likely that new recruits would be from the workers' familial and social worlds. In large part, such informality in recruitment through the use of family, community and workforce connections has often been viewed as a means of furthering management's control over the workforce (Brooks and Singh 1979; Hoel 1982; Jenkins 1986). Employers seeking certain qualities like 'reliability' and 'conformity' could guarantee these through family contacts and family discipline – it would not do to complain about the terms and conditions of employment, in part because this would reflect badly on those who introduced the worker to the employer (Hoel 1982). In my study there was substantial evidence in all three companies that core workers were prepared to be flexible in terms of their working hours in order to help the company cope with variable workloads, as is discussed below. Also, some core members even regret the growth of their companies simply because their core becomes diluted by 'outsiders'. Consequently, it is not only employers who govern the selection of new employees, but also existing employees. Although linked to Stanworth and Curran's (1973) 'particularistic succession', that is the appointment of individuals on the grounds of personal compatability with the *owner-manager*, the notion of core and transient workers also acknowledges the role of *other workers* in the recruitment and induction of new employees.

The utility to management of features like stability and discipline is beyond doubt and helps to explain the continued prevalence of informal recruitment practices even in large organisations (Collinson *et al.* 1990; Maguire 1988). However, informality can have unintended consequences which may militate against the very advantages that it is supposed to provide. By allowing the workforce such autonomy in attracting new workers, for instance, management in the study firms were effectively ceding considerable discretion over eventual recruitment decisions. Many of the workers from the case study companies had been with the firms for a number of years. They had developed their own norms, understandings and patterns of working. Given the dynamics of the production systems, which relied on the interdependence of workers for their effectiveness, it would have been extremely difficult for new recruits to survive for any length of time unless they fitted into existing configurations of social relations at work. Thus, those who did fit in became core or 'family' members and those who did not remained transient, that is they left after a short period. In some ways, then, small firm employees can be seen to be self-selecting in the long term.

The mutuality that such a recruitment process implies was evident in the case studies. There were instances where management felt an 'obligation' to employ family members despite there not being a pressing need for new workers in a strictly economic sense (see, for example, the case of the labourer who was taken on at Logos due to his relationship with the accountant's daughter). The 'family' therefore is not simply an undiluted resource; it can also constrain management in certain circumstances.

It must be noted here that family culture or symbolism is deployed in a largely unproblematic way by both small firm workers and by academics exploring the 'family' at work. Although Scase and Goffee (1980) have linked the promotion of a 'family' culture to autocratic management styles, the use of 'paternalism' as a control mechanism is largely unscrutinised. In fact, the family metaphor may be of greater application than those who have used it realise, if one begins to read in actual 'family' relationships in a more critical way. What kind of 'family' is being referred to in metaphors and analogies such as those abundant in small firms?

I would argue that the model of the 'family' upon which 'family firm' symbolism draws is that of the patriarchal nuclear family, with a male breadwinner whose wife cares for him and their children. This image of family does not chime with the actual relationships in either the family or the family firm. It exists only in nostalgic rhetoric and certain political ideologies and discourses. In fact, the processes at work within any family, actual or metaphorical, are far more complex, contingent and contested than the term initially suggests. This echoes Stanley and Wise's (1983) suggestion that there is a distinction between the family as an institution and real family life; in many cases the former is cast as an ideal against which the latter measures unfavourably. Mechanisms of control and support are not so clear-cut in reality – everything is negotiated through networks of affinity and antagonism. Thus, the amount of negotiation within a family is mirrored in the emotional bribery and calls to loyalty echoing round the case study firms. As Sarah Oerton (1993: 2) says, 'forms of rationality other than the purely calculative are important . . . especially in times of economic slump when formal rationality may be underscored in terms of appeals based upon family loyalties'. If one is a member of a 'family', one has obligations as well as rights. Oerton (1993: 3) goes on to point out that:

> Despite recognizing the importance of emotional and face-to-face rela-
> tions in small businesses, the research on 'family' firms in such settings

has not explored the gendered dimension of workers' familial orientations, nor issues of exploitation that are consequent upon such orientations.

WOMEN'S WORK

Management organisation is indeed further complicated by the role of gender, both in terms of the nature of women's jobs and in terms of the status attributed to them. Much of the actual management of the workplace in the case studies was the responsibility of women members of the 'family'. Women's management of the internal processes of the firm, however, often meant balancing a chaotic production system and the conflicting pressures of the shopfloor and management. Despite the rigours of these essentially managerial tasks, women were still supervisors rather than managers in these firms (and hence denied managers' status and pay).

Women in the small firm are thus often attributed roles that simulate the gendered division of labour within the family. These roles are in turn rewarded accordingly, influenced by the 'male breadwinner' and female 'actual or potential wife and mother' ideology (Phizacklea 1990: 23). Family orientations are thus 'a contradictory source of identity in the (paid) workplace as well as in the home' (Oerton 1993: 3) for women. Indeed, women in the study firms regularly expressed their frustration at not being taken seriously and being blocked from career progression. This was probably most evident at Logos where the pornographic calendars, the directors' refusal to interview women for engineering posts, women's talk being seen as gossip whilst men's was seen as legitimate, and Judy's frustration with her lower status and pay all confirmed the misogynistic culture. At FranTech women made similar complaints about not being taken seriously, not being listened to and being treated differently from their male colleagues.

Wellmaid was obviously different, as it was run and owned by women. However, there was still a strong insistence by some employees on its familial culture, even though they were unable to identify a 'father figure'. Instead, the three partners effectively took three different roles. One acted almost as an employee, working constantly alongside other employees but sorting out minor problems such as organising re-cuts and delivering garment pieces to machinists from the cutting room. Another director took charge of paperwork, sometimes helping with the studding of finished jackets, but concentrating on taking orders, organising dispatch and liaising with customers. The third director controlled the internal running of the factory and dealt with personnel issues such as hiring, firing and discipline. However, the way in which she carried out this function is worthy of note.

If she happened to see some aspect of malpractice taking place she would say, 'Don't let Sue [the third director] catch you doing that', or, 'Wait until Sue gets back – she'll have something to say about this'. However, in reality Sue almost never intervened and was perhaps the mildest of them all in temperament. As the owners were all women one might imagine that the firm could be run as a matriarchy, but in my opinion it was more reminiscent of a patriarchal family with an absent father. This could be because women entrepreneurs are even less likely to have management experience than their male counterparts (Watkins and Watkins 1986) and thus they impose the authority structures familiar to them outside of work – those found within the family. This is emphasised by the reference to women machinists as 'girls' and the concern of the directors about the women's personal problems and job security.

Other differences between the women-only firm and both Logos and FranTech include a higher degree of tolerance towards women's flexible work hours at Wellmaid. Thus, women were allowed to work around school hours if they had young children. It could be argued, however, that this has more to do with lack of availability of machinists in the local area and less to do with benevolence on the part of the owners. Nevertheless, this has become part of the company's culture and is put forward as a benefit associated with working at Wellmaid. The other factor which was specific to Wellmaid, in that it was voiced, was an expectancy that an all-women factory would be more emotional than a mixed or male one. This was considered a consequence of premenstrual tension by one of the directors. However, it is not my experience that emotional volatility was confined to this company. Indeed, Stanworth and Curran (1986) have pointed to the fact that small firms tend to provide greater opportunities for interpersonal conflict than large firms.

EMOTIONAL MANAGEMENT

In all the case studies I was witness to extreme emotional outbursts. As Scott *et al.* (1989) found, employment relations in any organisational setting are based on actual relationships. Thus, when an industrial relations problem could not be contained within other frames of reference, for example reduced to the personality of individual troublemakers, it erupted with extreme intensity. In Logos, for example, this manifested itself as a threatened fight between one worker and another who had borrowed his tools without consent. At FranTech one woman actually threw some papers at the owner after she had been wrongly accused of putting them in the wrong place. It appears that this was accepted and tolerated behaviour and perhaps gives further weight to the family analogy in that relationships are not straightforward but negotiated and contested. Power relationships are tolerated providing they are seen to be fair and reasonable. Unreasonable behaviour sometimes promotes violent outbursts which are tolerated by owners as they are by fathers. These types of authority relationships have led Ram (1992) to coin the term 'negotiated paternalism' to describe small-firm control structures.

Again, however, this is far from straightforward. Such behaviour may be accepted if it comes from a core ('family') member, but not from a transient one. Remember that core members are those who have been with the company for a long time. They enjoy the working styles and the social relations there and identify as 'part of the family'. Transient members, on the other hand, may find the working styles difficult, either through lack of relevant training or a preference for more structured work regimes. They may also find the existing social relations and company culture difficult to penetrate if they are not immediately liked by managers or co-workers in the firm. Thus, these members may describe themselves as 'large company people' or may not see themselves as part of the 'family'.

Another point about core workers is that they are allowed more leeway in their relationships with owners. This is primarily because they are more skilled and *au fait* with individual company working methods. Core workers may have built their jobs into such a complex array of unrelated tasks that they become irreplaceable. Thus, they are allowed time off, eccentric behaviour, and more personal and less autocratic relations with management, tending to accentuate the divisions between core and transient workers. This too is governed by what owners consider reasonable or unreasonable. For example, at Logos, Mike was allowed to chat for long periods of time without interruption whilst other workers were not. But at Wellmaid, when Anna took off too much time she was telephoned at home and told to come to work immediately. Core members were socially closer to owners, which meant a two-way relationship. Deviant behaviour was accepted provided it was not seen to abuse the special trust of the owners. However, core workers were seldom reprimanded for deviant behaviour – when Anna did arrive at work she was treated especially well in order to smooth over any possible rift in the relationship. Thus, core members obtain special privileges from their status, as they become too valuable to lose, but there are definite limits of reason beyond which they cannot go. In the case studies both workers and owners talked of betrayal and exploitation. The complexity of core worker–owner relationships derives in part from their ambiguity – whether a co-worker is treated as a friend, a colleague, an employee or a child appears to be contingent on the mood of the owner, the particular status of the employee, and the type or gravity of the situation.

There is also the issue for owners of keeping core workers. This is particularly complex in that salaries and benefits at larger companies cannot be matched by small firms. In all the case studies one strategy used to control this was emotional bribery. There were some benefits set up for employees to encourage a 'team spirit' and demonstrate that owners had their employees' best interests at heart. For example, at Logos, there was the company's holiday caravan, the jet-skiing and Christmas parties. At FranTech key members were allowed use of the company van or allowed time out during work hours. A second set of tactics emerges once an employee has been offered alternative employment – getting employees drunk and stressing the emotional bond between them and the owners, ignoring or not speaking to the employees, offering them huge benefits in a potential future when the company has grown, and launching a smear campaign against the potential new employer.

Thus, a family culture may be cultivated by owner-managers in order to promote trust and increase the degree of alignment of the goals of managers and employees. As a result, those who join the company must fit into the family culture or leave. Indeed, the family is a powerful and attractive model for relationships within a firm, as it is what we all already 'know' in some way or other; its features of openness, negotiation, flexibility, unspoken obligations, and especially loyalty and belonging, comprise a resonant set of identifying elements for management, particularly as it offers an alternative to the deployment of rigid managerial control. However, the maintenance of a family culture can also mean that valuable resources are wasted. For example, in the perpetuation of the gendered division of labour, the talents and skills of women are wasted, both in terms of their being blocked from certain jobs and because they become demotivated through continuing low pay in relation to their male co-workers. However, it must be recognised that women and other workers are not purely passive in the face of autocratic management, and that core workers can hold power over management in certain situations. Thus, in family firms employing family members, and those identified with a familial culture, power relationships are negotiated. A familial culture imposes obligations on owner-managers as well as affording them benefits. 'Negotiated paternalism' would therefore appear to have wider currency as it was equally applicable to my case studies.

PRIDE, LOYALTY AND CONTROL

Many employees in the case studies expressed pride in their work and the products which they produced. This was encouraged, at Logos for example, by adorning the walls with photographs of core employees standing with their completed products. In other ways, though, the loyalty of employees is difficult to explain. It is easier to see why owners are motivated to work long hours for low financial reward, as they have a high degree of personal investment in their companies. But why should employees do the same? In all the cases many employees worked very long hours when required to. In return they expected no time off in lieu nor excessive financial rewards for their efforts.

This implies a strong degree of loyalty to the companies, and this was shown in the case studies by core employees who expressed their ambitions not in terms of personal ambition but rather in terms of the development of their companies (this conflicts with Curran and Stanworth (1981), who suggest that small firm workers were less attached to their organisation than their large firm counterparts). Perhaps this was due to the long-standing 'comfortable' working relationships developed over many years. Some expressed satisfaction at being able to witness the outcome of their actions in a way that they perceived as impossible in larger organisations. Employees also appear to be motivated by a desire to become part of the family culture, which involves conforming to certain behaviour patterns. But all employees had a clear idea of the precariousness of their companies which was evident in the constant buzzing or panic atmospheres in which they worked. Thus, they realised that by contributing to the company goal of survival they were likely to safeguard their own jobs. This was shown clearly at FranTech where employees would battle with the owner to raise prices in order to increase the company's profitability. Thus, the knowledge that individual behaviour can effect job stability appears to inspire employees in a way lost in larger companies whose more complex goals and shareholder ownership confuse the issue of what (and whom) employees should be working for.

Control mechanisms deployed in the relationship between owner and transient members are in some ways much more straightforward. This would tend to be a more formal, managerial-style relationship. New employees were subject to close scrutiny, reinforcing the inherent power relationships. This too tends to reiterate the divisions between core and transient members.

Supervision in the companies did not appear to follow any rational pattern. At Logos, for example, shopfloor supervision was practically non-existent, whereas office supervision was intense. Shopfloor workers enjoyed their autonomy, whilst non-core office workers resented the tight control of their activities. This had created a degree of friction between office and shopfloor personnel. Shopfloor workers were seen by the office staff as being shirkers. At FranTech, however, there were two supervisors and three shopfloor workers. It seems likely that this situation had evolved simply to give the only man on the shopfloor enhanced status over the women workers. There appeared to be no logic employed in the determination of the degree of supervision or the deployment of management.

Finally, the owners of the companies should be examined in more detail. In all companies owners had problems delegating responsibility. At Wellmaid, this had led to two directors but no employees being able to use the electric cutter. Thus, if one director was absent and the other was busy, cutting was held up. At Logos, refusal on the part of the technical director to employ a supervisor left the shopfloor completely ungoverned apart from his hourly stroll around it. The consequence of this was not necessarily lower output, but rather a tendency for employees to take short-cuts regarding health and safety regulations. Furthermore, some functions were performed sloppily, which could compromise product quality. And, in attempting to develop a more bureaucratic system of management through distancing themselves from daily operations, the directors created a sharp rift between themselves and their employees. Employees fought this by constantly busying the directors with trivial problems, ensuring eventually that other managers were employed. It was seen as only 'fair' that long-serving employees should be allowed to share in the directors' success. Thus, in some respects this mirrored Burns and Stalker's (1966) 'pathological' systems where problems are constantly delegated upwards leading to an overload situation at the top management level. Further, as the directors retreated they decided to divulge less and less information to employees. The employees then obtained information through illicit sources.

At FranTech, the owner's intervention completely controlled the size of the company. A striking characteristic of the company was its almost ceaseless fluctuation in the size of the workforce. As was explained in the case study, this tended to be because as the company grew the owner neglected his sales duties and became more and more involved in production. As he concentrated his efforts in this area (which was not necessarily good for production, quite apart from having disastrous consequences for sales), the company would lose orders and consequently lay off workers. Thus, the company was perpetually expanding and contracting. This fits with Stanworth and Curran's (1986) finding that increasing marketing orientation in small firms results in owners spending less time with employees. However, it would be very difficult to fit this with current wisdom on stages of growth models (Churchill and Lewis 1983).

All of the directors dismissed the idea of trade unions in their companies.

Unions were seen as a sign of poor management and owners felt that their employees ought to be able to come to them directly if they had a problem. Thus, in two companies employees were labelled 'troublemakers' and dismissed for attempting to encourage union involvement. Such accounts are abundant in the small firms literature (Phizacklea 1990; Rainnie 1985; Scase and Goffee 1982).

Taken together, the issues raised in this chapter point to a picture of small firms industrial relations much more complex than aphorisms like 'small is beautiful' or 'small isn't beautiful' suggest. Crucially, in showing the web of social, familial and contractual relationships interplaying in the workplace, the material from the case studies suggests that Ram's (1992) 'negotiated paternalism' might indeed go some way to convincingly summing up the ways in which production and people are managed in small enterprises.

9 Quality, rationality and bureaucracy

In this chapter I hope to bring together a further set of theoretical issues through a reading of the case studies. My central concern is to understand the working of quality systems within the three study firms. As the detail in the case studies shows, not only was the operation of quality procedures radically different in each company, it also strayed considerably from the theory of quality management and, within the companies, there was a notable gulf between the ideal and the reality of quality control and assurance. By reviewing recent quality philosophy and method – notably total quality management and BS5750 – I hope to make clear that the ways in which quality is talked about by 'experts' is often inappropriate. Following a comparison of quality systems at Wellmaid, Logos and FranTech, I move on to explore quality through two theoretical lenses: rationality and bureaucracy.

QUALITY – IN THEORY AND IN PRACTICE

Quality control and assurance are central concerns of production. Total quality management (TQM) is currently the most fashionable quality philosophy, which Hill (1991) sees as the logical response to the rapidly changing product markets of the age. He argues that companies need to compete by working 'smarter not harder'. TQM is seen as creating a culture of quality and trust between management and employees, which in turn serves to satisfy customer demands. Similarly, Krause and Keller (1988) see TQM as a central ingredient of 'world class manufacturing', and one which they introduced in *just four years* to a small manufacturing company with sixty employees. A vital component of their success, Krause and Keller argue, was giving each and every employee a copy of Schonberger's book, *World Class Manufacturing: the lessons of simplicity applied*! Chase (1990: 247) sent the following message to readers of an edition of *Total*

Quality Management Magazine dedicated to small firms: 'To remain competitive means that you must manage change – and the only way to effectively manage change is through Total Quality Management'.

Thus TQM, as the latest management panacea, has inevitably found its way into the small firms world. TQM demands that all aspects of organisations are geared towards the continual improvement of quality, where quality is defined as satisfying customers (Drummond and Chell 1992). However, despite Chase's eulogising about the benefits of TQM to small firms, Anne Tomes (1989) has stated that, for all intents and purposes, quality in small companies is synonymous with the BS5750 system. Comparing these respective viewpoints and evidence from the case studies, it seems that while TQM might be seen as an 'ideal' way of managing quality, its demands in terms of creating 'a well-trained, multi-tasked workforce intent on meeting customers' needs [and working to] a corporate vision or mission' (Chase 1990: 247) simply cannot be met by small firms, who instead opt for more straightforward and seemingly attainable quality systems, such as BS5750. In addition, the 'badge of quality' which BS5750 provides – a badge increasingly demanded by customers – has a greater tangibility in the eyes of managers, employees and customers, and this tangibility is felt in terms of increased sales (Tomes 1989).

Davies (1990) has suggested that small firms might be reluctant to employ TQM since their owners believe that they are producing quality goods or services almost by virtue of their size: that employees all understand and adhere to the firm's 'mission'; that tasks are clearly defined; that communications within the company and with customers are excellent; that standards and measures are superfluous; and that small firm culture makes organisation and motivation of workers easy. Each of these claims he counters with the reality of small firms, and, as my case studies show, he is justified in doing so. This inevitably brings us on to the question of exactly how quality was managed within the case study companies.

QUALITY AT WELLMAID: VISUAL CONTROL

Each of the three companies studied employed some form of quality control system. At Wellmaid this was simply a visual inspection at various points in the production process. The system fell down at three points. Firstly, the quality of incoming material was not inspected upon arrival; secondly, re-cuts were unpopular and thus avoided; and thirdly, as the machinists were all working on a piece-rate system they devoted little time to inspection. Faults in the garments were almost always in the cloth rather than the stitching and yet were frequently missed until the final inspection point before packing.

The system attempted to correct this procedure and to ensure proper inspection throughout the progress of the garment's fabrication by identifying each garment with its machinist, using a tag sewn into the lining. When the relevant machinist was identified she would have to correct the error on hourly rate if it was a fault in the fabric or in her own time for stitching errors. However, machinists of faulty garments almost always removed their tag, thus rendering the item untraceable and it therefore fell to the partner/supervisor to correct the fault. This practice exactly replicates that noted by Ram (1992) in his study of small companies in the West Midlands clothing industry.

Vendor selection at Wellmaid was informal but effective. This is probably due to the fact that there are only three sources in Britain for their major procurement – the cloth. Cloth is purchased from one company until its quality begins to deteriorate, at which point orders are switched to another supplier. All suppliers charge more or less the same price.

QUALITY AT FRANTECH: MEETING THE STANDARD

At FranTech the quality control system was governed by BS5750. This included procedures and work instructions explaining the correct execution of some operations. However, there were many gaps in the system and most instructions were centred around shopfloor operations and ignored the processing of paperwork. Quality assurance in terms of static electricity control on the shopfloor was well maintained and supported by a programme of educational videos to emphasise its importance.

The inspection of shopfloor production work was carried out by operatives who swap pieces and inspect each other's output. The training for this was to have made similar items rather than more specific training in inspection procedures. On the whole, knowing the difficult areas in building the product does equip operatives to look for danger spots when inspecting. When the company is busier, however, other people, such as the accounts clerk, will be drafted in to inspect work. This introduces a greater possibility for error. Once the visual inspection is complete the item will move to 'Test' where it undergoes electrical testing.

One of the biggest threats to quality assurance at FranTech must be in the paperwork system. Engineers in the company show a particular lack of concern for filling it in properly. This leads to orders being taken incorrectly and to drawings and data sheets not being updated, and consequently products being designed to the wrong specifications or even to important items not being procured owing to their omission from parts lists, all of which reduce quality in terms of acceptable lead times.

Finally, the vendor selection procedure in the BS5750, which is supposedly in place at FranTech, is haphazard. Goods can only be purchased from approved vendors if the company has paid its previous debts to them. Otherwise materials must be sourced elsewhere. The system for evaluating vendors – whereby incoming goods are checked and defective items returned and noted – is also arbitrary. When the company has a full-time storekeeper she or he undertakes this task, but when it cannot afford a storekeeper then vendor appraisal is dropped. Further, criteria which decide whether or not an item should be accepted vary according to the urgency with which the item is needed, its replaceability, the customer for the finished product, and whether or not the company owes its vendor a 'favour'. At FranTech, then, the sophistication of the quality system is related to its current importance amongst other variables; its role as a sales tactic, however, is paramount: the BS5750 'badge of quality' adorns company notepaper, reassuring customers that 'quality products' are guaranteed.

QUALITY AT LOGOS: ADOPTING THE PURPOSE

At Logos the BS5750 system is also in operation. Here its implementation is more advanced. Among the staff there is a quality manager who is responsible for laying down quality procedures for every job; a documentation manager who ensures that all paperwork is current and all obsolete documentation is destroyed or filed; an inspector to monitor and test the quality of all operations carried out on the shopfloor; a certification clerk who checks all certification arriving with purchased goods; and a storekeeper who inspects a sample of all goods inwards. The sophistication of Logos's 'quality staff' is seemingly at odds with Tomes's (1989) assertion that a principal reason for poor application of BS5750 is the unavailability of personnel to carry out the necessary tasks. In fact, the document control manager and the quality manager spend at least half their time on other work within the firm not directly related to the quality system.

Training is organised and systematic and carried out with the aid of external bodies. However, despite the high level of organisation there are certain aspects of quality which are overlooked or ignored, such as the tendency of labourers to apply acid cleaner with a mop instead of a fine spray, and of operatives to ignore the guidelines laid down to prevent material contamination. Again these actions appear to relate to some aspect of shopfloor culture which prevents operatives from carrying out their function to the required quality specification despite having undergone relevant training.

A striking feature of Logos was the 'competition for quality' culture on the shopfloor. As the case study explains, operatives would congregate outside the inspector's office when test results from weld X-rays arrived, mocking those who had made mistakes. Thus, it would appear that this culture served to ensure a kind of quality assurance through social pressure (see also Sewell and Wilkinson 1992).

BS5750: TWO COMPANIES, TWO STANDARDS

One aspect of the case studies which is of particular interest is the contrast in the quality systems of the two companies with a BS5750 quality system. The BS5750 is used by potential customers to distinguish between the host of possible suppliers. It indicates a company which has achieved a certain level of quality both in its products and in its operations. It is, for those companies which possess it, a ticket to increased sales and as such many small firms seek to obtain it. However, contrasting the two firms in this study leads one to wonder what benefits purchasing from a BS5750-rated firm affords customers.

A striking difference between the companies was the varying degrees of sophistication of their quality systems. This aspect could have been linked simply to firm size or to product sophistication, but no doubt one important variable was the perspective of owner-managers to control systems. Particularly in relation to the BS5750 it is possible to see that the attitudes of managers at Logos and FranTech varied greatly. At both companies the system had been introduced with the sole objective of increasing sales, however the consequences of this varied to the extreme. At Logos, a quality manager and a document control manager were appointed to administer the system, although they also had other tasks to perform within the company. At FranTech, although a part-time quality manager set up the system, once this was in place it was monitored and controlled by the engineering manager.

At Logos the BS5750 has led to procedures and work instructions to cover virtually every operation. Furthermore, individuals are audited by the quality manager to ensure that they are working in accordance with the directions as laid down. If people are found not to be working in accordance with the procedures then the non-conformity is documented and action is taken to ensure that the discrepancy is rectified. At FranTech, however, no quality audits were carried out during my fieldwork. Furthermore, few activities are documented. For example, vendor selection and review is carried out at Logos in the form of files recording each vendor's rating. Visits are made by the purchasing manager to vendors where an inspection of the vendor's premises and working methods is carried out. Although the case study shows that there are loopholes in this system, major vendors are generally investigated.

None of this appears to be in evidence at FranTech. Moreover, I feel that this example can probably be generalised across the whole quality system. Thus it would appear that getting a BS5750 certificate provides no advantage to the quality systems of small companies but rather mirrors the general level of organisation and sophistication which already exists within the company. Hence, the BS5750 does far less for quality than for sales. Perhaps, though, the BS5750 is a self-fulfilling prophecy as it allows companies to move towards the manufacture of higher quality products through sales which in turn must have an effect on quality assurance procedures.

At Logos the emphasis was on making the BS5750 system thorough and ensuring that its potential for improving quality was maximised, whereas at FranTech the emphasis was most definitely on minimising both the paperwork and the 'interference' of the BS5750 on daily activities. In both companies, however, there was resistance to the implementation of the BS5750 by managers and employees. This, too, was based around an objection to the paperwork generated, as well as a feeling that people would be asked to accuse their colleagues of bad practice instead of being able to sort out problems between themselves. Objections tended to take the form of people complaining that the system was too rigid. Furthermore, there was a fear of audits, which were seen as a kind of policing. Overall, it appeared that the fear was of increasing bureaucratisation (this was seen as something which was bad about large firms, and which should thus be avoided by the smaller company).

A final point which potentially influences the quality of products at Logos is the lack of supervision. This in itself is not a problem as all the workers greatly appreciated their autonomy and were keen not to abuse the trust that had been placed in them. The problem was that some of the responsibility for supervision had informally come to rest on the shoulders of the inspector. This was because, although three lead hands had been appointed to deal with technical problems, they lacked the inspector's knowledge. This practice fits neatly with Gouldner's (1954) conception of conflict between administrative position and professional skill. In the first case authority is legitimised through hierarchy and status and in the second it is based on expert knowledge. This, Gouldner argues, gives rise to a conflict of authority. Such a conflict was very much in evidence at Logos, where only the time dimension had emerged as a quality consideration. Although Trevor was not formally given any role as supervisor it was expected by management that he would keep the work moving on the shopfloor. If he put an urgent item on hold pending tests this was seen by the engineering director as deliberately obstructive and thus Trevor felt under pressure not to do this. Trevor himself admitted that he was playing conflicting roles and that as a consequence his inspection duties were suffering.

This problem has no real solution, since it is linked to the development of the company from a very small entity. Many writers have pointed to the inability of owners to delegate responsibility as their company grows (e.g. Abdelsamad and Kindling 1978), and this is exactly what has happened at Logos. The consequence of this is that the shopfloor workers go un-supervised. This would not be a problem if the engineering director was always available, but as a director of a growing company he has other duties to perform. Giacchino *et al.* (1987) used case studies to show that with increasing firm size owner-managers became less involved in production and more involved in strategic monitoring of information. Thus, at Logos there is no one to whom the operatives can go with their problems. To try to rectify this, three lead hands have been appointed, but they lack authority and are not respected by other operatives. All the shopfloor workers spoke of their reluctance to work under a supervisor. This has probably developed as part of the shopfloor culture instilled by the engineering director. So, if a supervisor was taken on then he or she would probably be resisted by both the fabricators and the engineering director.

Although quality was something which was talked about considerably at Wellmaid, none of the owners had heard of terms such at TQM or quality circles. This is in sharp contrast with the other companies. At FranTech, for example, Raj attempted to introduce quality circles, a practice advocated by Brannen and Hranac (1983) and by Franklin (1980), who reminds readers that the sharing of any gains made through participative management styles is an integral part of their process. However, Raj displayed little real knowledge of what this technique usually involves and as a result members of the circles not only did not receive any kind of bonus for their efforts, but were also expected to stay behind after work without pay to participate in them. Furthermore, this was not considered the jurisdiction of shopfloor workers and so was comprised exclusively of managers and supervisors.

QUALITY AND RATIONALITY

In seeking to both understand and theorise the way in which quality systems operated in the study firms, I aim here to turn to notions of rationality, before moving on in subsequent sections to explore bureaucracy and surveillance.

In the context of small firms, we can clearly see the interplay of two forms of rationality, which we can label 'economic' and 'social'; indeed, the more we begin to think about the various rationalities at work in the small-firm setting, the more we begin to unravel the complexities therein. The way in which the 'family' ideology impacted upon work patterns, for example, shows the clash between these rationalities. The layout of shop-floors, the structuring of the production process, the mechanisms of control and management all highlight the interplay of the economic and the social. The very term 'negotiated paternalism' resonates with social rationality.

In addition, we can see that the rationale for doing a particular thing a particular way is often firm-specific or 'local': rather than obeying some general (global) rule or model of behaviour, each firm in the study has its own way of operating. While it would be my argument that it is difficult (maybe even impossible) to disentangle the economic and social reasonings in small firms, examples of firm-specific economic rationality can be drawn from the case study material, as the example of second-quality jackets at Wellmaid shows: while it could be argued that the company should pursue a policy of tightening quality to ensure a higher turnout of first-quality jackets, the fact that they can get greater remuneration from selling seconds direct to the public than from selling first-quality jackets through a vendor or intermediary means that the apparent 'slackness' in their quality procedure is actually more rational as it leads to greater profits.

Further, it is interesting to ponder the relevance of each quality system outlined above to the respective companies. For example, the system of visual inspection is sufficient to determine the quality of a wax jacket at Wellmaid. The system which they have developed, although crude, is sufficient for their needs providing they actually carry it out. The constraints are time and money. The cost of the time during which production is stopped whilst the fabric is inspected is easily covered by the wasted material saved if the fabric was faulty. However, money is more difficult to deal with. The company cannot afford to order material long in advance of production, therefore if there is only enough material in stock for two days' production and material which takes five days to replace is faulty then production must stop for three days. So the cost of the fabric wasted due to faults is less than the cost of three wasted production days. The constraining factor here is the amount of stock which the company can afford to keep, pending this sale.

This is one aspect which Wellmaid shares with FranTech. Quality becomes secondary to lead-time and need. Further, at FranTech every operation inevitably becomes urgent. The problem is that items cannot be ordered before products are sold owing to limited cashflow. Hence procurement is delayed until the last minute. If the goods which arrive are faulty then there is no time to return and replace them, therefore faulty components are often knowingly used. This aspect is intensified in small companies in two ways. Firstly, limited cashflow forces the acceptance of faulty goods onto the company which may in turn secure a lower price for its product because of the faulty part. Secondly, because the vendors to small companies are frequently larger entities and are not particularly bothered about the loss of a relatively small order, they are inclined to dump poor quality products onto their smaller customers. Thus, it may not always be possible to follow the guidelines advocated by Hill (1987), for example, on quality inspection and rejection of faulty items – the rationality of doing so is outweighed by the specific working patterns within the firms.

What I have hoped to suggest here is that the kinds of solutions offered by panaceas like TQM are inflexible and unworkable once one stops to consider the complex rationalities at play within an individual company. The possibility of employing economically rational systems – or for even applying seemingly commonsense quality control (chasing up second-quality products, for example) – is contradictory to the firm-specific working arrangements and local and social rationalities which actually dictate how quality is prioritised and managed. A closer look at the operation of BS5750 quality systems – supposedly response enough to be workable in small enterprises – reveals not only their fallibility in terms of failing to account for company specificities, but also shows how their very design – reliance on paperwork, accountability and systematisation – echoes with theoretical perspectives on bureaucratisation and surveillance.

QUALITY AND BUREAUCRACY

It is widely assumed that quality problems in small firms can be solved via the implementation of the BS5750. The BS5750 is a bureaucratic (paper-work) system which is supposed to ensure the accountability of individuals or materials to finished product quality. It is useful here to relate this to Alvin Gouldner's (1954) work on the nature of bureaucracies. Gouldner identified three patterns of bureaucratic behaviour, which he termed mock, representative and punishment-centred.

Mock bureaucracy refers to a system where rules are imposed by some outside agency. Neither superiors nor subordinates identify themselves with or participate in the introduction of rules, and nor do they see them as legitimate. The result of this can be high morale caused by a sense of conspiracy between superiors and subordinates in breaking the rules. Representative bureaucracy more closely mirrors Weberian notions of the concept. Thus, rules are installed by experts and seen as legitimate by those who must adhere to them, since the authority of the expert goes unchallenged. In this way the rules fit with existing norms and values prevalent within the organisation. The third form, punishment-centred bureaucracy, develops when rules arise in response to pressure from either management or workers. These rules are not seen as legitimate, but since they must be followed they emphasise authority and command. Thus, punishment-centred bureaucracies are most likely to lead to situations of conflict.

I would argue that these bureaucratic models can be applied to the implementation of BS5750. The motive of obtaining BS5750 status is often simply to increase sales. It is a marketing device which allows small firms to tap into vital larger or more 'up-market' customers and more profitable markets. Thus there is no incentive to improve *real quality* (of the product or service, as perceived by the customer) within the company, rather this choice is based on a desire to present a *quality image*. Thus, it is possible for a small firm to achieve BS5750 status without actually addressing any of its quality problems. All it must do is develop a manual and some procedures and 'tidy up' when the British Standards inspectors visit the factory. To all intents and purposes, this is the stage at which FranTech has remained. Thus, few procedures have been developed, and those that have are rarely implemented. A network of local firms ensures that Raj is informed with at least a week's notice when the BS inspectors will arrive. As a consequence of this, the factory is spring-cleaned, files are quickly updated and missing information is filled in on uncompleted paperwork. As soon as the inspectors have left, everything returns to normal, and the *ad hoc* practices return. Such visits cause much excitement within the firm, and employees collude with managers to 'fool' the inspectors.

At Logos, however, although two directors initially resisted the sales director's enthusiasm for BS5750, they eventually decided that if they had to have the system, then they would make the most of it. Thus, the system was adopted in a more thorough way than at FranTech. Initially, then, although the idea had been for a mock bureaucracy to increase sales, the system has developed as a representative bureaucracy. Procedures were designed around existing best practice, and rules were written around current methods whilst also drawing on suggested improvements from personnel and an 'expert' (a quality consultant who specialised in BS5750 implementation in small firms).

However, as the system developed, it became necessary to audit it. This is the process whereby employees are evaluated for their degree of conformance with the written procedures. Non-conforming employees are issued with NCRs and are given a limited period in which to amend their behaviour. If they do not, then further sanctions are taken. Thus the system becomes a punishment-centred bureaucracy. It is entirely possible that the system will eventually become dysfunctional as greater supervision will be needed to enforce and police the growing complexity of rules. Further, there are already clear signs of 'resistance' to the system developing within Logos, as described in the case study, and a growing animosity towards a system which apportions blame and accountability – precisely those roles the system is designed to fulfil.

The move to a punishment-centred bureaucracy also introduces notions of surveillance – and resistance to that surveillance. As has been noted by writers seeking to understand the organising cornerstones of modernity, and especially those from a broadly Foucauldian viewpoint (e.g. Dandeker 1990), bureaucracy and surveillance go hand in hand with the historical development of those forms of management, government and social and economic organisation seen as synonymous with modernity. A paperwork procedure like BS5750 operates as a surveillance system in that employees' performance is recorded and can be assessed. Thus, the very presence of the system serves to police the workforce almost panoptically (Sewell and Wilkinson 1992). As Dandeker (1990) notes, the rise of accounting procedures in the industrial revolution began this process of impersonal surveillance of working habits. His historical reading of the development of the business enterprise (see also Rose 1989), although relating to large organisations, shows clearly how bureaucratic systems are designed to facilitate the control of production without the necessity of constant personal supervision by employers (see also Edwards and Whitston 1994). And even in the small enterprise, where the distance between the boardroom and the shopfloor is often very short, such systems are often seen as vital to efficient operations, even if they end up becoming sites of conflict and resistance.

Thus, what we have here is a paradoxical situation. Small firms strive either to achieve a mock-bureaucratic application of BS5750, where the 'badge of quality' is worn, but little else changes and to all intents and purposes the actual quality system is irrelevant to workplace operations, or to use a model of representative bureaucracy to manage quality, where everyone absorbs both motive and the method, and improvements in quality are realised through the effective deployment of formal procedures. Falling into punishment-centred bureaucratic functioning plainly works *against* quality, creating friction and antagonism. Further, its reliance on surveillance and policing resonates with all the negative imagery of autocratic and coercive work environment something which small firm employees (and owners) almost universally profess to loathe.

Bureaucratic systems such as the BS5750, then, can be seen as both a help and a hindrance to the small organisation. Crucial here is the very fact that many small firms embrace an 'anti-bureaucratic' culture. This is generally thought to be for two reasons. Firstly, new entrepreneurs tend to express their satisfaction at getting away from the paperwork and departmentalism which they faced in large companies. Secondly, as Chapman (1989) has explained, paperwork is often done in a business owner's 'spare time' as it is not seen as something which directly contributes to production. In other words, paperwork is seen as impeding the process of getting finished products out of the door. Thus, the small business owner is often portrayed as someone who avoids bureaucracy at all costs. However, in my experience the situation is more complicated, and the pejorative sense of the word bureaucracy is countered by a perceived need to formalise, standardise and regulate – in short, to bureaucratise – operations. As a consequence of this paradoxical position, bureaucracy is despised on the one hand and actively sought on the other. At FranTech, one of the first things I was shown was the 'organisation chart'. The owner pointed out the various positions which he filled as part of his job. At Logos, my first job was to design a new 'organigram' which pinpointed every post-holder's position within the company. Perhaps this preoccupation with structure and systems is a derivative of the management literature which stresses the importance of offices, procedures, rules and structures – although many who own and work in small companies stress a dread of bureaucratisation, there is also a desire for it, partly because that is how 'proper companies' (for which read large organisations) operate, and partly because such systems offer clearly defined, 'rational' procedures. While large companies are being urged to thrive on chaos, the small firms held up as the embodiment of progressive working arrangements seek to survive through order.

10 Conclusion

In conclusion, there are a number of major themes which have been raised in this book which will now be reiterated. The literature on production management has been scrutinised and critically appraised. It was found that this literature comes from a logical–positivist philosophical tradition and that this produces two major problems. Firstly, in its search for panaceas such work neglects many of the contingencies of the workaday lives and conditions of small firms and is thus unreflexive and results-oriented. Secondly, the logical–positivist tradition seeks forms of order, rationality, validity and generalisability in such a way that it dismisses more qualitative projects. Thus, the very contingencies which render panaceas unworkable never come to light as quantitative methodologies by their very nature seek commonality instead of difference.

Next I examined some of the human resource management (HRM) principles raised by the study. Recruiting in the companies was informal, more often than not conducted by word of mouth. Training was very limited. In many cases employees were simply asked to watch another employee for a while and then do the job at similar skill levels and times as their more experienced colleagues. Some of the companies, however, did make use of further and higher education establishments or even other companies to train their staff, although this was often gendered or concentrated at higher levels of the companies. Owner-managers in all of the firms had fears about developing transferable skills in their employees. Flexibility, frequently extolled as a virtue of smaller companies, was shown to be more often numerical and not in terms of skills. Furthermore, all of the companies actively sought standardisation strategies at the expense of flexibility. Where flexibility was evident it was negative and forced, in the sense of not having the power to turn down orders even if these were well outside of the company's usual sphere of business and hence unprofitable.

Familial cultures existed in all three companies. Such cultures were shown to have wide-reaching implications for actual working conditions. Family metaphors were adopted by managers to promote a paternalistic style of control although this was found not to be as simple as some theorists have argued. Thus, such metaphors imposed obligations on as well as affording benefits to management. 'Negotiated paternalism' was found to be a more apt description of management patterns of control. The benefits of belonging to the 'family' were gendered, as buying into it frequently resulted in lower status for women whose caring roles were seen as 'natural' rather than skilled. Finally, family cultures were frequently exclusive, resulting in splits between so-called core and transient workers.

Quality systems within the companies were not necessarily based on 'economic' or global rationalities. Where they were then this tended to be shaped by BS5750, thus becoming bureaucratised. Different versions of bureaucracy tended to exist where the standard was adopted more or less wholeheartedly. For example, mock bureaucracies involved managers and workers colluding to fool inspectors as they visited factories to check that systems were thoroughly implemented. When they left, practices returned to normal. In punishment-centred bureaucracies employees were constantly monitored via audits, thus giving rise to surveillance systems of control.

The emphasis on multiple rationalities at work in small firms militates against the positivistic reasoning of much production research, which places all its emphasis on an unproblematic rationality. In the same way global rationalities are implicit in the kinds of quantitative methodologies which I have already critiqued. Thus all firms in a quantitative sample are thought of as operating within the same frame of reference. Small firms tend to be homogenised by quantitative studies, which fail to pick up on the subtleties that contribute to the way in which economic and social elements together define the working rationalities within each firm. Only a qualitative approach responds to the differences within and between firms with the necessary sophistication to begin the task of helping us understand exactly how these rationalities are played out to create the organisations which we study.

One vital conclusion of this book is therefore that the study of small firms is by its very nature inter- or multi-disciplinary as are qualitative enquiries. As long as production and other management research is carried out quantitatively it will probably remain uncritical and geared towards concepts of global and economic rationalities, since quantitative methods also fit this paradigm. Thus, management research produces global rationalities from methods which search for homogeneity whilst diversity remains problematic, both to the discipline and its chosen methods. In fact:

the very idea of a typical factory is a sociological fiction. It is the artificial construction of those who see only one mode of generalisation – the extrapolation from sample to population. There is, however, a second mode of generalisation, which seeks to illuminate the forces at work as a totality. . . . [This mode] is the extension from the micro context to the totality which shapes it . . . every particularity contains a generality.

(Burawoy 1985: 18)

In this sense, then, it is likely that as 'family firms' reflect the values of society as a whole then firms which adopt a familial culture will also reflect such values. Thus, such processes are generalisable from empirical study of the workplace to society as a whole and back again to other firms within that society, representing the commonalities of such firms in such a society.

I mentioned earlier that qualitative studies highlight the interdisciplinary nature of small firms and this book has certainly approached its data in such a way. I have also talked about paradigmatic problems associated with such interdisciplinary research. Thus production research frequently ignores the complexities brought to bear through the involvement of people, whilst reading some organisation studies literature one could be forgiven for thinking that production is a minor inconvenience in the social lives of working people. Thus interdisciplinary studies are often a way of showing workaday lives *as they are experienced* without the constraints of subject boundaries.

Finally, perhaps the study of small companies in this way has something more to offer. Often in larger companies researchers are constrained within specific departments or positions within a hierarchy. This inevitably leads to a skewed account of working lives. In some senses researchers in small companies face this problem to a lesser extent and therefore view the experiences of both management and employees at all levels. Thus, small firms research is important, not simply for its own sake, but also for the important issues which arise and are transferable to the wider working environment.

Bibliography

Abdelsamad, M. and Kindling, A. (1978) 'Why small businesses fail', *Advanced Management Journal* 9, 5: 28–29.

Adams, A. and Walbank, M. (1981) 'New product introduction in smaller manufacturing firms', SRC Report, Manchester: UMIST.

Adams, A. and Walbank, M. (1983) 'Research note: perceived and acted out training needs in small manufacturing firms', *International Small Business Journal* 2, 1: 46–52.

Adler, P. and Adler, P. (1987) *Membership Roles in Field Research*, London: Sage.

Amin, A. (1989) 'Flexible specialisation and small firms in Italy: myths and realities', *Antipode* 21, 1: 13–34.

Anon. (1985) 'Seamus Connolly: a market-oriented engineer', *European Journal of Marketing* 19, 5: 76–82.

Anon. (1990) 'Small firms have gone Boom! Boom! Boom!', *Employment News* 187, July: 1.

Anoochehri, G. (1988) 'JIT for small manufacturers', *Journal of Small Business Management* 26, 4: 22–30.

Appelbaum, S. and Hinds, D. (1984) 'The role of the management consultant in small business', *Business Quarterly* 49, Fall: 43–51.

Ashcroft, S. (1989) 'Applying the principles of optimized production technology in a small manufacturing company', *Engineering Costs and Production Economics* 17, 1–4: 79–88.

Atkin, I. and McArdle, L. (1992) 'Why flexible specialisation must "belong"', in R. Welford (ed.) *Small Business and Small Business Development – a practical approach*, Bradford: European Research Press.

Atkinson, J. (1984) 'Manpower strategies for flexible organizations', *Personnel Management* August: 28–31.

Bagguley, P. (1990) 'Post-Fordism and enterprise culture: flexibility, autonomy and changes in economic organization', in R. Keat and N. Abercrombie (eds) *Enterprise Culture*, London: Routledge.

Bannock, G. (1981) *The Economics of Small Firms*, Oxford: Blackwell.

Bennett, M. (1989) *Managing Growth*, London: Longman.

Berg, D. (1988) 'Anxiety in research relationships', in D. Berg and K. Smith (eds) *The Self in Social Inquiry: researching methods*, London: Sage.

Bernolak, I. (1981) 'To improve productivity in small business: why? how?' paper presented at the 11th European Small Business Seminar, 'Productivity', Helsinki, 15–18 September.

Berryman, J. (1983) 'Small business failure and bankruptcy: a survey of the literature', *International Small Business Journal* 1, 4: 47–59.

Binks, M. and Coyne, J. (1983) *The Birth of Enterprise: an analytical and empirical study of the growth of small firms*, London: Institute of Economic Affairs.

Birley, S. and Westhead, P. (1990) 'Private advertised business sales in the United Kingdom 1983–1988', *Area* 22, 4: 368–380.

Bolton, J. (1971) *Report of the Committee of Inquiry on Small Firms*, Cmnd 4811, London: HMSO.

Bosworth, D. and Jacobs, C. (1989) 'Management attitudes, behaviour and abilities as barriers to growth', in J. Barber, J. Metcalfe and M. Porteous (eds) *Barriers to Growth in Small Firms*, London: Routledge.

Brannen, K. and Hranac, J. (1983) 'Quality control circles for small business', *Journal of Small Business Management* January: 21–27.

Brooks, D. and Singh, K. (1979) 'Pivots and presents: Asian brokers in British foundries', in S. Wallman (ed.) *Ethnicity at Work*, London: Macmillan.

Bryman, A. (1988) *Quantity and Quality in Social Research*, London: Unwin Hyman.

Brytting, T. (1990) 'Spontaneity and systematic planning in small firms – a grounded theory approach', *International Small Business Journal* 9, 1: 45–63.

Burawoy, M. (1985) *The Politics of Production: factory regimes under capitalism and socialism*, London: Verso.

Burgess, R. (1984) *In the Field: an introduction to field research*, London: Unwin Hyman.

Burns, T. and Stalker, G. (1966) *The Management of Innovation*, London: Tavistock.

Cannon, T. (1989) 'The role of the small business in economic recovery: myth and reality', *Stirling Economics Teaching Papers*, Department of Economics, University of Stirling.

Carter, S., Faulkner, W., Nenadic, S. and Cannon, T. (1986) 'The nature, the role and the impact of small business research', in P. Rosa (ed.) *The Role and Contribution of Small Business Research*, Aldershot: Avebury.

Case, J. (1987) 'The enemy within', *Inc.* 9, 4: 32–38.

Chapman, T. (1989) 'The experience of running a small business in north Staffordshire', Occasional Paper, Staffordshire Polytechnic, Stoke-on-Trent.

Chase, R. (1981) 'A classification and evaluation of research in operations management', *Production and Inventory Management* 22: 49–58.

Chase, R. (1990) 'Commentary: who's next?', *Total Quality Management Magazine* 2, 5: 247.

Chell, E., Haworth, J. and Brearley, S. (1991) *The Entrepreneurial Personality: concepts, cases and categories*, London: Routledge.

Churchill, N. and Lewis, V. (1983) 'The five stages of small business growth', *Harvard Business Review* 61, 3: 30–50.

Clifford, D. (1973) 'Growth pains of the threshold company', *Harvard Business Review* 51, 5: 143–154.

Collinson, D., Knights, D. and Collinson, M. (1990) *Managing to Discriminate*, London: Routledge.

Connell, D. (1985) 'The management of growth in high technology companies', paper presented at the Institute of Electronic and Radio Engineers' Diamond Jubilee Conference.

Cooper, A. (1986) 'Technical entrepreneurship: what do we know?', in J. Curran, J. Stanworth and D. Watkins (eds) *The Survival of the Small Firm. 2: Employment, growth, technology and prospects*, Aldershot: Gower.

Cornell, B. and Shapiro, A. (1988) 'Financing corporate growth', *Journal of Applied Corporate Finance* 1, 2: 6–22.

Cowling, A., Stanworth, M., Bennett, R., Curran, J. and Lyons, P. (1988) *Behavioural Science for Managers*, London: Edward Arnold.

Curran, J. (1986) 'The width and the depth – small enterprise research in Britain 1971–1986', in P. Rosa (ed.) *The Role and Contribution of Small Business Research*, Aldershot: Avebury.

Curran, J. (1988) 'Training and research strategies for small firms', *Journal of General Management (UK)* 13, 3: 24–37.

Curran, J. and Burrows, R. (1987) 'Ethnographic approaches to the study of the small business owner', in K. O'Neill, R. Bhambri, T. Faulkner and T. Cannon (eds) *Small Business Development: some current issues*, Aldershot: Gower.

Curran, J. and Stanworth, J. (1979) 'Self-selection and the small firm worker – a critique and an alternative view', *Sociology* 13, 3: 427–444.

Curran, J. and Stanworth, J. (1981) 'The social dynamics of the small manufacturing enterprise', *Journal of Management Studies* 18, 2: 141–158.

Curran, J. and Stanworth, J. (1982) 'The small firm in Britain – past, present and future', *European Small Business Journal* 11, 1: 16–25.

Curran, J., Stanworth, J. and Watkins, D. (eds) (1986) *The Survival of the Small Firm. 2: Employment, growth, technology and prospects*, Aldershot: Gower.

Dandeker, C. (1990) *Surveillance, Power and Modernity*, Cambridge: Polity Press.

Davies, P. (1990) 'TQM in small firms', *Total Quality Management Magazine* 2, 5: 251–252.

Department of Trade and Industry (1983) *Robson Rhodes Report*, London: HMSO.

Dick, B. and Morgan, G. (1987) 'Family networks and employment in textiles', *Work, Employment and Society* 1: 225–246.

Dodgson, M. (1984/5) 'New technology, employment and small engineering firms', *International Small Business Journal* 3, 2: 8–19.

Donckels, R. and Dupont, B. (1987) 'New entrepreneurship and labour market conditions', *International Small Business Journal* 5, 4: 45–58.

Drummond, H. and Chell, E. (1992) 'Should organisations pay for quality?', *Personnel Review* 21, 4: 3–11.

Edwards, J. (1983) 'Social and political pressures upon the small firm: the role of the small business in future society', paper given at the EFMD Thirteenth Small Firms Conference, Vienna.

Edwards, P. and Whitston, C. (1994) 'Disciplinary practice: a study of railways in Britain, 1860–1988', *Work, Employment and Society* 8, 3: 317–337.

Elson, D. and Pearson, R. (1981) '"Nimble fingers make cheap workers"; an analysis of women's employment in Third World export manufacturing', *Feminist Review* 7: 87–107.

Ettkin, L., Raiszadeh, F. and Hunt, H. (1990) 'Just-in-time: a timely opportunity for small manufacturers', *Industrial Management* 32, 1: 16–18.

Filby, M. (1991) 'Ethnography, management research and masculinity: reflections on researching issues of gender and sexuality in a private service organisation', paper presented at the 'Qualitative Research' Conference, Strathclyde Business School, July.

Finch, B. (1986) 'Japanese management techniques in small manufacturing companies: a strategy for implementation', *Production and Inventory Management* 27, 3: 30–38.

Foster, J. (1990) 'Having a field day', *New Statesman and Society* 15 June: 28.

Frankenburg, R. (1963) 'Participant observers', *New Society* 1: 23–28.

Franklin, C. (1980) 'Improved productivity means increased profitability', *American Journal of Small Business* 5, 1: 3–5.

Friedman, A. (1977) *Industry and Labour*, Basingstoke: Macmillan.

Garsombke, T. and Garsombke, D. (1989) 'Strategic implications facing small manufacturers: the linkage between robotization, computerization, automation and performance', *Journal of Small Business Management* 27, 4: 34–44.

Gelsthorpe, L. (1992) 'Response to Martyn Hammersely's paper "On feminist methodology"', *Sociology* 26: 213–218.

Giacchino, J., Noseworthy, H., Moulton, T. and Miller, J. (1987) 'Presidential forum: monitoring company operations', *Small Business Report* 12, 2: 26–27.

Gibb, A. (1988) 'Enterprise culture: threat or opportunity?', *Management Decision* 26, 4: 5–12.

Gilder, G. (1984) *The Spirit of Enterprise*, Harmondsworth: Penguin.

Goss, D. (1991) *Small Business and Society*, London: Routledge.

Gouldner, A. (1954) *Patterns of Industrial Bureaucracy*, London: Macmillan.

Grablowsky, B. (1984) 'Financial management of inventory', *Journal of Small Business Management* 22: 59–65.

Grant, P. (1988) 'Industrial engineering: re-evaluation is necessary', *Small Business Report* 13, 1: 8.

Gregory, G., Klesniks, S. and Piper, J. (1983) 'Batch production decisions and the small firm', *Journal of the Operational Research Society* 34, 6: 469–477.

Griffith, J. and Dorsman, M. (1987) 'SMEs, new technology and training', *International Small Business Journal* 5, 3: 30–42.

Gupta, Y. (1988) 'Linking small business and modern management techniques', *Industrial Management and Data Techniques* March/April: 13–19.

Hammersely, M. and Atkinson, P. (1983) *Ethnography: principles in practice*, London: Tavistock.

Hankinson, A. (1987) 'Small firms pricing – the neglected art', *International Small Business Journal* 5, 4: 34–44.

Hankinson, A. (1989) 'Small firms' output determination: an attitude problem', *International Small Business Journal* 7, 3: 39–45.

Hill, S. (1991) 'How do you manage a flexible firm? The total quality model', *Work, Employment and Society* 15, 3: 397–415.

Hill, T. (1987) *Small Business Production/Operations Management*, Basingstoke: Macmillan.

Hoel, B. (1982) 'Contemporary clothing sweatshops: Asian female labour and collective organisation' in J. West (ed.) *Work, Women and the Labour Market*, London: Routledge & Kegan Paul.

Holland, G. (1984) 'MSC director wants changes to meet updating challenge', *Times Higher Education Supplement* 12 October: 4.

Holliday, R. (1992a) 'Cutting new patterns for small firms research', in K. Caley,

E. Chell, F. Chittenden and C. Mason (eds) *Small Enterprise Development: policy and practice in action*, London: Paul Chapman.

Holliday, R. (1992b) 'Pride and prejudice and participant observation', *Praxis* 24: 35–38.

Holliday, R. and Letherby, G. (1993) 'Happy families or poor relations: familial analogies in the small firm', *International Small Business Journal* 11: 54–63.

Jarillo, J. (1989) 'Entrepreneurship and growth: the strategic use of external resources', *Journal of Business Venturing* 4: 133–147.

Jeffcut, P. (1991) 'From interpretation to representation in organisational analysis: post-modernism, ethnography and organisational culture', paper presented at the 'Towards a New Theory of Organisations' Conference, University of Keele, April.

Jenkins, R. (1986) *Racism and Recruitment*, Cambridge: Cambridge University Press.

Johnson, F. and Aries, E. (1983) 'The talk of women friends', *Women's Studies International Forum* 6: 353–361.

Johnson, S. (1986) 'What sort of jobs do small firms create? – a review of the evidence', in P. Rosa (ed.) *The Role and Contribution of Small Business Research*, Aldershot: Avebury.

Keeble, D. (1990) 'Small firms, new firms and uneven regional development in the United Kingdom', *Area* 22, 3: 234–245.

Krause, P. and Keller, D. (1988) 'Bringing world-class manufacturing and accounting to a small company', *Management Accounting* 70, 5: 28–33.

Lawlor, A. (1988) 'Helping small companies to help themselves', *Industrial and Commercial Training* 20, 3: 18–21.

Lawrence, P. (1985) *Small Business Breakthrough*, Oxford: Blackwell.

Letherby, G. (1992) 'Treks, pies and audio-tape: a qualitative researcher's tale', *Praxis* 24: 47–49.

Liberatore, M., Titus, G. and Varano, M. (1990) 'Modelling the adoption of advanced manufacturing technology by small firms', *International Small Business Journal* 8, 2: 48–58.

Lin, E. (1980) 'Inventory control systems for small business', *American Journal of Small Business* 4, 4: 11–19.

Lockyer, K. (1983) *Production Management*, London: Pitman.

Lowden, J. (1988) 'Managerial skills for the entrepreneur', *Management Decision* 26, 4: 35–39.

MacMillan, I. (1975) 'Strategy and flexibility in the smaller business', *Long Range Planning* June: 62–63.

Maguire, M. (1988) 'Work, locality and social control', *Work, Employment and Society* 2: 71–87.

Marucheck, A. and Peterson, D. (1988) 'Microcomputer planning and control for the small manufacturer: part 1', *Production and Inventory Management* 29, 1: 34–38.

Mason, C. (1984/5) 'The development of new manufacturing firms', *International Small Business Journal* 3, 2: 33–45.

Mason, R. (1973) 'Product diversification and the small firm', *Business Policy* 3, 3: 28–39.

Massel, M. (1978) 'It's easier to slay a dragon than kill a myth', *Journal of Small Business Management* 16, 3: 44–49.

McKee, L. and O'Brien, M. (1983) 'Interviewing men: "taking gender seriously"', in E. Gamarnikow, D. Morgan, J. Purvis and D. Taylorson (eds) *The Public and the Private*, London: Heinemann.

McKeganey, N. and Bloor, M. (1991) 'Spotting the invisible man: the influence of male gender on fieldwork relations', *British Journal of Sociology* 42: 195–210.

Meyer, N. and Roberts, E. (1988) 'Focusing product technology for corporate growth', *Sloan Management Review* 29, 4: 7–16.

Mintzberg, H. (1979) 'An emerging strategy of "direct" research', *Administrative Science Quarterly* 24: 582–589.

Mulvihill, D. (1969) 'Inventory management', *Small Business Bibliography No. 75* November: 2–3.

Norgard, R. (1987) 'Forecasting corporate failure', *The Chartered Accountant in Australia* 58, 2: 44–46.

Oerton, S. (1993) '"It's our baby": familial orientations and collective exploitation in co-operative and collective organizations', paper presented at the annual conference of the British Sociological Association, University of Essex, 5–8 April.

Oi, W. (1983) 'Heterogeneous firms and the organization of production', *Economic Inquiry* 21, 2: 147–171.

Okeley, J. and Callaway, H. (eds) (1992) *Anthropology and Autobiography*, London: Routledge.

Orpen, C. (1985) 'The effects of long-range planning on small business performance: a further examination', *Journal of Small Business Management* 23: 16–23.

Perry, C. (1985/6) 'Growth strategies for smaller firms: principles and case studies', *International Small Business Journal* 5, 2: 17–25.

Peterson, R. and Schulman, J. (1987) 'Capital structure of growing small firms', *International Small Business Journal* 5, 4: 10–22.

Phizacklea, A. (1990) *Unpacking the Fashion Industry: gender, racism and class in production*, London: Routledge.

Piore, M. and Sabel, C. (1984) *The Second Industrial Divide*, New York: Basic Books.

Pollert, A. (1988) 'Dismantling flexibility', *Capital and Class* 34, Spring: 42–75.

Rainnie, A. (1985) 'Is small beautiful? Industrial relations in small clothing firms', *Sociology* 19, 2: 213–224.

Rainnie, A. (1989) *Industrial Relations in Small Firms: small isn't beautiful*, London: Routledge.

Ram, M. (1992) 'Management, control, ethnicity and the labour process: the case of the West-Midlands clothing industry', University of Warwick PhD thesis.

Ram, M. (1994) *Managing to Survive: working lives in small firms*, Oxford: Blackwell.

Ram, M. and Holliday, R. (1993) 'Relative merits: family culture and kinship in small firms', *Sociology* 27: 629–648.

Ramazanoglu, C. (1992) 'On feminist methodology: male reason versus female empowerment', *Sociology* 26: 207–212.

Rhodes, W. (1979) 'The ordering of raw materials and cash flow problems in a small firm concerned with batch production', Loughborough University of Technology MSc thesis.

Riggs, W. and Bracker, J. (1986) 'Operations management and financial performance', *American Journal of Small Business* 10, 3: 17–32.

Robinson, R. (1979) 'Forecasting and small businesses: a study of the strategic planning process', *Journal of Small Business Management* 17: 19–27.

Robinson, R. (1983) 'Measures of small firm effectiveness for strategic planning research', *Journal of Small Business Management* 21: 23–29.

Robinson, R., Pearce, J., Vozikis, G. and Mescon, T. (1984) 'The relationship between stage of development and small firm planning and performance', *Journal of Small Business Management* April: 45–52.

Rose, N. (1989) *Governing the Soul*, London: Routledge.

Rosen, M. (1991) 'Coming to terms with the field: understanding and doing organizational ethnography', *Journal of Management Studies* 28: 1–24.

Rothwell, R. (1988) 'The role of small firms in technological innovation', in J. Curran, J. Stanworth and D. Watkins (eds) *The Survival of the Small Firm. 2: Employment, growth, technology and prospects*, Aldershot: Gower.

Rothwell, R. (1989) 'Small firms, innovation and industrial change', *Small Business Economics* 1: 51–64.

Saladin, B. and Hoy, F. (1983) 'Cost efficient problem solving techniques for small business', *American Journal of Small Business* 7, 4: 4–14.

Scase, R. and Goffee, R. (1980) *The Real World of the Small Business Owner*, London: Croom Helm.

Scase, R. and Goffee, R. (1982) '"Fraternalism" and "paternalism" as employer strategies in small firms', in G. Day, L. Caldwell, K. Jones, D. Robbins and H. Rose (eds) *Diversity and Decomposition in the Labour Market*, Aldershot: Gower.

Scherer, A. and McDonald, D. (1988) 'A model for the development of small high technology businesses', *Journal of Product Innovation and Management* 5, 4: 282–295.

Schumacher, E. (1974) *Small is Beautiful*, London: Abacus.

Scott, M. (1986) 'The dangers of assuming homogeneity in small business research', in P. Rosa (ed.) *The Role and Contribution of Small Business Research*, Aldershot: Avebury.

Scott, M., Roberts, I., Holroyd, G. and Sawbridge, D. (1989) 'Management and industrial relations in small firms', Research Paper No. 70, Department of Employment.

Sewell, G. and Wilkinson, B. (1992) '"Someone to watch over me": surveillance, discipline and the just-in-time labour process', *Sociology* 26, 2: 271–289.

Shapero, A. (1975) 'The displaced uncomfortable entrepreneur', *Psychology Today* November: 83–88.

Sharp, J., Muhlemann, A., Price, D. *et al.* (1990) 'Defining production management core applications for smaller businesses', *Computers and Industrial Engineering* 18, 2: 191–199.

Smart, C. (1984) *The Ties That Bind: law, marriage and the reproduction of patriarchal relations*, London: Routledge & Kegan Paul.

Stanley, L. (1990) 'Doing ethnography, writing ethnography: a comment on Hammersley', *Sociology* 24: 617–627.

Stanley, L. and Wise, S. (1983) *Breaking Out: feminist consciousness and feminist research*, London: Routledge & Kegan Paul.

Stanworth, J. and Curran, J. (1973) *Management Motivation in the Small Business*, Epping: Gower.

Stanworth, J. and Curran, J. (1976) 'Growth and the small firm – an alternative view', *Journal of Management Studies* 13, 2: 95–110.

Stanworth, J. and Curran, J. (1986) 'Growth and the small firm', in J. Curran, J. Stanworth and D. Watkins (eds) *The Survival of the Small Firm. 2: Employment, growth, technology and prospects*, Aldershot: Gower.

Steiner, M. and Solem, O. (1988) 'Factors for success in small manufacturing firms', *Journal of Small Business Management* 26, 1: 51–56.

Steinmetz, L. (1969) 'Critical sizes of small business growth', *Business Horizons* February: 29–36.

Stockport, G. and Kakabadse, A. (1991) 'Using ethnography in small firms research', paper presented at the Fourteenth National Small Firms Policy and Research Conference, 'Small Enterprise Development: policy and practice in action', Blackpool, November.

Storey, D., Keasey, K., Watson, R. and Wynarczyk, P. (1987) *The Performance of Small Firms*, London: Croom Helm.

Strauss, G. (1974) 'Adolescence in organization growth', *Organization Dynamics* Spring: 3–17.

Tait, E. (1990) 'Owner-managers' perceived management education needs: an integrative framework', *International Small Business Journal* 8, 4: 33–48.

Tiler, C., Metcalfe, S. and Connell, D. (1990) 'The management of growth: negotiating transitions', paper presented at the 'Growth and Development of Small High Tech Businesses' Conference, Cranfield.

Tomes, A. (1989) 'Time for quality?: Implementing BS 5750 in small companies has its problems', *OR Insight* 2, 1: 4–6.

Van Maanen, J. (1979) 'Reclaiming qualitative methods for organizational research: a preface', *Administrative Science Quarterly* 24: 520–526.

Vozikis, G. and Glueck, W. (1980) 'Small business problems and stages of development', *Academy of Management Proceedings* 35: 373–377.

Ward, R. (1987) 'Resistance, accommodation and advantage: strategic development in ethnic business', in G. Lee and R. Loveridge (eds) *The Manufacture of Disadvantage*, Milton Keynes: Open University Press.

Warnes, B. (1987) 'Cashflow: the secret of flourishing businesses', *Certified Accountant* July/August: 17–18.

Watkins, D. (1983) 'Development, training and education for the small firm: a European perspective', *European Small Business Journal* 1, 3: 29–44.

Watkins, J. and Watkins, D. (1986) 'The female entrepreneur: her background and determinants of business choice – some British data', in J. Curran, J. Stanworth and D. Watkins (eds) *The Survival of the Small Firm. 1: The economics of survival and entrepreneurship*, Aldershot: Gower.

Williams, K., Cutler, T., Williams, J. and Haslam, C. (1987) 'The end of mass production?', *Economy and Society* 16, 3: 405–439.

Wright, D., Rhodes, D. and Jarret, M. (1983) 'Growth, survival and control in small manufacturing systems', *European Journal of Operational Research* 14, 1: 40–51.

Index

Numbers in *italics* represent pages
with diagrams.

Abdelsamad, M. and Kindling, A. 14,
    167
absenteeism 46, 49–50
Adams, A. and Walbank, M. 3, 144, 145
Adler, P. and Adler, P. 26
American Small Business
    Administration 4
Amin, A. 7
Anoochehri, G. 132, 135, 144
Appelbaum, S. and Hinds, D. 5
Ashcroft, S. 124
Atkin, I. and McArdle, L. 20
Atkinson, J. 7, 148, 149

Bagguley, P. 7, 148
Bennett, M. 11, 12
Berg, David D. 22, 23
Bernolak, I. 133
Berryman, J. 13
Binks, M. and Coyne, J. 9
Birley, S. and Westhead, P. 14
Bolton Report (1971) 1, 5, 150
Bosworth, D. and Jacobs, C. 9
Brannen, K. and Hranac, J. 167
Brooks, D. and Singh, K. 152
Bryman, A. 19, 21
Brytting, T. 10
Burawoy, M. 176
bureaucracy, mock 170, 172;
    punishment-centred 170, 171, 175;
    representative 170

Burgess, R. 24
Burns, T. and Stalker, G. 159

Cannon, T. 7–8, 124
Carter, S. *et al.* 20
Case, R. 13
Chapman, T. 10, 172
Chase, R. 125, 162
Chell, E. *et al.* 8
Churchill, N. and Lewis, V. 12, 159
Clifford, D. 5
Collinson, D. *et al.* 152
communication, ambiguities and
    misconceptions in 51–2, 55; as
    inadequate 82–3, 85; as poor 136–7
Companies Act (1981) 5
Connell, D. 15
control mechanisms 158; delegation
    159, 167; intervention 159;
    supervision 158–9, 166; trade
    unions 159–60, *see also* culture and
    control
Cooper, A. 9, 146
core ('family') workers 151, 152,
    156–7
core-periphery workers 6–7, 148, 149
core-transient workers 146–7, 149,
    158, 175
Cornell, B. and Shapiro, A. 11
Cowling, A. *et al.* 142
culture and control, and
    concentrations of management
    106–7, 109, 113; and differing
    gender viewpoints 108–9, 113; and

external image 47–8; familial
46–50, 54; and internal image 48;
and owner-manager attitude 9–10,
11; patriarchal and paternalistic
77–82, 85; and sexual harassment
82, *see also* control mechanisms
Curran, J. 19, 20, 142; and Burrows,
R. 19; and Stanworth, J. 5, 147,
150, 158

Dandeker, C. 171
Davies, P. 162
decision-making, by consensus 138;
informal 50–1; lack of employee
involvement 138
Department of Trade and Industry 5
development, cost of 123–4; and
design 122–3
Dick, B. and Morgan, G. 151
Dodgson, M. 16, 130
Drummond, H. and Chell, E. 162
Dun & Bradstreet Reports 13

education 10
Edwards, J. 123
Edwards, P. and Whitston, C. 172
Elson, D. and Pearson, R. 141
emotional management 22–4, 153,
155–7
entrepreneurs 8–10, 142, 172
equal opportunities 148–9
ethnographic studies 19–22
Ettkin, L. *et al.* 135

familial ideology 46–50, 54, 149, 150,
151–4, 156, 157, 174–5
field roles 27–8
fieldwork, experience of 17–18; and
gender 28–30
Filby, M. 24, 25, 30
finance 11–12, 14, 126–7, *128*, 169
Finch, B. 4
flexible firm 7, 140, 147–9, 174
Foster, J. 21
Frankenburg, R. 19
Franklin, C. 167
FranTech Ltd, culture and control in
106–9, 113; described 86;
equipment and technology in

100–2, 112; inventory control in
98–100, 112; layout 86–7, *88*, 111;
production process in 89–94,
111–12; quality in 94–8, 112;
recruitment in 102–3, 112;
scheduling in 9, 87, 111; strategic
operations in 110–11, 113; training
103–6, 112–13
Friedman, A. 6

Garsombke, T. and Garsombke, D. 15,
131
Gelsthorpe, L. 21
Giacchino, J. *et al* 167
Gibb, A. 8
Gilder, G. 7
Goss, D. 7
Gouldner, A. 170
Grant, P. 3
Gregory, G. *et al.* 130
Griffith, J. and Dorsman, M. 146
Gupta, Y. 3, 125, 131

Hammersley, M. and Atkinson, P. 21,
26, 28
Hankinson, A. 6, 119, 122, 124, 132
Hill, S. 13, 115, 121, 161, 169
Hoel, B. 152
Holland, G. 146
Holliday, R. 116; and Letherby, G.
151

Institutionalist School 7
inventory control, and action research
124; and annual stocktake 128–9;
as chaotic 99–100, 112; and
finished goods 41, 100; and
inefficient layout 69–70, 84; and
owner attitudes 124–5; and
purchasing 125–7; as thorough
98–9; and use of computers 133;
use of just-in-time (JIT) 69; as
visual 40–1, 127–8, 129; and
work-in-progress 41, 70, 100, 129

Jarillo, J. 9
Jeffcut, P. 22
Jenkins, R. 152
Johnson, F. and Aries, E. 25

Johnson, S. 6

Keeble, D. 13, 14
Krause, P. and Keller, D. 161
Lawlor, A. 2, 15, 114, 134, 136
Lawrence, P. 11
layout, constraints on 116–17;
    inefficient 58–9, 84; logical 86–7,
    111; poor 32–*33*, 53; process 115;
    product 115
Letherby, G. 22
Liberatore, M. *et al.* 15, 130
Lin, E. 127
Lockyer, K. 117
logical-positivist tradition 173
Logos Ltd, culture and control in
    77–82, 85; described 56–7;
    equipment and technology in 70–2,
    84; inventory control in 69–70, 84;
    layout of 57–9, *58*, 83; production
    process in 62–5; quality system in
    65–9, 84; recruitment and training
    in 72–7, 84–5; scheduling in 59–2,
    84; strategic operation in 82–3, 85
Lowden, J. 10, 144
loyalty 158

McKee, L. and O'Brien, M. 23
McKeganey, N. and Bloor, M. 29
MacMillan, I. 12
Maguire, M. 152
management process, firm-specific
    rationalities 115
Marucheck, A. and Petersen, D. 133
Mason, R. 8, 11, 144, 150
Massel, M. 13
Meyer, N. and Roberts, E. 15, 131
Mintzberg, H. 20
Mulvihill, D. 124, 125

negotiated paternalism 150, 156, 160,
    168, 175
Norgard, R. 14

Oerton, S. 153, 154
Oi, W. 3, 130, 142, 146
Okeley, J. and Callaway, H. 22

paper-work 10, 89–92, 94–7, 111–12,

121–2, 126, 129–30, 172
participant observation 19–20
Perry, C. 11
Phizacklea, A. 6, 15, 141, 154, 160
Piore, M. and Sabel, C. 7, 148
Pollert, A. 7, 148, 149
Post-Fordism 6–7
pricing 122
pride 157
production process 114–15; and
    BS5750 121; dependent on
    specialist knowledge 35;
    disorganisation of 120; and fault
    rectification 37; flexibility in 37;
    and forced development work 91;
    and job knowledge 92; matching
    process to product 121; and piece
    rate payment 36–7; and processual
    inertia 35–6, 53, 64–5, 84; and
    redundancies 92–3; reliance on
    paper-work 89–92, 111–12; studies
    of 2–3; and sub-contract work
    92–3; theory and practice 62–4
promotion, internal 143
pull–push effects 9
purchasing, and cashflow limitations
    126–7, *128*; and need for minimum
    stock-holding 125–6; and problem
    of paperwork 126; reliance on the
    person rather than function 127

qualitative/quantitative methods
    18–22, 175
quality circles 167
quality control 161–2, 175; *ad hoc*
    system 38–9, 53; and BS5750
    65–9, 84, 94–5, 112, 163–8, 170–2;
    and bureaucracy 170–2; and
    cash-flow 169; constraints on
    inspection 97–8; inadequacy of
    stores function 95–6; and
    inadequate paper-work 94–7, 112;
    and lack of supervision 66–7; and
    lead-time 169; and materials
    handling 68–9; and rationality
    168–9; and vendor rating 95; visual
    162–3

Rainnie, A. 6, 142, 150, 151, 160

Ram, M. 10, 22, 25, 115, 117, 120, 141, 150, 156, 160, 163; and Holliday, R. 142, 151
Ramazanoglu, C. 21
recruitment 173; and ability to 'fit in' 142; of the already trained 144; external 12; gender bias in 74–5, 141; as haphazard 42–3, 54; inadequacy of 142; informal 72–4, 102–3, 112, 140–1, 152; internal 12; and price of labour 142–3; processual inertia of 143–4
reflexivity 22–4
research methods 1–16; theory and practice 18–19
Rhodes, W. 124
Riggs, W. and Bracker, J. 2, 133
Robinson, R. 5, 133–4; *et al.* 134
Rose, N. 171
Rosen, M. 21
Rothwell, R. 8, 124

Saladin, B. and Hoy, F. 125
satisficing 145
Sausbauer, 2
Scase, R. and Goffee, R. 150, 151, 153, 160
scheduling 117; as automatic 119; as chaotic 129; during busy/slack periods 34–5, 53; haphazard 59–62, 84, 87, 89, 111; poor 119–20; as problematic 118–20
Scherer, A. and McDonald, D. 121
Schumacher, E. 150
Scott, M. 4, 20; *et al.* 4, 155
Sewell, G. and Wilkinson, B. 165, 171
Shapero, A. 8, 9
Sharp, J. *et al.* 2
small firms, ability to innovate 7–8; access to 25–7; co-operation as alien 148; failure of 13–15; and friendship 24–5; helping 3–4; homogeneity 4, 9; and job creation 5–6; patterns of growth 11–13, 15; relationships in 6; role and contribution 1–2; size 3, 4–5; ways of researching 1–16
Smart, C. 23
Stanley, L. 21; and Wise, S. 153

Stanworth, J. and Curran, J. 5, 12, 152, 155, 159
Steiner, M. and Solem, O. 131, 140
Steinmetz, L. 12
Stockport, G. and Kakabadse, A. 19, 20–1, 24, 25, 26
Storey, D. *et al.* 13 strategic operations, and BS5750 110; confused aims and objectives 52–3; and growth 134–5; importance of planning 133–4; and market niche 137–8; and standardisation 110–11, 135–6; and survival strategy 110
Strauss, G. 12
surveillance 171

Tait, E. 10, 145
technology, high usage of 70–2, 84, 100–2, 112, 131–2; implementation of 15–16; low usage of 41–2, 54; use of new 130–1
Tiler, C. *et al.* 11
Tomes, A. 162, 164
total quality control (TQM) 161–2, 169
training 10, 174; as expensive 145; initial 76; as internal and inadequate 144–5; limited 43–5; low wage for 43, 44; needs of 146; office 75–6, 84; on-going 76–7; organised and systematic 164; and owner-manager attitudes 146; reluctance in 144; and restriction of opportunities 145; shopfloor 75, 84; and transferable skills 77, 103–4, 174; as variable 103–6, 112–13; wastage in 45
triangulation techniques 20

Van Maanen, J. 22
Vozikis, G. and Glueck, W. 12, 14

Ward, R. 151
Warnes, B. 14
Watkins, D. 11, 114–15, 142, 146
Watkins, J. and Watkins, D. 155
Wellmaid Clothing, culture and control in 46–50, 54; described 31–2; equipment/technology 41–2, 64; inventory control in 39–41, 54;

layout 32–*33*, 53; production
process 35–7, 53; quality in 38–53;
recruitment/training 42–6, 54;
scheduling 34–5, 53; strategic
operations in 50–3, 54–5
Williams, K. *et al.* 7
women, how treated 154–5
Wright, D. *et al.* 13